Nurturing the Imperial Presidency

Theory Workshop

NEW FRONTIERS IN SOCIAL AND POLITICAL THEORY

Series Editors

Filipe Carreira da Silva, *University of Lisbon* and
Selwyn College, University of Cambridge

Mónica Brito Vieira, *University of York*

Editorial Board

Benjamín Arditi, *Universidad Nacional Autónoma de México*
Said Arjomand, *State University of New York, Stony Brook*
Patrick Baert, *University of Cambridge*
Peter Beilharz, *Curtin University*
Duncan Bell, *University of Cambridge*
Gurminder Bhambra, *University of Sussex*
Marta Bucholc, *University of Bonn*
Robin Celikates, *University of Amsterdam*
José Maurício Domingues, *State University of Rio de Janeiro*
Roberto Frega, *CEMS Paris*
Axel Gosseries, *University of Louvain*
Paul Joosse, *University of Hong Kong*
Wolfgang Knobl, *Hamburg Institute for Social Research*
Patchen Markell, *Cornell University*
Mihaela Mihai, *University of Edinburgh*
Marcus Morgan, *University of Bristol*
Véronique Mottier, *University of Cambridge*
Sofia Näsström, *Uppsala University*
Daniel Silver, *University of Toronto*
Marta Soler Gallart, *University of Barcelona*
Rob Stones, Western *Sydney University*
Mathias Thaler, *University of Edinburgh*
Frederic Vandenberghe, *State University of Rio de Janeiro*
Miguel Vatter, *Flinders University*

VOLUME 1

The titles published in this series are listed at *brill.com/wspt*

Nurturing the Imperial Presidency

A How-to Manual in Eight Essays

By

Brien Hallett

BRILL

LEIDEN | BOSTON

Cover illustration: Created by Floor Boissevain | Eijgen Stijl.

Library of Congress Cataloging-in-Publication Data

Names: Hallett, Brien, author.
Title: Nurturing the imperial presidency : a how-to manual in eight essays / by Brien Hallett.
Description: Leiden, The Netherlands : Koninklijke Brill NV, [2021] | Series: Theory workshop - new frontiers in social and political theory, 2590-1869 ; volume 1 | Includes bibliographical references and index.
Identifiers: LCCN 2020031332 (print) | LCCN 2020031333 (ebook) | ISBN 9789004439252 (hardback) | ISBN 9789004439269 (ebook)
Subjects: LCSH: Executive power. | Presidents. | War and emergency powers. | War, Declaration of. | War and emergency legislation. | Legislative power.
Classification: LCC K3340 .H35 2020 (print) | LCC K3340 (ebook) | DDC 342/.062–dc23
LC record available at https://lccn.loc.gov/2020031332
LC ebook record available at https://lccn.loc.gov/2020031333

Typeface for the Latin, Greek, and Cyrillic scripts: "Brill." See and download: brill.com/brill-typeface.

ISSN 2590-1869
ISBN 978-90-04-43925-2 (hardback)
ISBN 978-90-04-43926-9 (e-book)

Copyright 2021 by Koninklijke Brill NV, Leiden, The Netherlands.
Koninklijke Brill NV incorporates the imprints Brill, Brill Hes & De Graaf, Brill Nijhoff, Brill Rodopi, Brill Sense, Hotei Publishing, mentis Verlag, Verlag Ferdinand Schöningh and Wilhelm Fink Verlag.
All rights reserved. No part of this publication may be reproduced, translated, stored in a retrieval system, or transmitted in any form or by any means, electronic, mechanical, photocopying, recording or otherwise, without prior written permission from the publisher. Requests for re-use and/or translations must be addressed to Koninklijke Brill NV via brill.com or copyright.com.

This book is printed on acid-free paper and produced in a sustainable manner.

LiLi, Victoria, Kekoa
水滴石穿, 繩鋸木斷

Contents

Preface XI
Acknowledgments XV
List of Figures XVI

1 The Moral and Procedural Structure of Declarations of War
    An Introduction 1
    1   A Brief Overview of the Theory of Speech Acts 5
    2   Charles V of France, the Wise, and the Congress of the United States 14
    3   Perceptual Issues: Legislative Capacities and Incapacities 16
    4   Definitional Issues: a Lexical vs. a Performative Definition 19
        4.1 *War as a Performative Speech Act* 20
    5   The Four and a Half Lexical Declarations of War in American History 23
        5.1 *Absolute vs. Conditional Declarations of War* 25
        5.2 *Reasoned vs. Unreasoned Declarations of War* 27
        5.3 *The Organizational Capacity and Incapacity for Declaring War* 29

2 Executive War Making from George H. W. Bush to Gilgamesh
    Invariant State Practice 32
    1   An Elected Constitutional Monarch 32
    2   An Invariant State Practice 34
    3   Explaining the Rise of Elected Constitutional Monarchies: the "Power of the Purse" 36
    4   From Majesty to Sovereignty 39
    5   Primus Inter Pars 40
    6   Parsing Sovereignty 43
    7   Conclusion: Imagining an Alternative after Five Thousand Years 48

3 The Congressional Incapacity to Declare War
    Legislative Sins of Omission vs. Executive Sins of Commission 50
    1   Two Examples of War Making Procedures in Kingless Assemblies 51
        1.1 *The Second Continental Congress* 51
        1.2 *The Security Council* 53
    2   War and Non-War: Two Examples of Congressional Incapacity 55
        2.1 *Non-Authorization by the 112th Congress* 55
        2.2 *Authorization by the 107th Congress* 61

3   James Madison and the Power to Declare War   63
     3.1   *The War of 1812: Sins of Commission and Sins of Omission*   65
4   Conclusion   69

4 Defining War and the Declaring of War
Performative Speech Acts and Ontological Guillotines   70
1   Part 1: Declarations as Performative Speech Acts   70
     1.1   *Defining the Indefinable*   73
           1.1.1   Defining "Armed Conflict"?   74
     1.2   *Codependency: the Speech Act Character of War*   76
           1.2.1   Three Thought Experiments   78
           1.2.2   Rule of Law and the Outlawing of War   79
           1.2.3   Erasing the Codependent Relationship   80
           1.2.4   An Imperfect "Perfect"   82
2   Part 2: Declarations as Ontological Guillotines: Transforming the Subjective into the Objective   83
     2.1   *Functional Equivalent Ways to Declare War*   86
           2.1.1   Positively Missing the Point   86

5 The Declaring of War as a Conflict Resolution Strategy   92
1   The Shortcomings of Hague Convention III   94
2   Unconditional Cynicism and Bad Faith   95
3   Parliamentary vs. Executive Decision-Making: the Decision Is the Declaration vs. the Decision Is Not the Declaration   98
4   The *Jus Fetiale*: Procedural Justice Sustains Substantive Justice   105

6 The United Nation's Security Council
An "Original Understanding" vs. "Original Intentions"   110
1   Original Irrelevance: Perceiving a Separation of Powers   111
     1.1   *John Yoo's "Original Understanding"*   111
     1.2   *Arthur Schlesinger, "Original Intent," and "Collective Judgment"*   116
2   Searching for Suitable Textual Models   118
     2.1   *The Security Council and the Exercise of a Functionally Equivalent Power to Declare War*   119
3   Conclusion   124

7 A Monarchial vs. a Republican Constitution
Misplacing Ends and Means   126
1   Constitutional Symmetry: the Road Not Taken   134

2   Procedural Legitimacy and the Ontology of Policy Ends and
     Means   137
     2.1   *The Ontology of a Procedurally Legitimate Declaration of Policy
            Ends in a Republic*   138
     2.2   *The Ontology of a Procedurally Legitimate Ordering of Policy
            Means in a Republic*   141
 3   Conclusion   143

8 Ends and Means or Checks and Balance?
  Obscuring Agency by Authorizing War in the Unites States and Europe   145
  1   Clausewitz *On War*   147
  2   The Just-Interaction Criteria   148
  3   The Federal Convention of 1787   150
  4   Obscuring Agency by Authorizing War in the Unites States and
      Europe   151

Appendices

Appendix A   The Declaration of Independence and Twelve Congressional
             Declarations of War   159
Appendix B   British Declaration of War against France, 7 May 1689   169
Appendix C   Two Modern, Procedurally Imperfect Declarations
             of War   172
Appendix D   A Model Constitutional Amendment   175
Appendix E   A Joint Resolution to Establish a Joint Congressional
             Drafting Committee of 20xx   179
Appendix F   Re-evaluating the Traditional Just-War Criteria   185

Bibliography   187
Index   194

Preface

Ronald Reagan is responsible for this book. In response to the June 1982 Israeli invasion of Lebanon, President Reagan deployed Marines to Beirut in August 1982 to serve with the Multinational Force. The Multinational Force was a "peacekeeping force." Consequently, the Marines were busy keeping the "peace," President Reagan insisted. They had not been introduced "into hostilities, or into situations where imminent involvement in hostilities is clearly indicated by the circumstances," in the words of the 1973 *War Powers Resolution*.

Many people, however, felt that President Reagan was being disingenuous. Instead of "peacekeeping," the newspapers reported daily that the Marines and the other troops in the Multinational Force received hostile fire. The fire came from various Lebanese militia groups engaged in a very hot war among themselves and with the invading Israeli. If the newspapers were to be believed, the Marines had most certainly been introduced "into hostilities, or into situations where imminent involvement in hostilities is clearly indicated by the circumstances."

Lead by Speaker of the House, Tip O'Neil, a year-long dispute ensued over whether or not the hostile fires received by the Marines met the provisions of the *War Powers Resolution*. After much back and forth, a compromise was reached over a year later, on Wednesday, 12 October 1983, with the passage of Public Law 98–119; 97 Stat. 805, "*Providing statutory authorization under the War Powers Resolution for continued United States participation in the multinational peacekeeping force in Lebanon in order to obtain withdrawal of all foreign forces from Lebanon.*" Eleven days later, on Sunday, 23 October 1983, a truck bomb destroyed the Marine barracks, killing two hundred and forty-one. President Reagan announced the withdrawal of the Marines on Tuesday, 7 February 1984. They returned to their ships on Sunday, 26 February 1984. This ended the dispute.

As this year-long controversy filled the newspapers, I became interested not so much in President Reagan's disingenuity as in Tip O'Neil's call for an authorizing resolution. Why an "authorization" instead of a "declaration of war?" Article 1, Section 8, Clause 11 reads that "The Congress shall have the power ... to declare war." Did this clause not trump a "statutory authorization under the War Powers Resolution?" Would such a constitutionally mandated declaration not settle the dispute decisively? After some thought, I concluded that both Reagan and O'Neil were begging the constitutional question.

Had I been trained in the law; I would have immediately recognized just how naïve I was. Reagan and O'Neil were not begging the constitutional question.

Rather, they were disputing the finer points of James Madison's doctrine of the "separation of powers," and how this "separation" leads to his doctrine of "checks and balances." President Reagan wanted to widen the "separation" and minimize the "checks." Speaker O'Neil wanted to narrow the "separation" and maximize the "checks." Untrained in the nuances of constitutional interpretation, however, I looked, not at the dispute, but at the Declare War Clause, and saw two different problems: What is a declaration of war? And, what is war such that it must be declared?

Realizing that the second question was very much more complex than the first, I decided to look into the first. Moreover, "What is a declaration of war?" seemed directly relevant to Reagan and O'Neil's question begging. After all, the entire dispute would evaporate the instant that the Ninety-eighth Congress simply declared war, as the Constitution suggested that it should.

In pursuit of answers, I did what I was trained to do. I went to Government Docs in the basement of the library and rummaged around until I had collected the relevant data—all twelve of the congressional declarations of war, 1812–1941. I then added the *Declaration of Independence*, for a total of thirteen. Owing to much duplication, the number of congressional declarations can be reduced to five or, better, to four, depending on how one classifies the 1846 Mexican-American War. Upon reading the texts, I immediately saw that the *Declaration of Independence* was very different from the congressional declarations of war, as can be read in Appendix A. Obviously, more than one way existed to declare war. Equally obvious from even a glance the data I had collected, some of the ways were very much better than others. Thus, one way to read this book is as a continuation of my effort to explain why and how the texts of the congressional declarations are so radically different, and so unsatisfactorily so, than the text of the *Declaration of Independence*.

With the raw data in hand, I, first, wrote an exploratory study, *The Lost Art of Declaring War* (1995), and, then, pushed the research further in *Declaring War* (2012). The principal discoveries of *The Lost Art* were two. The first discovery was to confirm the complete incapacity of the Congress to *exercise* "the power … to declare war." The lesser reasons for this incapacity is the insuperable collective action problems of the large, majority-rule, bicameral Congress operating under standing-committee rules. The greater reason for this incapacity is the fact that an assembly organized and structured to set domestic policy and make domestic laws is ill-suited to set foreign policy and declare war. Different functions require different organizations and structures.

The second discovery was the *jus fetiale* of the early Roman Republic. Although now lost, enough of the *jus fetiale* survived so that Renaissance scholars could piece it together. Their reconstruction is important for two reasons: First, it provides a terminology for talking about the why and how of declarations of war. Second, it introduces the Roman concept of *pium* ("piety" in the Roman sense of decorum), which allows one to talk about the relationship between procedural justice and substantive justice. Namely, how a strict, solemn or "pious" adherence to proper procedures in the declaring of war vouchsafes the substantive justice of both the declaration and the war.

For example, because the Second Continental Congress made a procedurally perfect, solemn declaration of war, this procedural justice vouchsafes the substantive justice of both the declaration and the revolution. In stark contrast, owing to the fact that the United States Congress has made only unsolemn, procedurally imperfect declarations of war, this fact undermines both the procedural and substantive justice of the wars so declared, as can be read in Appendix A.

The principal discovery of *Declaring War* was the fact that John Austin's performative speech act theory essentially mirrors the *jus fetiale*, which, in turn, mirrors the traditional just-war criteria. For, declarative speech acts may be performed solemnly, in a procedurally perfect, "pious" manner or unsolemnly in a procedurally imperfect and "impious," functionally equivalent manner. Further, owing to the fact that speech act theory mirrors both the *jus fetiale* and the traditional just-war criteria, it provides the tools for exposing not only the procedural structure of the declarative speech act, but, of much greater importance, its moral structure. The critical importance of this "mirroring" is that speech act theory forces one to look at and analyze the authority to do—whether legitimate or illegitimate—instead of the power to do. And, as soon as one begins to the analyze authority to speak, one is also forced to look at and analyze human interactions in terms of the coherence of ends and means instead of interests or costs and benefits. Hence, a second way to read this book is as a continuation of my effort to explain and understand the procedural and moral structure of performative speech acts, in general, the declarative speech act, in particular. Namely, as a continuation of my effort to explain and understand the entire incapacity of legislative assemblies, in general, and of the Congress, in particular, to *exercise* "the power ... to declare war."

Before turning to the second more complex question raised by the Declare War Clause, "What is war such that it must be declared?" I realized that I had left a number of loose ends on the table. I could have said several things better, and I had not addressed several others, at all. In particular, I had been so absorbed in confronting the American experience that I had neglected the rest of the world and the universal experience of declaring war. In Appendix II in *Declaring War*, The Fœderative Powers in Parliamentary Governments, I had touched on the larger issues, but more was needed. Hence, the present book. My initial exploration had led to tentative discoveries, which I developed further, but, in this book, I am endeavoring to apply what I have learned more generally.

Sheltering in place, Honolulu, May 2020

Acknowledgments

Once again, I must acknowledge Peter Manicas for the precision of his insights, Manfred Henningsen for his insistence that I re-read Machiavelli's *Discourses*, and pay attention this time, and, very especially, Manfred Steger for his provocative conversations and his probing counter-arguments that search out every flaw of logic and tendentious assertion. And most of all, I must thank my family for their heroic forbearance. All of the tortured syntax and twisted logic that remain are due only to the tin ear and stubbornness of the author. And, finally, I plead guilty to a penchant for sarcasm. It is, I believe, a defense against cynicism.

List of Figures

1. A system of checks and balances 38
2. The asymmetric structure of a constitutional monarchy (hereditary or elected) 49
3. The symmetric structure of a republican constitution 49
4. Conflict resolution potential of the manifestive moment 94
5. Performative structures: time, agent/speaker, and quality 136

CHAPTER 1

The Moral and Procedural Structure of Declarations of War
An Introduction

Abstract

Declarations of war are declarative speech acts. Hence, the primary purpose of this chapter is to move beyond the lexical or dictionary meaning so as to discover the moral and procedural structure of declarative speech acts. To do this, the point of departure is a brief exploration of the relationship between the declaring and waging war. Why declare war if most wars are "undeclared?"

A secondary purpose is to explain and understand the moral and procedural implications of various foundational American texts: the American Constitution's Declare War Clause and the declarations of war reproduced in Appendix A, as well as those reproduced in Appendices B and C.

The declaring and waging of war are intimately connected. During the last five thousand years of recorded history, this intimate connection has been embodied in the person of either an hereditary or an elected war leader. The war leader embodied this connection, first and foremost, because of the raw physical and political power of the commander of the nation's armed forces: If the nation's war leader wished to go to war, few could or would oppose him. As an example, reconsider how President George W. Bush and Prime Minister Tony Blair initiated the 2003 invasion of Iraq. Conversely, if the nation's war leader did not want to go to war, even fewer could force him to do so. As an example, reconsider President Grover Cleveland's refusal to initiate war with Spain over Cuba in 1894 and 1895.

To be sure, this raw power is usually cloaked in mystical and mythical reasons and justifications. The nation's hereditary or elected war leader is said to declare and wage war as a matter of imperial or divine right or as his royal prerogative or, more legalistically, as an "inherent executive power." Thus cloaked, the war leader might decide to initiate a "war" declared in due form; or, he might decide to initiate an "undeclared" "armed conflict" by ignoring the procedures and ceremonies required by due form. The *decision* as between a procedurally perfect or a procedurally imperfect declaration was entirely his, and he most frequently chose a procedurally imperfect "undeclared" "armed conflict." But, either way, few doubted the locus of the powers to declare and wage war. That is, until the end of the eighteenth century.

At the time of its writing in 1787, the American Constitution was unusual, but unexceptional, with respect to the waging of war. Unusual, because the war leader was elected, and not hereditary. Kings and emperors were more usually hereditary monarchs, especially in the seventeenth and eighteenth centuries, so an elected chief executive officer and war leader was most unusual at the time, although not now. The American Constitution was unexceptional because the chief executive officer, the president, was also the nation's war leader, the commander-in-chief of the nation's armed forces, "The president shall be commander in chief of the army and navy of the United States, and of the militia of the several States, when called into the actual service of the United States" (II. 2. 1). Kings and emperors had always exercise both civil and military functions simultaneously, so this constitutional provision was exceptionally unexceptional.

The case, however, was different with respect to the declaring of war. With respect to the declaring of war, the American Constitution was both unusual and exceptional. Both, because this power was not explicitly vested in the nation's war leader, the president/commander-in-chief. Instead, the declaring of war, but not the waging of war, was explicitly vested in the nation's legislative assembly, the Congress, "The Congress shall have power … to declare war" (I. 8. 11).

This explicit vesting was unprecedented. It had literally never been done before, and for excellent reasons. First and foremost, such a vesting had always before been impossible, and, hence, unimaginable. Impossible, because representative legislatures functioning within a three-branch system had simply not existed until just recently in human history. With the first stirrings at the end of the twelfth century, various west European Councils of the Realm, Parliaments, Estates General, and Cortes had fought their kings so as to institute themselves as recognizably modern legislatures. This struggle was more or less successful by the end of the eighteenth century. But nowhere had the ruling elite ever heard of such a literally unprecedented idea as separating the war leader's power to declare war from his power to wage war. Consequently, this separation of powers was literally unimaginable. Neither John Locke nor Baron de Montesquieu could have imagined such an unprecedented idea.

In addition to being unprecedented and unimaginable, how was one going to overcome the raw physical and political power of the nation's war leader? As long as the army and navy were the king's army and navy, as long as the army and navy took an oath of allegiance to the king, who was going to tell the king that he could no longer declare war? The Royal Armies and Navies obeyed the king's orders, not the wishes of novel and not-yet-firmly established representative legislatures.

One must, therefore, stand in awe at the audacity of this unusually exceptional and unprecedented American vesting of "the power ... to declare war" in the nation's legislature. Yet, a shadow of a precedent did exist; an inkling of an idea did exist. During the past five thousand years of recorded history, virtually all, but not all, societies have been ruled by either an hereditary or an elected war leader who both declares and wages war. Notwithstanding, "kingless" societies were not entirely unknown. Needless to say, a "kingless" society is not a good precedent for a modern three-branch polity with a "king," an elected war leader with both civil and military responsibilities. Nonetheless, only a "kingless" society negates the raw physical and political power of a nation's war leader. Negation is not a precedent, but it does cast an intriguing shadow. And, as a matter of fact, three such "kingless" polities have existed in the past.

The first of these "kingless" polities is the democracies of ancient Greece. In these democracies, a single assembly of citizens created various subcommittees to exercise various executive functions. Notably, the office of commander of the armed forces did not exist. Instead, the assembly elected a war leader, a *strategos*, to lead each campaign as needed. More fully, in order to *exercise* "the power ... to declare war," the assembly would propose, draft, debate, amend, and, finally, *decide* the question of war or peace with a vote. When the vote was for war, the assembly next elected the *strategos* to lead the campaign, and only that campaign. In this manner, no permanent office of commander-in-chief existed, and no individual could accumulate permanent control of and power over the armed forces. The obvious difficulty with ancient democracies, however, is that this form of organization is neither viable nor feasible for complex modern societies.

The second of the "kingless" polities is the Roman Republic, which was "kingless" until Augustus transformed the old Republic into an empire. In the Roman Republic, the declaring of war was a cooperative enterprise. The Senate drafted, debated, amended, and, finally, voted a draft declaration of war. This draft was then vetted by the *collegium fetialis*, before being taken to the people of Rome for a final vote up or down. Again, if the vote was for war, the Senate would either elect a general to command or, more usually, authorize the consuls to command. In this manner, no permanent office of commander-in-chief existed, and no individual could accumulate permanent control of and power over the armed forces, until Augustus did just that. As with the Greek democracies, however, the obvious difficulty with the Roman Republic is that this form of organization is neither viable nor feasible for complex modern societies.

The third of the "kingless" polities is a revolutionary society. Examples of assemblies in revolt against their kings or oppressors are numerous since the end of the sixteenth century. They include the Dutch Estates General in revolt against Philip II of Spain, the English Long Parliament in revolt against

Charles I, the American Second Continental Congress in revolt against George III, the French National Assembly in revolt against Louis VI; or more recently, the Indian National Congress in revolt against British rule, the African National Congress in revolt against the apartheid government of South Africa, the Central Committee of the Chinese Communist Party in revolt against the government of the Republic of China, the Southern Christian Leadership Conference in revolt against the segregated South in the United States, the Mau Mau Movement in revolt against British rule of Kenya, the Central Committee of the Vietnamese Workers Party in revolt against French rule, and the like. In these and many more cases, the absence of the king, forced the assemblies to both declare and wage war against oppression. Yet, again, as with the Greek democracies and the Roman Republic, no revolution is permanent, despite what Mao Tse-tung might have said. At some point the revolution must end, and a regular, three-branch constitution must be ordained and established.

The net result is that the verdict of six thousand years of human history is decisive. Three, and so far only three, different constitutional structures are conceivable with respect to the declaring and waging of war. First, almost always in human history, societies have constituted themselves such that either an hereditary or an elected "king" sits at the apex of the political and social hierarchy. Owing to this fact, the hereditary or elected monarch functions simultaneously as both the chief executive officer and the commander-in-chief of a standing army. Possessed of the raw power of the combined roles, this individual both wages and declares war. His raw power, however, is camouflaged by speaking of it mystically as an imperial or divine right or as his royal prerogative or, more legalistically, as an "inherent executive power."

Second, exceptionally in human history, a few ancient or revolutionary societies have constituted themselves without a "king." In such cases, the various executive functions are exercised by a number of sub-assemblies and, as a result, no individual is in possession of the power to both declare and wage war. While inspiring, these few examples are, to repeat, neither viable nor feasible for complex modern societies.

And, finally, more recently in human history, since the end of the sixteenth century, progressively more societies have adopted mixed constitutions. The "king's" legislative functions are usurped by an assembly, a parliament, without infringing upon his twin powers to declare and wage war, what John Locke called the sovereign's foederative powers—"the power of war and peace, leagues and alliances."

Thus, to repeat, one must stand in awe at the audacity of the Federal Convention to propose vesting of "the power ... to declare war" explicitly in the nation's legislative assembly. This had never been done before. To disassociate

the "the power ... to declare war" from the power to wage war was a leap into the unknown. This leap of faith, needless to say, was based on three complimentary, but unexamined, propositions:
1) That executive war-making could be frustrated by separating the power to wage war from "the power ... to declare war."
2) That relocating the latter to a non-executive branch of government would be both possible and effective.
3) That the legislative branch was the non-executive branch that could best *exercise* "the power ... to declare war," in addition to discharging its primary legislative function as the nation's "giver of laws."

Over two hundred years of American history have proven the third proposition invalid because infeasible. Nevertheless, this historical verdict in no way diminishes the aspiration of the first or the plausibility of the second. Audacious experiments often fail. For all the reasons argued in the chapters that follow, the United States Congress, in particular, and all legislative assemblies, in general, are completely incapable of *exercising* "the power ... to declare war." Yet, to repeat, this fact does not mean that a properly located and properly structured decision-making assembly could not frustrate executive war-making, the "Imperial Presidency" in Arthur Schlesinger's words. And, indeed, Appendices E and F propose two possible solutions.

The fact that the third proposition is not viable, therefore, is of less importance than what can be leant from the unique experiment in constitutional design that is the Constitution of the United States. In particular, one needs to be mindful of the fact that "the power ... to declare war" is a universal human phenomenon that is independent of any given social organization or constitutional framework. Thus, by toggling between the universality of "the power ... to declare war," on the one hand, and, on the other hand, the specificity of the American experiment with its rich mine of insights and examples, one is better able to map out a path that might possibly lead to frustrating executive war-making. The first step along such a path is to recognize and acknowledge that "the power ... to declare war" is, above all, an *exercise* of the power to do things with words.

1 A Brief Overview of the Theory of Speech Acts

This book relies upon John Austin's Speech Act Theory to undergird its multifaceted historical and constitutional analyses. In the chapters that follow, the history of waging and declaring war is filtered through a practical application of the moral and procedural structure of performative speech acts, in general, and of declarative speech acts, in particular. This appeal to Speech Act Theory is made in order to explain and understand the historical failure the legislative branch to wrest "the power ... to declare war" away from the executive branch of government, from kings and Imperial Presidents. The basic argument of this book, therefore, is that the future of executive war-making is bright and untroubled as long as the speech act character of war and the declaring war is ignored. Until the Theory of Speech Acts is taken into account, the future of both executive war-making, in general, and the Imperial Presidency, in particular, is smooth sailing.

In broad strokes, the declarative act can be performed by either one of two declarers of war in either one of two different manners: War may be declared by either an individual or a collectivity. To reiterate, individual declarers of war have traditionally included kings, emperors, presidents, prime ministers, and similar war leaders. Collective declarers of war have traditionally included the assemblies of the Greek city-states, the Roman Republic, revolutionary assemblies, and similar "kingless" political organizations.

Putting the identity of the declarer aside for a moment, the utterance of the declarative act may be performed in either one of two different ways. It may be performed either in a procedurally "perfect" manner or in a procedurally "imperfect" manner. When performed in a procedurally "perfect" manner, the performance is also "solemn" *i.e.* performed with *pium*, "piety" in the Roman sense of decorum (see Chapter 5.). When performed in a procedurally "imperfect" manner, the performance is, naturally, "unsolemn" *i.e.* performed with *impium*, "impiety." The difference between *pium* and *impium* has been partially codified in Article 1 of Hague Convention III of 1907, *Relative to the Opening of Hostilities*, "The contracting powers recognize that hostilities between themselves must not commence without previous and explicit warning, in the form either of a reasoned declaration of war or of an ultimatum with conditional declaration of war."

Needless to say, when performed with a procedurally perfect, solemn manner in accordance with Hague Convention III of 1907, an internationally recognized "war" comes into existence. Alternatively, when performed with a procedurally imperfect, unsolemn, functionally equivalent manner that is not in accordance with Hague Convention III of 1907, an internationally recognized "armed conflict" comes into existence.

Recurring to the identity of the declarer, a difficulty now arises. *Ought* the declarer of war be an individual or a collectivity or either indifferently? Empirically, historically, traditionally, the answer is either, indifferently. Either an individual or a decision-making assembly may indifferently *decide* and *declare* war, according to Hague Convention III. The obvious reason, of course, is that virtually all the wars during the past six thousand years have been *decided* and *declared* by an individual, the nation's war leader. Wars *decided* and *declared* collectively by the ancient democracies or republics, including revolutionary assemblies, are few and far between. Collectively declared wars must, therefore, be considered as anomalies, marginal phenomenon of little impact on or of interest to international law. Moreover, wars *decided* and *declared* collectively by revolutionary assemblies have always been illegitimate, fomented by "terrorists," unless the rebellion was successful, of course.

However, this indifference on the part of history and international law is not without its drawbacks. It, unmistakenly, prejudices the search for a path that might possibly lead to frustrating executive war-making: On the one hand, if the declarer of war may be either an individual or a collectivity, indifferently, then no reason exists to object to individual war leaders both declaring and waging war as their imperial or divine right, their royal prerogative or, more legalistically, as their "inherent executive power." On the other hand, if the declarer of war *ought not to* be an individual, but *ought to* be a collectivity, then a moral, if not an empirical, reason exists to object to individual war leaders both declaring and waging war.

In short, the eternal battle between *is* and *ought* reappears. The empirical facts of the matter are that wars can be *decided* and *declared* either by an individual or by a decision-making assembly, indifferently. Further, war has almost always been *decided* and *declared* by an individual, the nation's war leader. And, pushing the point one more step, all the empirical evidence shows that the nation's war leader may *decide* and *declare* war either in Hague compliant or non-compliant forms and procedures. When in compliance, the war leader initiates an internationally recognized "war." When in not compliance, he initiates an internationally recognized "armed conflict." Given the raw physical and political power of a nation's war leader, neither morality nor *ought* are of any relevance as far as international law is concerned.

One possible argument for disputing the indisputable empirical facts of the matter is that war is a social interaction and, hence, it *ought to* be *decided* and *declared* socially. As such, no individual, no matter how physically and politically powerful, *ought to decide* and *declare* war. This argument is, of course, an analogue to the claim that individual chief executives *ought not to* both make and execute the nation's laws. That, instead, the nation's laws *ought to* be enacted collectively in a decision-making assembly, in a parliament; but that the nation's laws *ought to* be overseen and executed by an individual chief executive. Overseen and executed, but not also enact by him. The moral foundation upon which both claims stand is a belief that no individual *ought to* impose his individual intentions and decisions upon others, especially, upon the collective other. As John Stuart Mill has observed, "it is as little justifiable to force our ideas on other people, as to compel them to submit to our will in any other respect" (Mill 1867, III: 166–7).

On the assumption that Mill has articulated a morally decisive, if empirically contested, reason for collective decision-making in both law- and war-making, then one *ought not to* be indifferent as to the identity of either the lawgiver or the declarer of war. Morally, if not empirically, only collective decision-making assemblies can legitimately speak in solemn, procedurally perfect form so as to *decide* on and promulgate laws. Morally, if not empirically, only collective decision-making assemblies can legitimately speak in solemn, procedurally perfect form so as to *decide* on and *declare* war. Critically and crucially, then, even when a society has constituted itself so as to delegate "the [collective] power … to declare war" to its war leader, his utterances must now be recognized and understood as morally, if not empirically, illegitimate, a functionally equivalent speech act. And, this is the case even when the declarations appear to be Hague Convention III compliant.

This moral claim suggests, one might note, that virtually all of the wars waged in the past five thousand years were illegitimate, if not immoral, precisely because *decided* and *declared* by individuals, by the nation's war leader, in place of a decision-making assembly. Some may find this claim extreme, if not irrelevant.

A second possible argument for disputing the indisputable empirical facts of the matter is that the absolutely necessary condition for the existence of war is a declarative speech act. As such, it possesses an inherent and intrinsic physical and moral structure. This moral structure is constituted by means of four different acts of two different kinds, namely, two mental acts—an *intention* and a *decision*—and two physical acts—a *draft* and a *declaration*. From this quadruplex, four different procedural scenarios arise. More precisely, as a matter of empirical, but not moral, fact, the quadruplex enables an individual war leader to initiate armed hostilities in either one of three illegitimate, functionally equivalent, procedurally imperfect scenarios. As a matter of moral, but not empirical, necessity, the quadruplex also enables a decision-making assembly to initiate war in one and only one procedurally perfect scenario. Need it be mentioned, vice travels many ways and byways; virtue takes only the high road.

The moral difference between an individual and a collective declarer of war notwithstanding, the structural logic of the four scenarios, requires both an individual and a collective declarer to form an *intention*, in the first instance. Subsequently, the declarer must *decide* to act on its *intention*. The moral and structural point, of course, is that one cannot, or, at least, should not *decide* on an interaction without first *intending* to accomplish some end, purpose, or goal. Intentionless decisions are problematic.

The two moral and mental acts, however, are without effect or practical consequence unless and until they leave the declarer's mental or psychological world and are manifested in his physical world as a communication to others. Consequently, the structural logic of the four scenarios, requires both an individual and a collective declarer to *draft* a text, which text is published and *declared*, in the second instance. The moral and structural point, of course, is that one cannot, or, at least, should not *declare* without first *drafting* the words to be uttered. Wordless declarations are problematic.

Once the four inherent and intrinsic elements of the declarative speech act have been isolated, one immediately recognizes that they may be performed by different speakers at different times in different orders. This flexibility is crucial to the nurturing of executive war-making. If one and only one procedural scenario were possible, as is the case with decision-making assemblies, functionally equivalent utterances producing "undeclared" "armed conflicts" would also be physically impossible. This, in turn, would make executive warmaking impossible. These four procedural scenarios are illustrated in the following authority-tracing schematics.

1. Unsolemn Functionally Equivalent Declarations by an Individual, not in due form:

    Scenario 1: A Socially Sanctioned Declarative Act by the Nation's Hereditary or Elected King:

    At (t^1), the war leader *intends/decides* to go to war on his personal authority.

    At (t^2), the text of the declaration is *drafted*, usual by a clerk.

    At (t^3), the text is published and *declared*, either by the war leader himself or by his heralds.

    At (t^4), military orders are issued.

    (See Appendix B: British Declaration of War against France, 7 May 1689.)

    Scenario 2: An Unsolemn Functionally Equivalent Declarative Act by the Nation's Hereditary or Elected King:

    At (t^1), the war leader *intends/decides* to go to war on his personal authority.

    At (t^2), the text of a military order is *drafted*.

    At (t^3), the text of a *public announcement* is *drafted*.

    At (t^4), military orders are issued.

    At (t^5), a *public announcement* of the execution of the military order is made by the war leader, most recently in a televised address

(See a more detailed schematic of President George H.W. Bush's *Operation Just Cause*, the 1989 invasion of Panama, in Chapter 8.)

Scenario 3: An Unsolemn Functionally Equivalent Declarative Act by the Nation's Hereditary or Elected King that Involves a Legislature:
At (t^1), the war leader *intends/decides* to go to war on his personal authority.
At (t^2), the text of a resolution of "authorization," "approval," or general "support" is *drafted* and presented to a legislative assembly.
At (t^3), the legislative assembly ratifies the resolution.
At (t^4), the text of a military order is *drafted*.
At (t^5), the text of a *public announcement* of the execution of the military order is *drafted*.
At (t^6), military orders are issued.
At (t^7), the *public announcement* of the execution of the military order is made by the war leader, most recently in a televised address.
(See a schematic in Chapter 3 and Appendix C: President George W. Bush and Prime Minister Tony Blair's public announcement of the 2003 invasion of Iraq.)

In sharp contrast to executive war-making by the nation's war leader, a procedurally perfect, solemn declarative act uttered by a purpose-built, collective, decision-making body is both simpler and less flexible. One and only one procedural scenario is possible:

II. Solemn Declarations by a Collective Decision-Maker, in due form:
Scenario 4: A Solemn Collective Declaration in due form:
At (t^1), a purpose-built, collective decision-making body *drafts, debates,* and *amends* the text of a declaration of war.
At (t^2), the purpose-built, collective decision-making body simultaneously *intends, decides,* and *declares* war with a vote.
At (t^3), the commander of the nation's armed forces is therewith morally and legally authorized and empowered to oversee the execution of the military means to achieve the *declared* political objectives of the war.
This moral and legal authorized empowerment is analogous to the manner in which a chief executive officer is morally and legally authorized and empowered to oversee the execution of the political objectives of domestic legislation.
(See the schematic in Chapter 8 and Appendix A: *The Declaration of Independence*.)

Four, comments are perhaps appropriate: First, as will be discussed many times over in the following chapters, legislative assemblies simply lack the capacity to *exercise* "the power ... to declare war" in a procedurally perfect, solemn declarative act. The issue here is not that legislative assemblies lack "the [empirical] power ... to declare war" in a procedurally imperfect, unsolemn declarative act. That is not the issue, as can be read in Appendix A. Naturally, this incapacity nurtures executive war-making, in general, and an Imperial Presidency, in particular. Be they styled as congresses, diets, dumas, national assemblies, parliaments, or the like, legislative assemblies are, therewith, part of the problem, and not part of the solution.

This point is illustrated in *Scenarios 3* at (t^3) and (t^4). For beyond cavil, to "authorize," "approve," or offer general "support" is clearly not "to declare war." One demonstrates the capacity "to declare war" by "declaring war" in a procedurally perfect, solemn (*pium*) Hague compliant manner. To "authorize," "approve," or offer general "support" at the behest of the nation's war leader is only to demonstrate an incapacity "to declare war." This incapacity derives from two sources: The more obvious source is the all but overwhelmed by collective action problems inherent in legislative assemblies. This means that they are too easily either ignored or "managed," as Commanders-in-Chief James Madison discovered in 1812 and as William McKinley did, once again, in 1898 (Hallett 2012, Ch 2 and 3 respectively).

The less obvious source of legislative incapacity is function. The primary function of legislatures is to legislate domestic laws and policies. But foreign policy, in general, and the declaring of war, in particular, are neither domestic policy nor domestic laws. Hence, to ask a domestic policy assembly to declare war and make foreign policy is ask it to do a job for which it was not designed. And, to compound the problem, this design flaw is exacerbated by the legislative branch's collective action problems.

If, therefore, one objects to executive war making and an Imperial Presidency, then one must design a purpose-built, collective decision-making assembly. Such an assembly must minimize its collective action problems by restricting its membership to fifty or fewer delegates, on the one hand, and limit its functions to the making of foreign policy and the declaring of war, on the other hand. In other words, one must turn to the Second Continental Congress or the United Nations Security Council for the design of a collective alternative to executive war-making, as will be discussed in following chapters.

The second appropriate comment is to remark upon is the variety and complexity of the *intends-decide-draft-declare* structure of the declarative act. This variety and complexity, needless to say, creates ample room for executive branch manipulation, as is illustrated in *Scenarios 1 to 3*. In contrast, normal parliamentary procedures impose a strict *draft*-then-simultaneously-*intend*/

decide/declare discipline upon any collective *exercise of* "the power ... to declare war." When not jammed up by collective action problems, this parliamentary discipline sharply reduces the room for executive branch manipulation. Variety and complexity nurtures executive war-making; parliamentary discipline in a purpose-built, suitably sized decision-making assembly does not nurture executive war-making.

The third appropriate comment is to observe the temporal sequencing of performative speech acts. The temporal sequencing draws out and makes explicit the structural and moral mechanics of both procedurally imperfect, unsolemn, executive decision-making and, equally, procedurally perfect, solemn, collective decision-making. With respect to the declarative acts in *Scenarios 1 to 3*, a national war leader always *intends/decides* before he *drafts/declares*. Hence, his mental acts are separated from his physical acts by an interval of time, by a temporal lag. Inversely, in *Scenario 4*, a purpose-built, collective decision-making body *drafts*, debates, and amends the text of the declarative act before it votes on the *draft* text, therewith simultaneously *intending, deciding,* and *declaring*. Hence, an indecisive and contingent collective physical act—the *drafting, debating,* and *amending* of a text—is now separated by an interval of time from the decisive and simultaneous collective performative acts of *intending, deciding,* and *declaring*.

This relocation of the temporal lag is of critical importance for two reasons: First, it defines performatively the difference between executive and parliamentary acts, in general. Second, and equally important, it defines performatively the difference between an individual and a collective declarer of war, in particular. Thus, an individual declarer of war is he who *intends/decides* before he *drafts/declares*. This temporal sequence, in turn, defines executive procedures. Conversely, a collective declarer of war is that which *drafts* before it simultaneously *intends/decides/declares*. This temporal sequence, in turn, defines collective, parliamentary, procedures. Since the text of a declaration of war should be coherent and well-reasoned, as is the *Declaration of Independence, drafting* the text and ensuring its coherence and clarity before *intending, deciding* and *declaring* makes good sense. In short, executive *intending/deciding* before *drafting/declaring* puts the cart before the horse.

To highlight the obvious, putting the cart before the horse is the wrong, perhaps, the immoral, way to do things. Most especially, it is the wrong, perhaps, the immoral, way to do things with words. A procedurally perfect, solemnly uttered declarative act *ought to* be a clear and coherent text. Consequently, it *ought to* be *drafted*, revised, and vetted before the *intending, deciding* and *declaring*, as was the case in 1776 with the Second Continental Congress. Conversely, *intending* and *deciding* before *drafting* and *declaring* produces a profoundly illogical, procedurally imperfect, unsolemnly uttered declarative act, as is illustrated with the 2003 presidential and prime ministerial public announcements of George W. Bush and Tony Blair in Appendix C.

In sum, the Roman procedural distinction between *pium* and *impium* effectively measures much, if not all, of the moral content of performative speech acts. Procedurally perfect, solemn ceremonies and rites establish a foundation of procedural justice that vouchsafes the substantive justice of the speech act. Procedurally imperfect, unsolemn ceremonies and rites undermine the foundations of procedural justice and, therewith, destabilizes the substantive justice of the speech act, as history amply demonstrates.

And, finally, like all performative speech acts, declarative acts serve a fundamentally ontological function. They are, as John Austin said, *How To Do Things with Words* (1975 (1962)). As such, performative speech acts are empirical and moral phenomena that bridge the gap between the mental acts of *intending* and *deciding* to do something and the physical acts of actually doing that which is *intended/decided*. Performative speech acts serve, therefore, as the absolutely necessary mental and physical condition to bring that which is *intended/decided* into existence. Unless some individual or some collectivity utters either a solemn declaration of war in due form or an unsolemn functionally equivalent speech act not in due form, "the power ... to declare war" cannot possibly be exercised. Consequently, to repeat, any *exercise* of the power to "authorize," "approve," or offer general "support" is not an *exercise* "the power ... to declare war."

To rephrase and summarize what has been said so far in a more technical language, like many other performative speech acts, declarative acts combine and recombine two mental acts, *intending* and *deciding*, with two physical acts, *drafting* and *declaring*. In consequence, the empirical and temporal logic of the declarative speech act is that the *declaring* of war is physically impossible unless and until the text of the declarative act has been *drafted*. Without words, without a text, no performative speech act is physically possible. Wordless utterances are not performative speech acts. That is, more technically, wordless utterances may be a communication, but they are not locutionary acts in the required performative sense.

Yet, the physical acts of *drafting* and *declaring* cannot possibly come into existence unless and until the moral and mental acts of *intending* and *deciding* are undertaken by the declarer of war. In consequence, the moral and temporal logic of the declarative speech act is that the *deciding* to go to war is physically impossible unless and until the moral content of the declarative act has been *intended*. Without an *intention*, without a purpose, end or goal, no performative speech act is possible. Intentionless or purposeless utterances are not performative speech acts. That is, more technically, without a well-reasoned and fully justified *intention*, the utterance may be a communication, but it will be without a morally credible illocutionary force.

Hence, given the physical and moral complexity of the declarative speech act, precisely where in the ceremony or procedure *ought* the declarer of war *decide* upon the *intention* of the war? Empirically, as the four *Scenarios* demonstrate, *intending* and *deciding* can occur either simultaneously with the *declaring*, as in Scenario 4. Or, the *intending* and *deciding* can occur at (t^1) before the *drafting* and the *declaring* the text, as in *Scenarios 1 to 3*. Morally, however, only *Scenario 4* produces procedurally perfect, solemn declarations of war uttered by a decision-making assembly collectively. Perversely, *Scenarios 1 to 3* produce unsolemn functionally equivalent speech acts uttered by an individual war leader. Thus, on the one hand, *Scenario 4* is *pium* in the sense that it vouchsafes the procedural justice the locution's illocutionary force, whereas, on the other hand, *Scenarios 1 to 3* are *impium* in the sense that they destabilize the procedural justice of the locution's illocutionary force. This moral logic may be outlined and summarized as:

I. Unsolemn Functionally Equivalent Declarations by an Individual, not in due form: *Scenarios 1* to 3:
   At (t^1), an individual does the mental act of *intending/deciding*.
   At (t^2), an individual does the physical act of *drafting*.
   At (t^3), an individual does the physical act of *declaring*.

II. Solemn Declarations by a Collective Decision-Maker, in due form: *Scenario 4*:
   At (t^1), a decision-making assembly *drafts* a well-reasoned text that justifies the moral imperative of the *decision* to go to war.
   At (t^2), a decision-making assembly votes on the draft declaration, therewith simultaneously enacting the *intention/ decision/ declaration*.

2 Charles V of France, the Wise, and the Congress of the United States

War leaders possess the raw physical and political power to initiate war on their own personal authority. This is a given. But wise war leaders avoid this option. Wise war leaders "consult" with—in the sense of "co-opt"—their elders, their bishops and barons, their privy council, their viziers or ministers, and, with increasing frequency since the thirteenth century, their legislative assemblies. The political wisdom of developing wider support for a war before initiating armed hostilities is just too obvious.

Since the advent of more or less modern legislative assemblies in Western Europe, European war leaders have focused their "consultations" on their tax-authorizing legislatures. An excellent example of this is found in Christine de Pisan's praise for the politically astute conduct of Charles v of France, the Wise. After he had *decided* to renew war against Edward III of England in 1369, Charles v:

> ... assembled at parys [Paris] at his parliament the forsaid foure estates/ .../and to theym purposed his reasons ayenst thenglyssh men [against the English men] demaundyng theyr aduys/yf he had cause to bygynne warre/for without iuste cause/the regarde & deliberacion emonge theym/and the consente & wylle of his good subgetts in no wyse he wold doo it at whiche counseyl by long deliberacion was concluded that he had good & iuste cause to begynne agayn the warre & thus the good wise kynge entreprysed it/(1937, I, V).

To be sure, the Four Estates did not issue the official declaration of war. Charles v did. But the Four Estates did enact a functionally equivalent speech act. They voted war taxes as a sign of their "grete loue" of Charles, which the King much appreciated—both the love and the tax revenue.

What is of the greatest significance in the example is how Charles v wisely exploited his advantages as a first mover and agenda setter. Charles v *decided* to reignited the Hundreds Years War on his own authority and convened the Four Estates so as to "consult" with it. The Four Estates did not *decide* and *declare* war, therewith authorizing Charles v to wage the war under its collective authority. In 1369, the first mover advantage of Charles v was considered right and proper because everyone agreed that Charles v both declared and waged war as his divine right and royal prerogative. Artfully hidden behind this customary agreement is the unrecognized fact that no legislative assembly has ever demonstrated a capacity to *decide* and *declare* war in any meaningful way. More precisely, this incapacity to *exercise* "the power ... to declare war" does not lie in an inability to *declare* war in a minimal, lexical or dictionary manner; rather, the incapacity is located in an all but total incapacity to *intend* and *decide* the question of war or peace and *draft* a text.

For example, as can be read in Appendix A, the Congress of the United States has *declared* war in a minimal, lexical or dictionary manner four times—in 1812, 1898, 1917, and 1941. But it has done so only after Commanders-in-Chief James Madison, William McKinley, Woodrow Wilson, and Franklin Roosevelt had first made the *decision* to go to war. Then, the *intention* and *decision* having been made, each of the Commanders-in-Chief ordered the State Department to *draft* the text of an absolute declaration of war that conforms to the minimal, dictionary definition of a declaration of war. One partial exception does exist with the 1898 declaration against Spain over Cuba. This partial exception is discussed in a moment, just below. Next, after an interval of time, each of the Commanders-in-Chief wisely requested that their respective Congresses ratify the State Department *drafted* text. Needless to say, each Congress faithfully complied with these requests. Each Congress *declared*, "That war be and the same is hereby declared to exist between x and The United States of America."

The incapacity of all legislatures to *draft*-then-simultaneously-*intend/decide/declare* war on their own *initiative* is critical, first, because the *capacity* of the nation's war leader to act imperially depends entirely on this legislative *incapacity*. If any legislature had ever possessed this *capacity*, then that *capacity* would have immediately *incapacitated* the imperial ambitions of the nation's war leader. No Caesar could have ever crossed the constitutional Rubicon. Be that as it may, recognizing and acknowledging this legislative *incapacity* is not difficult. The newspapers provide a daily stream of uncontested evidence, although other, more academic, sources are available (*e.g.*, Fisher 1995; Hallett 1998 and 2012; Wormuth and Firmage 1989). Further evidence is given in Chapter 3, where are retold the remarkable examples of the 107th Congress in "authorizing" the 2003 invasion of Iraq and the 112th Congress in not "authorizing" the 2011 no-fly zone over Libya.

After recognizing and acknowledging this legislative incapacity, the next step in *not* nurturing executive war-making is to take a closer look at the Declare War Clause, Article 1, Section 8, Clause 11. This is done more fully in Chapter 4. With a closer look, one is able to draw out and highlight the basic constitutional flaws that sustains executive war-making, on the one hand; and, on the other hand, one is able to envision several possible constitutional or statutory remedies, such as those suggested in Appendices D and E.

To do this, one must investigate at least two different issues: issues of perception and of definition.

3   Perceptual Issues: Legislative Capacities and Incapacities

In order to nurture executive war-making, one must accept at least three misperceptions. The first misperception is to believe in the capacity of parliaments and congresses to exercise two very different functions. It is to believe that they can make both domestic and foreign policy in spite of their overwhelming collective action problems. If "misperception" is too strong a tea, one may downgrade this issue from "misperception" to one of "decisive impetus." This, of course, was Arthur Schlesinger's tactic:

> [T]he imperial Presidency received its decisive impetus, I believe, from foreign policy; above all, from the capture by the Presidency of the most vital of national decisions, the decision to go to war. ... It [the growth of the imperial Presidency] was as much a matter of congressional abdication as of presidential usurpation. As it took place, there dwindled away checks, both written and unwritten, that had long held the Presidency under control. ... [But b]y the early 1970s the American President had become on the issue of war and peace the most absolute monarch (with the possible exception of Mao-Tse-tung of China) among the great powers of the world (1973, ix).

Note Schlesinger's finely tuned balance: The growth of the imperial Presidency "was *as much* a matter of congressional abdication as of presidential usurpation." Yet, still, "its decisive impetus" was "*above all*, from the capture by the Presidency of the most vital of national decisions, the decision to go to war. ..."

But to say that both branches were more or less responsible is to misperceive the gross incapacity of the one and the overwhelming capacity of the other. For, the fact of the matter is that the parliaments and congresses of the world could not possibly "abdicate" a power they have never had. As already noted, the parliaments and congresses of the world most certainly possess the capacity to pass resolutions of "authorization," "approval," or of general "support." They also possess the capacity to raise war taxes. But in no case has a parliament or congress ever *exercised* "the power. ... to declare war" in the full sense of *drafting* and then simultaneously *intending/ deciding/ declaring* war with a fully reasoned, Hague III compliant declaration.

Equally, the war leaders of the world have never had any need to "capture" "the *power.* ... to declare war." For over five thousand years, they have exercised this power not only as their divine right and royal prerogative, but also because they commanded a standing army. When the commander-in-chief tells the army to go to war, it goes to war.

The second misperception required in order to nurture executive warmaking is to believe that modern constitutions are "democratic," and not "republican." Which is only to say that headline-grapping, day-to-day politics are one thing, but that a nation's three-branch constitutional regime or institutions are another thing. For example, American politics have been "democratic" since roughly the 1830's with the arrival of universal suffrage for adult, white, males. Hence, the "democratic" quality of American politics is not in question. The question is whether the Constitution as a text and a document is best viewed as "democratic" or "republican." This question is best engaged by evaluating the following dilemma with regard to the *exercise* "the power. ... to declare war":

1) If the constitutional text is viewed as "democratic," then the principal problem to be solved is ensuring maximum participation, if not of the entire population, at least of the members of the nation's parliament or congress.

   This means, as is discussed in Chapter 6, that the main issue for Senator Jacob Javits and the other drafters of the moribund *War Powers Resolution of 1973* was ensuring timely "consultation" so as to promote the "collective judgment" of the president and the Congress.

   The purpose of the 1973 *Resolution*, therefore, is not to ensure a congressional *exercise* of the Congress's Article I "*power*. ... to declare war," but to promote a minimum of "democratic" participation by the Congress in the president's "inherent executive power" to wage and declare war.

2) Inversely, if the constitutional text is viewed as "republican," then the principal problem to be solved is structural. Most fundamentally, the paramount problem of any "republican" constitution is to determine how the sovereign's "unitary" rights and powers are to be divided. Namely, what are the number of primary governmental functions or branches. Are they two, three, four, or more?

   In terms of the *exercise* of the "power. ... to declare war," this means that the main "republican" issue is a very practical empirical question: Is the legislative branch both competent to and capable of *exercising* "the power. ... to declare war?"

   In turn, this question gives rise to a second dilemma:
   a) Beyond question, a large, majority-rule, bicameral legislature operating under standing-committee rules can discharge its primary function to make laws, despite its nearly overwhelming collective action problems.
   b) But can this same large, majority-rule, bicameral legislature operating under standing-committee rules also discharge a secondary function and *exercise* "the power. ... to declare war," despite its nearly overwhelming collective action problems?

c) Or, can "the power. ... to declare war" be exercised *collectively* only by a small, majority-rule, *monocameral* assembly operating under committee-of-the-whole rules, owing to its relatively manageable collective action problems?

Without attempting to answer the dilemma here, the principal effect of viewing the Constitution as "democratic" is to deflect attention away from issues of republican constitutional structures, and onto issues of "participation," which is the paramount democratic value. This unresolved tension is taken up in Chapter 3, among others.

The third misperception required in order to nurture executive war-making is to limit the discussion to the two hundred years of American history. The principal disadvantage of this shortsighted misperception is the way in which it directs attention away from issues concerning the republican structures of *deciding* and *declaring* war to irrelevant issues about "checks and balances" and "the separation of powers." Indeed, after more than two hundred years of back and forth, Institutionalists like Terry Moe and William Howell make much more sense, "The actual powers of the three branches, then, both in an absolute sense and relative to one another, cannot be determined from the Constitution alone. They must, of necessity, be determined in the ongoing practice of politics" (1999, 853).

Still, framing the dispute in terms of Hamiltonian "inherent executive" powers versus Madisonian "inherent legislative" powers is not without great polemical value. In particular, this framing of the dispute is very helpful in misperceiving the Constitution as "democratic," and not as "republican." Arguing about "inherent" powers and the dynamics of the system of "checks and balances" implicates "democratic" values by equating "participation" with "the ongoing practice of politics." Such debates imply that the principal desideratum of a well-functioning government and constitution is the "participation" of the two political branches in all decision-making, including the *deciding* and *declaring* of war, as the 1973 *War Powers Resolution* suggests. In an attempt to restore a modicum of "republican" perspective, Chapters 2 and 3, reach back five thousand years for insight and information. Beginning with the Sumerian epic *Agga and Gilgamesh*, the customs, laws, and practices that have governed the *deciding* and *declaring* of war over the millennia are sought out and analyzed.

4 Definitional Issues: a Lexical vs. a Performative Definition

The critical definitional issue for nurturing an hereditary or elected war leader who commands a standing army is to define the key terms, "to declare" and "declaration." For those who prefer an inadequate "original understanding" of the constitutional terms, one must cite Samuel Johnson's 1775 *Dictionary of the English Language*:

To Declare. *v. a.* 1. To clear, to free from obscurity. 3. To publish; to proclaim.

To Declare. *v. n.* To make a declaration; to proclaim some resolution or opinion, some favour or opposition.

Declaration: 1. A proclamation or affirmation; oral expression; publication" (*s.v.* 1775. *Cf.* Yoo, 2005, 145).

For those who are less fastidious about an "original understanding" of the terms, one might cite the *New Oxford American Dictionary*:

declare, verb, 1 [reporting verb] say something in a solemn and emphatic manner: {a} [with obj.] formally announce the beginning of (a state or condition).

declaration, noun, a formal or explicit statement or announcement: *they issued a declaration at the close of the talks | declarations of love.* {1.} the formal announcement of the beginning of a state or condition: *the declaration of war | a declaration of independence.* (*s.v.* 2010).

The inadequacy of both lexical definitions is not that they are false or confusing in some sense. Not at all. Indeed, they are good and true definitions of the two lexical items. If one's objective is simply to understand the two lexical items, then either the "original understanding" or the modern variation is more than adequate. However, the constitutional issue is *not* simply about understanding the two lexical items "to declare" and "declaration." Rather, the constitutional issue is to understand the *exercise* of "the power. ... to declare war." How, in point of fact, does one *exercise* this power?

In order to answer this question, one must understand that Article I, Section 8, Clause 11, does not *just* say that "The Congress shall. ... declare war." Simply meeting the lexical criteria of the dictionary definitions is clearly inadequate. To be sure, as already noted, the Congress has met this minimal, lexical criteria in a manner of speaking on four occasions—in 1812, 1898, 1917, and 1941—as can be read in Appendix A and as is analyzed in the next section of this chapter. Fortunately or unfortunately, the *exercise* of "the power. ... to declare war," requires very much more than simply making "a formal or explicit statement or announcement." But what more?

4.1 *War as a Performative Speech Act*

The following chapters of this book attempt to give a full answer to the question. Briefly, however, in order to move beyond the lexical definitions, the first step is to recognize and acknowledge that one cannot make a "declaration" in due form about nothing. Something has to be said. What?

In response, the *text* or *content* of the "declaration" must "proclaim some resolution or opinion, some favour or opposition." Further, the public announcement must "formally announce the beginning of (a state or condition)." For a disaster declaration, the *text* or *content* of the "declaration" must be "a formal announcement of the beginning" of the moral state and the material condition of a "disaster," as is discussed more fully in Chapter 4. For a "declaration of war," the *text* or *content* of the "declaration" must be "a formal announcement of the beginning" of the moral state and the material condition of a war. And, so on for other types of "declarations."

But to say this much is only to meet the standards of a lexical definition. The lexical standard, however, is clearly inadequate because "moral states and the material conditions" are not *powers*. Rather, they are the consequences of the *exercise* of a *power*. Critically and crucially, then, simply meeting the lexical definition of either the noun, "declaration," or of the verb, "to declare war," is entirely inadequate. Where, after all, is "the *power*. ... to declare war" be found?

The performative definition of an *exercise* of "the *power*. ... to declare war" is found in the structure of a declarative speech act itself. It culminates in what John Austin called the "transmissible authorities" of the "total speech situations" (1979, 100; 1975, 52). Hence, "the *power*. ... to declare war" is found in the four different procedures outlined above by means of which a declarative speech act may be uttered. To flesh out these "power" generating procedures, reconsider two of the four scenarios in greater detail:

Scenario 3: An Unsolemn Functionally Equivalent Declarative Act by the Nation's Hereditary or Elected King that Involves a Legislature:
- At (t^1), a nation's war leader *intends/decides* to go to war on his personal authority. He, therewith, creates the moral or immoral *intention* of the declarative speech act, its illocutionary force.
- At (t^2), a nation's war leader *orders* the *drafting* of a secret operational plan for the war by his staff. This *order* to draft is his initial locutionary act.
- At (t^3), a politically astute war leader *orders* the *drafting* of the text of a resolution of "authorization," "approval," or general "support" and presents it to his legislative assembly.
- At (t^4), the legislative assembly *votes* to ratify the resolution of "authorization," "approval," or general "support."
- At (t^5), the staff of a nation's war leader *drafts* the text of a public address *announcing* the execution of his secret military *order*.

At (t^6), a nation's war leader *announces*, publicly, the execution of his secret military *order*, most recently in a televised address. This public announcement is his second locutionary act.

The combination of the *public announcement* and the *military order* constitute a procedurally imperfect, unsolemn functionally equivalent locutionary act.

In greater detail, this procedurally imperfect, unsolemn functionally equivalent locutionary act:

1) *communicates* to the world the moral or immoral *intentions* that are said by the war leader to justify the resort to war and, simultaneously,
2) also *transmits* to military and civilian officials:
    a) a statement of the political objectives/*intentions* of the war and,
    b) the war leader's personal *authority* to do and accomplish that which was articulated in the text of military *order* and/or the *public announcement*.

(See Appendix B: British Declaration of War against France, 7 May 1689.)

⁝

Scenario 4: A Solemn Collective Declaration in due form:

At (t^1), a competent and legitimate purpose-built, collective decision-making body debates and amends a *draft* text of a declaration of war, the locution.

At (t^2), the competent and legitimate purpose-built, collective decision-making body simultaneously *intends, decides,* and *declares* war with a vote on the *draft* text. This simultaneous *intention, decision* and *declaration* constitutes a procedurally perfect, solemn declarative speech act. In greater detail:

1) If passed, the content of the text of this "clearly" articulated and solemn locutionary act generates or creates the moral or immoral *intention* of the declarative speech act, its illocutionary force.
2) If passed, the illocutionary force of the procedurally perfect, solemn locution, i.e., the declarative speech act, simultaneously:
    a) *communicates* to the world the moral or immoral *intentions* that are said to justify the resort to war and, and
    b) also *transmits* to military and civilian officials:
        i) a "clearly" articulated statement of the political objectives/*intentions* of the war and, simultaneously,
        ii) the collective *authorities* of "the good People of these Colonies" to do and accomplish that which was articulated in the content of the text.

At (t^3), the commander of the nation's armed forces is therewith morally and legally authorized and empowered to oversee the execution of the military means to achieve the *declared* political objectives of the war.

This moral and legal empowerment is analogous to the manner in which a chief executive officer is morally and legally authorized and empowered to oversee the execution of the political objectives of domestic legislation. (See the schematic in Chapter 8 and Appendix A: *The Declaration of Independence.*)

In sum, beyond Samuel Johnson's lexical definitions of the key terms, the raw "power. ... to declare war" may be *exercised* in two different ways. The fundamental difference between the two ways is the location of the initial moral act that creates the speaker's *intention/decision* to do something. And, then, once created, this moral act then drives or propels the illocutionary force of the speech act.

Thus, whensoever the illocutionary act occurs as part of the (t^1) mental act of an individual commander-in-chief, this moral act of *intention/decision* brings into existence an *exercise* of "the power. ... to declare war" by means of a procedurally imperfect, unsolemn, functionally equivalent speech act of one sort or another. Significantly, when uttered in this procedurally imperfect manner, the unsolemn functionally equivalent speech act does not conform to the moral, empirical, or temporal logic of the act of declaring war.

Inversely, whensoever the illocutionary act occurs as part of the (t^2) vote in a purpose-built, collective decision-making assembly, this moral act of *intention/ decision/ declaration* brings into existence an *exercise* of "the power. ... to declare war" by means of a solemn declarative speech act. Significantly, when uttered in this collective manner, this solemn declarative act does conform to the moral, empirical, and temporal logic of the act of declaring war. In short, both speakers possess "the [empirical] *power.* ... to declare war." But the one does so in violation of the moral, empirical, and temporal logic of declarative speech act, whereas the other does so in conformity to that logic.

Troublesomely, the illogical way is the historical norm, while the logical way is the exceptional aberration. Even more troublesomely is that a nagging moral intuition suggests that only the aberrant collective declarative act is the truly legitimate way to *exercise* "the power. ... to declare war." The next section is a brief an attempt to understand the historical strength of the "norm." Chapter 3 takes up the discussion in greater detail.

5   The Four and a Half Lexical Declarations of War in American History

The incapacity of all legislative assemblies to *exercise* "the *power.* ... to declare war" makes executive war-making inevitable. This incapacity is the nettle that

Arthur Schlesinger and many others have failed to grasp. Fortunately, the lexical and performative definitions can be put to work grasping the nettle. As an example of this, the four and a half lexical declarations of war in American history provide concrete instances. They represent two specific data points. First, they clarify the difference between the lexical and performative definitions of war. Second, they identify the multiple opportunities for a war leader to manipulate a legislative assembly.

But before doing that, however, one needs to do the math. All toll, one may generously say that the United States Congress has declared war twelve times, which is rather fewer than the total number of wars fought by the United States, however one might count the wars. For example, the Civil War was declared by the Confederate Congress, but not by the United States Congress. As can be read in Appendix A, the twelve lexical declarations are distributed over four wars:

One absolute declaration against Great Britain for the War of 1812.

An appropriations act for the Mexican-American War, 1846.

Two declarations for the Spanish-American War, 1898, one conditional and one absolute declaration.

Two absolute declarations for World War I, one against Imperial Germany and one against the Imperial and Royal Austro-Hungarian Government.

Six absolute declarations for World War II:

   one against the Imperial Government of Japan,

   one against the Government of Germany,

   one against the Government of Italy,

   one against the Government of Bulgaria,

   one against the Government of Hungary, and

   one against the Government of Rumania.

As will be discussed in a moment, the fact that the Fifty-fifth Congress declared war both conditionally and absolutely is of considerable interest. Still, this means that only one Congress has done so, and only for one war. Also of interest is the fact that, for World Wars I and II, the Sixty-fifth and Seventy-seventh Congresses declared war lexically multiple times. Still, these multiple lexical declarations were for only one war each. Subtracting the redundant declarations, one is left with basically five American wars for which the nation's war leader employed *Scenario 3*. But that brings one to the wondrous 0.5 "declaration" of 1846. Owing to the fact that this "declaration" is actually an appropriations act, the five is reduce to four and one half. Consider the 0.5 "declaration" first, before the other four.

An Act providing for the Prosecution of the existing War between the United States and the Republic of Mexico of 1846 is a marvel. Indeed, even its title betrays its fraudulence. Instead of "formally announc[ing] the beginning of (a state or condition)," as the *New Oxford American Dictionary* says it should, the act "provides for the prosecution of an existing war," a war that already exists, but, apparently, was never declared. Despite this, the 1846 act is usually included in lists of congressional declarations of war. However, this is over generous to a fault. Yes, it is a "declaration" of war in the sense that it is functionally equivalent declarative act, but, actually, it is an appropriations act, as can be read. It is of a kind with the war taxes that his Four Estates voted Charles V in 1369. Because of this, the best one can say is that the 1846 act counts as not more than half of a declaration.

More specifically, the act was a mundane appropriation's bill for the raising of volunteers. It was languishing in the Twenty-ninth Congress at the behest of President James Polk and the more hawkish members, until May, when President Polk made the sensational announcement that the Mexicans had attacked General Zachary Taylor on the Texas border. Later, the truth came out that Mexicans had not attacked General Taylor. Rather, General Taylor had attacked the Mexicans. However, the truth was not known in May of 1846. The 1846 act is, therefore, a Gulf of Tokin Resolution a hundred years before that infamous congressional enactment. Less than accurate information, however, panics the Congress as effectively as accurate information. Consequently, a panicky Twenty-ninth Congress quickly added a new preamble and a new purpose to the appropriations bill. Its passage made President Polk, if not an Imperial President, at least a president waging an imperial war of conquest.

If that explains the 0.5, what is one to make of the remaining four congressional enactments? To make sense of them, one must evaluate them under three different main heads:

1) Is the text absolute or conditional?
2) Is the text reasoned or unreasoned?
3) And, of the greatest importance, is the United States Congress a purpose-built body that possesses the capacity to *exercise* the "power. ... to declare war," as was the Second Continental Congress? Or, was the United States Congress purpose-built body to serve other, law-making, functions? Consequently, does the United States Congress possess the organizational capacity of the Second Continental Congress or does it not?

5.1 *Absolute vs. Conditional Declarations of War*

Most conveniently for executive war-making, absolute declarations of war do not require either reasons or justifications. At the point in a dispute when war is declared absolutely, reasoning has been exhausted during the negotiations and, hence, can too easily be ignored as merely repetitious. However, conditional declarations are necessarily uttered before this point of last resort is reached. As a result, reasons or "conditions" must be articulated in any conditional text. A conditional declaration of war without conditions is a contradiction in terms.

By happenstance, the only conditional declaration in congressional history is the *House Resolution 233 of 18 April 1898* for the Spanish-American War, which the Senate gutted and replaced with *Senate Amendment of House Resolution 233 of 20 April 1898*. The House acceded to the Senate's gutting of its text, and, thus, after approval by President William McKinley, the Senate draft became the operational text. Both resolutions can be read in Appendix A. The conditional clause in the operative section of the Senate Act is the second clause. The third clause is the authorizing clause:

> Second. That it is the duty of the United States to demand, and the Government of the United States does hereby demand, that the Government of Spain at once relinquish its authority and government in the Island of Cuba, and withdraw its land and naval forces from Cuba and Cuban waters.
>
> Third. That the President of the United States be, and he hereby is, directed and empowered to use the entire land and naval forces of the United States, and to call into the actual service of the United States the militia of the several States to such extent as may be necessary to carry these resolutions into effect.

The importance of the "demand" is its conditional quality. Absolute war will not occur, if Spain agreed to the "conditions" stipulated in the second clause. Namely, had "the Government of Spain at once relinquish[ed] its authority and government in the Island of Cuba, and withdraw its land and naval forces from Cuba and Cuban waters," an absolute war would not have commenced.

When Spain did not agree to the "conditions," President McKinley ordered the State Department to draft an absolute declaration, which the Fifty-fifth Congress passed on 25 April 1898. As expected, the absolute declaration complies with the lexical definition for a declaration of war. It "formally announce[s] the beginning of (the state or condition)" of war: "That war be, and the same is hereby, declared to exist, and that war has existed since the twenty-first day of April, anno Domini eighteen hundred and ninety-eight, including said day, between the United States of America and the Kingdom of Spain. ... "

The importance to this exceptional 1898 sequence of a conditional declaration followed by an absolute declaration is that it exemplifies two long neglected aspects of the *deciding* and *declaring* of war. First, it exemplifies the not unimportant fact that declarations of war come it two different degrees or types—conditional and absolute. This aspect is taken up in Chapter 4 when the codification of the laws and customs of war under Hague Convention III of 1907, *Relative to the Opening of Hostilities* is discussed. Second, it exemplifies the conflict resolution potential of the declaring of war, when the traditional laws and customs of war are followed. This conflict resolution potential is addressed in Chapter 5.

5.2   *Reasoned vs. Unreasoned Declarations of War*

The *Declaration of Independence* and the two versions of the conditional declaration of 1898 are the only reasoned declarations in American history. The others are all unreasoned, in addition to being absolute and lexical. The main difference, to repeat, is that the three reasoned declarations of war state reasons that are believed to justify the resort to war. To do this, they not only indict the gravamina, but also articulate the peace terms/war aims, therewith articulating the "reasons" that are said to justify the *decision* to go to war. Inversely, all of the absolute and lexical congressional declarations are unreasoned. Since unreasoned declarations give no reasons, one is forced to conclude that, officially, the war is waged for no reason at all. This conclusion, need it be said, is to the enduring benefit of executive war-making. The war leader *decides*. He drafts the text. And, the Congress declares, as any good Town Crier would.

The contrast between reasoned and unreasoned declarative acts, therefore, is significant. For example, in order to know the official reasons and justification for the American Revolution, one has only to read the text of the *Declaration of Independence*. This is possible because the text of the *Declaration of Independence* is fully reasoned and justified. In order to learn of the official reasons and justifications for any of the many American wars since 1776, one must read a variety of functionally equivalent presidential statements, addresses, press conferences, and the like. All one will ever learn from the unreasoned congressional declarations is that the nation's war leader was astute and employed *Scenario 3* and the Congress faithfully passed his draft expeditiously.

The crucial point here is that the unreasoned quality of the absolute, lexical declarations testifies to the fact that the respective congresses did not declare war in any meaningful sense. This is the case because they had no direct, institutional role in either the *intention/decision* or the *drafting*. Their only institutional function was to *declare*. But, of course, the three declarative specifications are not of either equal moral or equal political weight. He who answers the question of war or peace and drafts the text controls the process, not the

Town Crier. Hence, one must conclude that the respective congresses did not *exercise* the "power. ... to declare war" in any meaningful sense.

To drive home the critical importance of a reasoned text, reconsider next the three declarations of war, which are reasoned texts: In accordance with the ancient laws and customs of war, the Second Continental Congress and the Fifty-fifth Congress drafted texts that gave an explanation of and a justification for declaring war against Great Britain and Spain, respectively. The Second Continental Congress did this in an absolute declaration. The House of Representatives and the Senate in the Fifty-fifth Congress did so in two very different drafts of a conditional declaration. The differences between the two drafts are that the House draft was reasoned, if not fully so, whereas the Senate version was a masterpiece of political rhetoric in the worst possible sense owing to the fact that it was a travesty of logic and reason. Nonetheless, all three texts 1) indicted the gravamina that constituted the *casus belli*, 2) denounced both the gravamina and those responsible for them, and, 3) declared the nation's peace terms/war aims. In addition, because it was an absolute declaration, the 1776 declaration also 4) declared war. In this manner, all three articulated a just cause, right intention, and last resort criteria (Hallett 1998, 53). An outline of the just-war criteria, reinterpreted as the just-interaction criteria, is found in Appendix F.

Thus, the Fifty-fifth Congress did meet the formal requirements for a reasoned conditional declaration of war. However, it was unable to do so without playing political games (Hallett 2012, Ch 3). For, the final Senate version of the 1898 conditional text was reasoned in form, but not in substance. Indeed, to repeat, its substance is a travesty. The extent of the perversion can be gaged by comparing the final Senate text with the House draft, and the House draft with the *Declaration of Independence*. The House draft cannot really be compared with the *Declaration of Independence*. It lacks the elegance and fullness of explanation of the 1776 text, but it is still of some substance. In particular, "the death by starvation of more than 200,000 innocent noncombatants" is a significant indictment of how Spain had conducted its war in Cuba. It points to a humanitarian *casus belli* of a not negligible importance.

But whatever the shortcomings of the House draft, it is a stunningly persuasive document when compared to the Senate text. To begin with, the Senate's indictment is bombastic. The overwrought indictment, however, is the Senate's lesser sin. The unforgiveable travesty is located in the first operational clause, "That the people of the Island of Cuba are, and of right ought to be free and independent." As was pointed out by Senator George F. Hoar, Republican from Massachusetts, the clause "contains an affirmation contrary to the fact when it affirms that the Republic of Cuba is now free and independent ..." (*Cong.*

Rec.: 1898, 3992). In other words, if "the people of the Island of Cuba" not only "ought to be free and independent," but "are" actually free and independent, then the purpose of the war has already been achieved. What, then, is the purpose of waging a war to accomplish a purpose that has already been achieved?

In sum, the incapacity of the Congress to *exercise* its constitutional power to *decide* and "to declare war" is complete. When faced with the option of choosing between a less than elegant, but still plausible text, and a counterfactual, illogical perversion of a text, the choice is not in doubt.

5.3   *The Organizational Capacity and Incapacity for Declaring War*

The capacity to *exercise* "the power ... to declare war" is not a problem for monarchs. By ancient custom and divine right, if not raw power, their royal prerogative makes of them the one and only speaker entitled to *intend/decide*, *draft*, and *declare* the commencement of the moral state and material condition of war. Conversely, the capacity of decision-making assemblies is very much problematic. Beyond collective action problems, as already noted, the problem has two aspects: The fact that no viable models exist and the fact that different organizational structures are required to accomplish different functions.

To repeat and re-emphasize, no modern parliament possesses the capacity to *exercise* "the power ... to declare war" on its own *initiative*. Yet, neither the kingless Roman Republic nor the kingless Athenian democracy is a suitable model upon which to organize a large, complex modern society with a chief executive who commands a standing army, an elected constitutional monarchy. The only other examples of kingless political structures are revolutionary assemblies. But, again, a revolutionary assemble is not a viable model for a large, complex modern society.

Be the deficiencies of revolutionary assemblies as it may, no one will deny that different organizational structures are required to accomplish different functions. Consequently, much can be learned from the organizational structures of revolutionary assemblies, most especially from the Second Continental Congress. More precisely, one can compare the organizational structures of the Congress with the organizational structures of the Second Continental Congress:

1) The enactment of the fully reasoned *Declaration of Independence* was performed by a small, *monofunction*, majority-rule, unicameral assembly operating under committee-of-the-whole rules.

    In terms of size, the Second Continental Congress consisted of fifty-five delegates, not all of whom were present at any given moment.

    In terms of function, the Second Continental Congress was responsible for all of the foreign affairs and virtually none of their domestic affairs of the thirteen colonies, soon to be states, including the declaring of war.

2) The enactment of the unreasoned congressional declarations was performed by a large, *bifunction*, majority-rule, bicameral assembly operating under standing-committee rules.

In terms of size, the Congress of the United States has ranged from one hundred and seventy-six members in 1812 to five hundred and thirty-five in 1941.

In terms of functions, the Congress of the United States is responsible for all of the domestic affairs and several, but not all, of the nation's foreign affairs.

Not incidentally, the Congress of the United States does not function in a "kingless" political system. Rather, it functions in a system with an elected constitutional monarch in all but name. As a result, the president/commander-in-chief is widely recognized to possess "the constitutional authority to conduct U.S. foreign relations and as Commander in Chief and Chief Executive," in the words of the *War Powers Resolution* of 1973.

As is discussed in Chapters 2 and 3, but principally in Chapter 6, the Second Continental Congress performed all three declarative specifications of *Scenario 4*. It *decided* the question of war or peace on its own initiative, and it drafted, amended, and voted on the text of the declaration on its own initiative. It also published and declared war on its own initiative. Conversely, the United States Congress has never *decided* the question of war and peace on its own initiative and has drafted only the conditional declaration of 1898 on its own initiative. However, the 1898 travesty is better seen as a display of congressional incapacity, than of congressional capacity.

To re-emphasize the obvious, then, the well-known reasons for the capacity of the Second Continental Congress and the incapacity of the United States Congress can be summarized as:

1) In a small, *monofunction*, majority-rule, unicameral, assembly operating under committee-of-the-whole rules:
   a) collective action problems are tractable;
   b) dysfunction caused by inappropriate, additional functions do not exist, and
   c) information asymmetries do not exist.
2) Conversely, in a large, *bifunction*, majority-rule, bicameral assembly operating under standing-committee rules:
   a) collective action problems are all but intractable;

b) dysfunction caused by inappropriate, additional functions paralyzes, and

c) information asymmetries with executive offices are overwhelming.

In conclusion, because of its unmanageable size and multiple functions, legislative assemblies, such as the United States Congress, possess only the capacity to meet the lexical definition of "to declare war," and this if and only if the nation's war leader provides the required leadership and agenda setting, as is discussed throughout, but mainly in Chapter 3.

CHAPTER 2

Executive War Making from George H. W. Bush to Gilgamesh

Invariant State Practice

Abstract

An historical account of executive war-making and the rise of elected constitutional monarchies is used to distinguish democratic politics from republican constitutions. The account moves from the ancient concepts of power and majesty to the medieval concept of sovereignty. Jean Bodin, John Locke, and Montesquieu's confusion over the functional analysis of "sovereignty" is then leveraged to explain, in part, the incapacity of legislatures to *decide* and *declare* war.

Winston Churchill and Franklin D. Roosevelt are positive examples of modern, elected war leaders. The list of negative examples is very much longer. Still, why are the modern president, prime minister, or chancellor still revered as the nation's war leader? Why is the modern chief executive officer still responsible for making foreign policy and war, as kings have always done? Strange is it not?

Even stranger, why does a lopsided asymmetry exist between foreign and domestic affairs? In domestic affairs, a legislature possessed of the "power of the purse" makes policy, while the president, prime minister, or chancellor executes the policies so made. This is precisely what the term, executive, implies. But in foreign affairs the case is different. The modern president, prime minister, or chancellor not only executes foreign policy; he makes it as well. He functions basically as an elected constitutional monarch, restrained by a legislature in domestic affairs, virtually unrestrained in the conduct of foreign affairs, including war. To respond to questions such as these, one must begin at the end of the story, before turning to the beginning.

1   An Elected Constitutional Monarch

In the afterglow of his liberation of Kuwait from Saddam Hussein, President George H. W. Bush was invited by Princeton University to preside over the dedication of its new Social Science Building. The ceremony took place on Friday, 10 May 1991, at 11:45am, during which time President Bush took the opportunity to explain his understanding of how the war powers of the Congress and the presidency were separated and how this system of separated powers checked and balanced each other:

> This does not mean that the executive may conduct foreign business in a vacuum. I have the greatest respect for Congress and I prefer to work cooperatively with it wherever possible. Though I felt after studying the question that I had the inherent power to commit our armed forces to battle [in Kuwait] after the U.N. resolution, I solicited congressional support before committing our forces to the Gulf war. So while a President bears special foreign policy obligations, those obligations do not imply any liberty to keep Congress unnecessarily in the dark.
> BUSH 1992, 497. See also *ibid.*, 19–20

Basically, President Bush's view is that no separation of war powers exists between the presidency and the Congress because the Congress has no war powers. Critically, President Bush did not come this view casually. Only after much "study," did he conclude 1) that the president as commander-in-chief possesses the "inherent power to commit our armed forces to battle," as kings and emperors have always done, and 2) that the only relevant congressional roles are a) to work cooperatively with the president and b) to support our troops before they enter battle.

But, if no separation of powers exists in this constitutional domain, then no system of checks and balance exists in this domain, either. Neither cooperation with the president nor support of the troops counts as a check to balance the president's "inherent power to commit our armed forces to battle." Curiously, though, the U. N. Security Council does have the power to authorize an American president to go to war to liberate another country. In June 1950, this "authorizing" power was first used by President Harry Truman to liberate South Korea.

As an expression of congressional "cooperation," President Bush, of course, welcomed the congressional *Authorization for Use of Military Force Against Iraq Resolution of 14 January 1991* (Pub. L. No. 102-1. 105 Stat. 3). Still, the congressional gesture was really unnecessary. After all, the president's "inherent" powers had already been "*authorized*" by Security Council *Resolution 678 of 29 November 1990*. In sum, the proper place for the United States Congress in both foreign affairs and war is on the sidelines, where it is to be kept *not* "unnecessarily in the dark."

While President George H. W. Bush has stated the matter much more baldly than other presidents, it is not difficult to imagine that every president since George Washington would agree with him. The only difference other presidents might add is to remark how reckless and politically incorrect was President Bush's statement. For example, President Woodrow Wilson was much more circumspect and diplomatic in his Monday, 26 February 1917 address to the Sixty-fourth Congress requesting authority to arm American merchant ships, "No doubt I already possess that authority [for "armed neutrality"] without special warrant of law, by the plain implication of my constitutional duties and powers; but I prefer, in the current circumstances, not to act upon implications" (Wilson 1917). Charles V, the Wise, would concur.

In sum, the distillation of over two hundred years of American history yields a superficial contradiction. On the one hand, one sees the repeated exercise of the very real "inherent powers" of the presidency in foreign affairs and war; while, on the other hand, one hears the evergreen, aspirational words of the Constitution. Yes, of course, Article I, Section 8, Clause 11 of the Constitution implies that the Congress possesses the power "to declare war." Yet, the reality is otherwise. The invariant pattern is of presidential war making, accompanied by assiduous efforts not "to keep Congress unnecessarily in the dark." This invariant pattern, as John Yoo (2005) has, in effect, argued, transforms an otherwise republican constitution into a constitutional monarchy. Not a hereditary constitutional monarchy as in Britain, but an elected, constitutional monarchy (Nelson, 2014). Still, of very much greater interest is the fact that this pattern of "inherent" executive war power is not just invariant during the brief two hundred and thirty years of American history. The invariance stretches back at least five thousand years to where the story begins.

2 An Invariant State Practice

For over five thousand years, foreign affairs, in general, and the question of war or peace, in particular, have always and everywhere been determined by the nation's war leader on his own "inherent power." Of course, the war leader's "inherent power" does not mean that he acts entirely alone. He almost always seeks cooperation and support from his council or councils, which he seldom keeps "unnecessarily in the dark." This has been the case since at least the time of the five-thousand-year-old Sumerian epic, *Agga and Gilgamesh* (Pritchard 1955, 44–7). Interestingly, this epic contains the earliest recorded declaration of war.

The epic begins with the arrival of heralds from Agga of Kish with an official, open and determined, conditional, procedurally perfect declaration of war. Gilgamesh, as the nation's war leader, seeks first the cooperation and support of his council of elders. His initial attempt with this council is unsuccessful. Desiring peace, it resolves to " ... submit to the house of Kish, let us not smite it with weapons" (l. 14). Rebuffed, Gilgamesh goes next to the council of "men," probably meaning "young or armed men," which is more receptive. After a second debate in that council, Gilgamesh secures its support and cooperation, "Do not submit to the house of Kish, let us smite it with weapons" (l. 29). The heralds of Kish having returned with this defiant and absolute, procedurally perfect declaration from Gilgamesh, "Agga, son of Enmebaraggesi besieged Erech" shortly thereafter (l. 49). The epic ends, naturally enough, with a celebration of Gilgamesh's victory over Agga.

Note, first off, that the epic is also a classic case of a war leader "venue shopping," consulting with one council after another other until he finds a cooperative council. As already noted, President Harry Truman revived the tactic in 1950 for the Korean War. Anticipating trouble with the Eighty-first Congress, President Truman went instead to the new United Nations Security Council to obtain a functionally equivalent declaration of war, a Security Council "authorization," in this case. Several presidents, including George H. W. Bush, have used the tactic since.

To the surprise of no one, kings, emperors, presidents, prime ministers, and chancellors—the war leaders of the nations of the world—have seldom deviated from Gilgamesh's example. All war leaders know that they possess the "inherent power to commit our armed forces to battle," but astute war leaders also know that going to war without the cooperation and support of their councils needlessly increases the risk of failure. For astute war leaders, therefore, not keeping their councils "unnecessarily in the dark" is a rule not to be violated. Hence, whether the realm is a minor kingdom or a major empire, whether in China, India, the Americas, or somewhere in between, all war leaders have followed Gilgamesh's example. In abbreviated form, they first *decide* the question of war or peace. Second, they "consult" with their council or councils to ensure cooperation and support by not keeping them "unnecessarily in the dark." And, lastly, they obtain some form of "approval," "authorization," or budgetary support from their council or councils. After that, the war leader himself may or may not declare war solemnly. Agga and Gilgamesh both chose to declare war solemnly, but many war leaders, as for example George H. W. Bush, do not.

Such is the invariant state practice of the millennia. To imagine that American war leaders would act any differently is to gainsay the force of five thousand years of history and the experience of all the cultures and nations of the world.

As a result, what Arthur Schlesinger mistakenly called *The Imperial Presidency* in 1973 is in truth only business as usual, when viewed from the standpoint of world history. For over five thousand years, the invariant pattern of monarchial rule of foreign affairs, if not domestic affairs, has been all but universal. The two hundred years of American history provide no exception to this invariant pattern of state practice. The Imperial Presidency is, therefore, not an anomaly. Rather, the stunning and startlingly anomaly would be a congressional capacity to *decide* and *declare* war.

What needs to be explained, then, is not the reality of executive war making. What needs be explained is the origins of the bizarre notion that a legislative assembly could usurp the "inherent power" of the nation's war leader to go to war. To explain this, one must undertake two separate, but related tasks. First, one must come to terms with the legislative "power of the purse" and the rise of modern, elected constitutional monarchies. Second, one must come to terms with the confused and confusing concept of "sovereignty." More precisely, one must come to terms with the internal origins of sovereignty as a mode of functional analysis of the constitution of government. Once sovereignty has been established internally, it has various external or international affects and effects. But these international affects and effects are of no interest here. The only concern here is for the internal origins of sovereignty and the functional analysis that falls out of the establishment of a sovereign within a nation-state.

3   Explaining the Rise of Elected Constitutional Monarchies: the "Power of the Purse"

The reality of the nation's war leader conducting foreign affairs, including war, is and has always been recognized universally. Critically, the existence of a legislature possessed of the "power of the purse" is a recent West European invention. The point, of course, is that a legislature with the "power of the purse" is the defining difference between true monarchies and constitutional monarchies. In true monarchies or dictatorships, any legislature that might exist is no more than a rubber stamp. All powers belong to the monarch or dictator. The simplicity and elegance of this all-encompassing unity of power in the hands of one person is, of course, the main reason most nations across the world for most of the last five thousand years have been ruled as true monarchies or dictatorships.

In a very dissimilar manner, constitutional monarchies lack the elegant unity of true monarchies principally because a legislature exists that *exercises* the "power of the purse." This separation of power affords the legislature considerable leverage to determine and direct the domestic affairs of the realm. Since most people are most interested in domestic affairs most of the time, the constitutional monarch's subjects have always been content to leave the conduct of foreign affairs, including war, in the capable hands of the nation's war leader—its king, emperor, president, prime minister, or chancellor. But, if the "power of the purse" is the defining difference, how did this deviation from the simplicity and elegance of a true monarchy arise?

As is well known, the seeds of constitutional monarchies were planted in Western Europe after the fall of Rome. The Germanic tribes that filled the vacuum left by Imperial Rome bought with them a surprising system that made their war leaders into non-absolute, often elected kings. The prime example of this occurred on Monday, 15 June 1215, on the field at Runnymede. On that day, the hereditary King John of England was forced by his bishops and barons to sign the *Magna Carta*. Among its many other provisions, Clauses 12 and 14 reiterated that only with the consent of the common counsel of the realm could taxes be levied and assessed.

This early thirteenth century "common counsel of the realm" was not yet a full parliament nor a modern representative assembly, but it was a good start. Good enough so that, four hundred years later, in 1641, during the English Civil War, Parliament could defend its refusal of supply to Charles I for his Scottish war by observing "how many of our parliament rolls do record that the king advised with his parliament about his foreign wars, and could not undertake them without the advice and supplies of the parliament." Indeed, between 1323 and 1639, "the king advised with his parliament" for every significant war, save one. On that occasion, he had promised to go without a new subsidy during the coming year (Joseph 2013, 96–7).

Ironically, then, the key to the evolving power of a common council of the realm over domestic affairs was the king's preoccupation with foreign affairs and war. Funding foreign wars usually required domestic taxes, which only the common council could provide. The salient contrast in this regard is Philip II Augustus' defeat of the combined forces of England, Flanders, and the Holy Roman Empire during the summer of 1214. Phillip II, unlike King John, was not constrained by a deficiency of personal resources. He did not need new taxes to support his wars. His immediate military entourage included 250 knights, an equal number of horse sergeants, almost 100 mounted crossbowmen, 133 foot crossbowmen, 2,000 foot sergeants and 300 mercenaries. This was a significant force, especially, when supplemented by the levees of his loyal bishops and barons (Bradbury 1998, 252). As a result, Philip II Augustus was able to meet the two-pronged invasion by King John of England and the combined force of the Holy Roman Emperor, Otto VI, and the Ferdinand, Count of Flanders, from his own resources. Dividing his forces, Prince Louis defeated King John's army at Roche-au-Moine on Wednesday, 2 July 1214, while, farther north toward the River Lys just south of Lille, Phillip caught up with Otto IV and Ferdinand on Sunday, 27 July 1214 at the bridge at Bouvines. There, he defeated Otto and Ferdinand in a rout that is one of the decisive battles in the history of the construction of the French state. It is also one of the decisive battles of English history. His defeat at Roche-au-Moine not only destroyed King John's plans to increase his French possessions, but further antagonized his bishops and barons, who, in the next year, demanded he sign the *Magna Carta*.

In sum, over succeeding centuries, war and the limits of the king's personal resources to wage war were the ironic axis upon which the common council of England leveraged its "power of the purse" into effective control of domestic affairs. Slowly, then, these constitutional monarchies developed their modern three-branch configuration: 1) An elected legislature that dominates the making of domestic policy because it controls the purse strings. 2) An elected executive with two unbalanced responsibilities: a) the execution of the domestic policies made by the legislative and b), in addition, the conduct of foreign affairs, including war, as the "inherent power" and right of the nation's war leader since the time of Gilgamesh. 3) An appointed judiciary that adjudicates disputes in law.

Yet, the legislature not only had to break the monarch's monopoly on domestic political power in fact, it also had to justify its power conceptually, intellectually. In time, this ideational need led to development of a doctrine of "separation of powers," which, in turn, made possible a doctrine of "checks and balances." Still, the doctrines themselves are only explanations, not justifications. The two doctrines explain the idealized dynamics of the three-branch structure, as illustrated in Figure 1. They answer the question, "How might the structure work, ideally?" Ideally, it works by separating 1) the "power of the purse" from the execution of domestic policy, 2) the power to conduct foreign policy from the power to make domestic policy, and 3) the power to adjudicate domestic causes of action from the first two. Then, once separated, these powers ideally serve to check and balance each other in the conduct of domestic affairs.

FIGURE 1   A system of checks and balances

Explanation, however, is a very weak form of justification. In this regard, "sovereignty" became the critical concept. Neither "sovereignty" nor any other abstract concept is needed to justify true monarchy. True monarchies are justified by raw power, not by abstract conceptions. This, after all, is the meaning of Caesar's crossing of the Rubicon. Power, not rule of law, would henceforth prevail in Rome. Hence, the "inherent power" of the nation's war leader is a full and complete justification for a true monarch, as George H. W. Bush has articulated most clearly. Inversely, though, any form of government that consists of more than one part, requires a conceptual justification. This conceptual justification has been provided by "sovereignty." For, without a concept of "sovereignty," the functional analysis essential to any justification for dividing governing institutions into two, three, four, or more branches is impossible.

4   From Majesty to Sovereignty

As already noted, the constitutions of ancient Greece and Rome cannot and have not served as models for large, modern societies. One of the principal reasons for this is that the Greeks and the Romans lacked any justificatory concept even remotely as powerful as "sovereignty." Instead of sovereignty, the Greeks spoke of *krateisis*, power, and the Romans spoke of *majestas*, majesty. The more interesting and important of the two terms is *majestas*. "*Majestas*" derives from *magnus*, great, and refers to the power, amplitude, and dignity of the Roman Senate and People. The often-told story that captures the meaning of "majesty" tells of Gaius Popillius Laenas, a special Senate legate to Egypt in 168 BCE. At the time, Antiochus IV Epiphanes, the Seleucid emperor, was busy conquering Ptolemaic Egypt, the main supplier of grain to Rome. Instead of sending an army to defend Rome's grain supply, the Senate sent Popillius, who met Antiochus IV outside of Alexandria. Without shaking the Emperor's hand, the story goes, Popillius used his staff to draw a circle in the sand around Antiochus VI. He, then, demanded a firm response to the Senate's demand that Antiochus VI end his conquest of Egypt before the Emperor stepped out of the circle. Recognizing the power and dignity of Rome, her majesty, Antiochius IV immediately affirmed his desire for peace, ended his conquest of Egypt, and returned to Syria (Livy 1919, xlv, 12). Rome's reputation, her majesty, had proven the equal of several legions.

Reputation or majesty, however, is not an analytic concept, not any more than *krateisis*, power. A government may or may not possess these qualities, but neither the constitution nor the structure of a government can be derived from either. Descriptively, majesty was a very useful term; analytically it leads nowhere. In this sense, the ancient Greek and Roman anomalies are just as conceptually barren as all the absolute monarchies of history. Neither regime type provides any useful analytic purchase on the elements of a well-constituted government, especially a republican government.

5 Primus Inter Pars

In search of a way out of this conceptual *cull de sac*, the only other place to look is the non-absolute Germanic monarchs of Western Europe, and the best time to look is at the dawn of the thirteenth century. In the decades surrounding 1200, three consequential events occurred: First, Philip II, Augustus, set in motion what would eventually become the modern French state with his double victories in 1214. Second, King John set in motion what would eventually become modern, constitutional monarchies with his signing of the *Magna Carta* in 1215, from which every modern, non-dictatorial government descended in the fullness of time. And, finally, the dawn of the thirteenth century also saw the birth of a new and conceptually interesting term, *souverain*. In succeeding centuries, this new term would prove critical in justifying and shaping both the modern nation-state and modern constitutional monarchies, both hereditary and elected. Unlike majesty, sovereignty is not a comparative term. Instead, sovereignty exists only internally within the state and is a personification of the rights and powers of the state.

This last point is critical. Before "sovereignty" is able to acquire or express any external qualities or meanings, it must firmly establish itself internally. Incipient and inchoate at first, the term has come to describe and express extremely complex and contested external relations between and among the nation-states of the world. Indeed, in recent centuries, the concept has metastasis to such a degree that our current understanding is well summarized in the subtitle of Stephen Krasner's excellent book, *Sovereignty: Organized Hypocrisy* (1999).

The term's future hypocrisy and misadventures aside, the key to understanding sovereignty is to realize that the word derives from Vulgar Latin, and not classical Latin. It derives from *superanus* and is formed on the classical Latin base *super-*, above. It describes the character or quality of one (a sovereign) who is superior to or above others. The fact that sovereignty comes from vulgar, and not classical, Latin is important because it means that it is not an ancient term with classical roots in Plato, Aristotle, Cicero, or any another of the ancient political philosopher. Rather, it is a new, thirteenth century medieval term to describe, not the king's power or majesty, but an unanticipated, nascent political hierarchy found only in the non-absolute Germanic kingdoms of Western Europe. It arose and could only arise in feudal kingdoms that possessed a common council of the realm exercising the "power of the purse."

As with any new term, *souverain* was a very shaky and unstable concept at first, and for many centuries thereafter. First attested in c.1150 in the *Oxford Psalter*; its second attestation in 1286 illustrates both its political foundation and its initial ambiguity (s.v. *Dictoinnaire de L'Académie Française* 1935–1938). This second attestation is found in Philippe de Beaumanoir's 1286, *Coutumes De Beauvaisis*:

> *1043* Pour ce que nous parlons en cest livre en pluseurs lieus du souverain et de ce qu'il puet et doit fere, li acun pourroient entendre pour ce que nous ne nommons conte ne due, que ce fust du roi; mes en tous les lieus la ou li rois n'est pas nommés, nous entendons de ceus qui tienent en baronie, car chascuns barons est souverains en sa baronie. Voirs est que li rois est souverains par desus tous (p23) et a de son droit la general garde de tout son roiaume, par quoi il puet fere teus establissemens comme il li plest pour le commun pourfit, et ce qu'il establist doit ester tenu. Et si n'i a nul si grant dessous li qui ne puist ester tres en sa court pour defaute de droit ou pour faus jugement et pour tous les cas qui touchent le roi. Et pour ce qu'il est souverains par desseur tous, nous le nommon quant nous parlons d'aucune souraineté qui a li apartient (1899–1900 [1286], t. 2, 1043).
>
> *1043* Because we speak in several places in this book of the sovereign and what he can and should do, some might think that because we do not mention a count or a duke that this is the king; but anywhere we do not mention the king we are referring to those who hold directly from him [*tienent en baronie*], for each baron is sovereign in his barony. It is true that the king is sovereign over all and lawfully has his whole kingdom in his general care; so that he can make what laws for the common good, and what he legislates must be observed. And below him there is none so great that he cannot be haled into the king's court for default of judgment or false judgment, and in any other case where the king's interest is involved. And because he is sovereign over all, we mention him when we are speaking of some sovereignty which belongs to him.
>
> BEAUMANOIR 1992 [1286], 1043

First, one must note that Beaumanoir is not talking about power *per se*. Nor is he talking about majesty. Rather, he is talking about a structure of rights and duties that creates an hierarchy. The king is "above," not because his power radiates majesty, nor because "might makes right," but because he "has his whole kingdom in his general care; so that he can make what laws for the common good." All others are below and must obey his justice and laws. But notice the tension, if not the contradiction: On the one hand, the king is sovereign and above all such that "there is none so great that he cannot be haled into the king's court for default of judgment or false judgment, and in any other case where the king's interest is involved." And yet, on the other hand, the barons are sovereign in their baronies? Is this not the anarchy of *imperia in imperium*? Yes, it is. Consequently, does this "States within the State" anarchy not destroy the very hierarchy that Beaumanoir has just defined? It most certainly does. Yet to say so is only to recognize that the concept is as incipient and inchoate as the emerging nation-states of thirteenth century medieval Europe. If Philip II of France were not truly sovereign, four hundred years later, Louis XIV would be.

But consider again the contradiction between power and right, between the reality of medieval anarchy and Beaumanoir's aspirational hierarchy. Notice how the contradiction opens up a new and differentiated conceptual space. Philip II of France, King John of England, and the other Germanic rulers were clearly not absolute monarchs. They lacked an undisputed power or majesty. They were boxed in from above and below. From above, their power was continually disputed by their barons, who were also "sovereign in their baronies." At the same time, from below, their power was divided such that they were answerable in some measure to a "common counsel of the realm" for domestic affairs, most particularly, for the levying of taxes. Hence, they did not possess the undifferentiated majesty with which the Roman Senate and People described their power. Nor were they true, absolute monarchs who held the mandate of heaven. Instead, the Germanic kings were *primus inter pars*, the first among the nation's several warlords.

The upshot was that the claim of sovereign rights and duties clashed annually with the reality of baronial power in medieval Europe. Neither the absolute emperors of history, nor the city-states of Greece, nor the Roman Republic would have been able to imagine such an anarchic state of affairs. This *imperia in imperium* instability naturally fostered the internecine warfare of the Hundred Years War (1337–1453), but, slowly over the next four hundred years, the nation-states of Western Europe began to emerge, as did modern constitutional monarchies. The full potential of the concept of "sovereignty" to produce a functional analysis of government also emerged equally slowly. Indeed, its justificatory potential did not bear fruit until the sixteenth and seventeenth centuries. Then, the pressure of the French Wars of Religion (1562–1598) and the English Civil War and Restoration (1640–1689) drew out the analytic potential of the term.

6 Parsing Sovereignty

This process of functional analysis began in earnest toward the end of the sixteenth century with the publication of Jean Bodin's *The Six Bookes of a Commomweale* in 1576. Published in the midst of the French Wars of Religion, *The Six Bookes* were Bodin's philosophical response to the appalling bloodshed then tearing France apart. Ignoring the potential of the barely functioning French parliaments of the time, Bodin argued that only a true, absolute sovereign could bring order, stability, and peace to the realm. Only a true sovereign could end the French Wars of Religion and construct an orderly *imperium in imperium* out of the anarchical *imperia in imperium*.

He began his argument in true Renaissances style by first assimilating the new concept, "sovereignty," into the ancient concept, "majesty," in Book I, Chapter VIII, "Sovereignty is that absolute and perpetual power vested in a commonwealth which in Latin is termed *majestas* ... " (1992, 1). With this, Bodin suggested that both "majesty" and "sovereignty" were abstractions vested in the people as a whole. But abstractions cannot govern. To govern, Bodin reasoned, both "majesty" and "sovereignty" had to be embodied in the person of the king. But, if the barons were also "sovereign," as Beaumanoir wrote, if the king was only *primus inter pars*, then how was one to identify or define the characteristics that made the king the uniquely righteous "sovereign." What distinguished the *primus* from the *pars*?

To be an absolute "sovereign prince," Bodin argued in Book I, Chapter X, that person must meet two criteria: The first criterion was the person's hierarchical status. Not surprisingly, Bodin could not escape completely from the prejudices of his time. Even in the midst of a bloody religious war, he argued that a "true sovereign" must be the God-chosen and Church-consecrated ruler of the realm:

> Since there is nothing greater on earth, after God, than sovereign princes, and since they have been established by Him as His lieutenants for commanding other men, we need to be precise about their status (*qualité*) so that we may respect and revere their majesty in complete obedience, and do them honor in our thoughts and in our speech. Contempt for one's sovereign prince is contempt toward God, of whom he is the earthly image. That is why God, speaking to Samuel, from whom the people had

demanded a different prince, said "It is me that they have wronged ... (1992, 46).

But, then, Bodin made a stunning break with ancient and medieval political philosophy and took a giant leap into the modern world. He settled on a much more solid and modern criterion. He reasoned that the "sovereign prince" must be a person who was not *primus inter pars*. The "sovereign prince" was *primus* because he was markedly different from all his subjects, including his bishops and barons. Hence, Bodin defined the "sovereign prince" in a non-essential, empirical manner as he who is different from his subjects, as he who possesses a status, attributes, or properties (*qualité, marques, nota*) not shared by any of his subjects:

> To be able to recognize such a person—that is, a sovereign—we have to know his attributes (*marques, nota*), which are properties not shared by subjects. For if they were shared, there would be no sovereign prince. Yet the best writers on this subject have not treated this point with the clarity it deserves, whether from flattery, fear, hatred, or forgetfulness (*ibid.*).

Bodin's non-essential methodology, consequently, enabled him to define Beaumanoir's hitherto ambiguous term, "*souverain*," with precision. More important, though, he defined "sovereignty" in functional terms. Neither undifferentiated power nor majesty was any longer the issue. Neither God's favor nor consecration by the Church counted any longer. Political actors were now to be known for what they did, by their constitutional functions and duties, and not by how many men-at-arms paid homage and liege to them. The results of his breakthrough were listed in his Book I, Chapter X, *Of the true markes of Soueraigntie,* which speaks of more than one hundred and fifty regalian rights. Of these, the first four marks are the most consequential:

I. Primary Governmental Functions:
    A. Legislative: "This then is the first and chiefth marke of Soueraignty, to be of power to giue laws and commaund to all in generall, ..." (Bodin 1962, 162 [161]).
    B. Foreign Affairs: "... to denounce warre, or treat of peace, one of the greatest points of soueraigne maiestie: ..." (*ibid.*, 163 [162]).
    C. Executive: "The third marke of Soueraigne maiestie is to be of power to create and appoint magistrats, ... , especially the principall officers, which are not vnder the commaund of other magistrats" (*ibid.*, 166).

D. Judicial: "But now let vs speak of the fourth marke of Soueraignetie, that is to wit, of the *Last Appeal*, which is and always hath beene one of the most principall rights of soueraignetie" (*ibid.*, 168).

In the wake of the War of Religion, Louis XIII (1601–1643) and Louis XIV (1638–1715) effectively imposed their sovereignty on the nobles of France by means of their power and majesty. By the time of Cardinal Mazarin's death on Saturday, 9 March 1661, the centralized French states was a reality, and the Sun King's place at the pinnacle of French politics and society was undisputed. The nobles had been domesticated; the fortifications of their chateaux had been torn down, and *Les États-Généraux* had been prorogued in 1614. It was not recalled until 1789 at the beginning of the French Revolution and the end of the French experiment with absolute monarchy.

Meanwhile, across the English Channel, during the seventeenth century, Charles I's efforts to imitate the French experiment with absolute monarchy led to the English Civil War and the rise of an almost modern, hereditary constitutional monarchy. In response to these tumultuous events, John Locke took up again the question of defining governmental functions from where Bodin had left it. In his 1690 *Second Treatise*, Chapter XII, *Of the Legislative, Executive, and Federative Power of the Common-wealth* was devoted to the question. But he had a problem. Whereas Bodin imagined an *absolute* monarchy, Locke needed to explain how the newly emerging *constitutional* monarchy functioned. A simple listing of the four or five primary functions of the sovereign would not work for Locke, as it had for Bodin. The oxymoronic character of a *constitutional* monarchy ensured complexity and befuddlement.

In particular, Locke had to contend with two different sets of overlapping roles and functions. In order to reflect English practice at the time, he had to merge Bodin's judicial function and his foreign affairs function into the king's executive powers. This amalgamation reduced Bodin's four primary marks of sovereignty to three. Yet, because the English king exercises three of Bodin's four primary functions, Locke's "three" functions can be looked at two different ways. When looked at in terms of the location at which the function is exercise (*i.e.*, at home or abroad), one gets:

I. Primary Governmental Functions 1:
    A. Domestic Affairs:
        1. Legislative,
        2. Executive/Judicial (*i.e.*, "of the municipal laws of the society within its self").
    B. Foreign Affairs:
        1. Fœderative (*i.e.*, "the power of war and peace, leagues and alliances").

When looked at in terms of which institution exercises the function (i.e., the king or the Parliament), one gets:
1. Primary Governmental Functions 2:
    A. The King:
        1. Executive/Judicial (*i.e.*, Domestic Affairs),
        2. Fœderative (*i.e.*, Foreign Affairs).
    B. Parliament:
        1. Legislative (*i.e.*, Domestic Affairs).

Whereas Bodin's non-essential, functional approach to defining "sovereignty" is undoubtedly a breakthrough, the confusion introduced by Locke's functional analysis of Britain's emerging constitutional monarchy is clearly problematic. Are the primary marks of sovereignty three, as Locke implies, or four, as Bodin implies? Until the number of primary functions is fixed, how can one separate governmental powers or design a system of checks and balance? How is one to check and balance an indeterminate number of powers?

To pause for a moment before continuing, while George H. W. Bush is an unlikely scholar of Lock's *Second Treatise*, one cannot avoid noticing that he has come to the same conclusion as Locke on the structure of constitutional monarchy. The difference is that, whereas Locke based his analysis upon centuries of medieval practice in England and Western Europe, George H. W. Bush based his analysis upon presidential practice over the past two hundred years of American history. As long as the legislature is *not* kept "unnecessarily in the dark," the management of America's foreign affairs is a fœderative power and the exclusive domain of the king/executive, according to both George H. W. Bush and John Locke. To be sure, as in any constitutional monarchy, the management of America's *domestic* affairs is a split responsibility, shared as between the executive and the legislative, according to both John Locke and George H. W. Bush. But this only acknowledges that the American president is a modern, elected constitutional monarch in the Western European tradition. More, this Western European tradition is built on over five thousand years of invariant state practice since at least Gilgamesh. Hence, to imagine that a few aspirational words written on parchment in 1787 could change five thousand years of executive control of foreign affairs and war is surely naïve, if not hubris. But I digress.

In his 1748 *De L'Esprit Des Loix*, Baron de Montesquieu did much to magnify the confusion created by Locke. When he came to describe the English constitutional monarchy, he found Locke's analysis less than comprehensible. As a result, throughout most of his book, Montesquieu divided the primary governmental functions into three in an undefined way:

1. Primary Governmental Functions:
    A. legislative,
    B. executive,
    C. judicial.

However, in Book XI, Section 6, *Of the Constitution of England*, he opted for four primary marks, which, coincidentally, paralleled those of his compatriot Jean Bodin:

1. Primary Governmental Functions in England:
    A. Legislative (*i.e.*, enacting laws),
    B. Executive (*i.e.*, executing public resolutions),
    C. Fœderative (*i.e.*, conducting foreign and military affairs),
    D. Judicial (*i.e.*, trying the causes of individuals).

As is well known, the 1787 Federal Convention appeared to resolve the confusion by ignoring both Locke and Montesquieu of Book XI, and adopting Montesquieu's more frequent number of three. Since 1787, the gold standard for the number of primary governmental functions into which the sovereign's power should be separated has been fixed as three:

1. Primary Governmental Functions:
    A. legislative (*i.e.*, Article I of the Constitution of the United States),
    B. executive (*i.e.*, Article II of the Constitution of the United States),
    C. judicial (*i.e.*, Article III of the Constitution of the United States).

What is one to make of all this? In the first place, the Federal Convention's choice of three primary functions was natural because three had become the common consensus by the end of the eighteenth century, as evidenced by Montesquieu's more frequent use of three. In the second place, constitutional monarchies—either hereditary or elected—*do* possess a three-branch structure. No other way exists to describe their structure. In the third place, the three-branch structure also conformed to the American experience. Since the founding of Jamestown in 1607, both proprietary and royal charters had established colonial governments consisting of three branches: a London appointed governor, an advisory council or later a legislature to deal with colonial affairs, and a judiciary. As colonies, foreign policy was made and conducted from London by the king. Thus, the Founding Fathers had no need to sort out Montesquieu's indecision as to whether the primary functions of government were three or four. They already had thirteen well-functioning, three-branch governments to hand as their models. For nearly two hundred years their colonial governments had managed the domestic affairs of the colonies most successfully on a system of three: executive, legislature, and judiciary. True, the new national government would also have to manage foreign affairs, but this changed little from the perspective of the delegates to the Federal Convention in 1778. Foreign affairs could easily be conducted by the president as chief executive and war by the president as commander-in-chief, as kings and emperors have done since the time of Gilgamesh. Should anyone be surprised at the overwhelming power and force of over five thousand years of history?

7   Conclusion: Imagining an Alternative after Five Thousand Years

Had the Congress proved capable of actually *exercising* the power to *decide* and "to declare war," the five-thousand-year invariant pattern set by Gilgamesh would have been broken. But this was not to be. The actual never managed to replicate the ideal. Still, are the republican values of the constitution to be forsaken?

For, indeed, might the twenty-first century not be the proper moment to break with the invariant state practice of the past? Might the twenty-first century be the moment to imagine an alternative to five thousand years of the nation's war leader making foreign policy and *deciding* the question of war or peace? To do so, one must reevaluate Bodin's functional analysis of "*souverain*" and reimagine the structure of a fully republican government, a government wherein the nation's war leader does not make foreign policy and does not *decide* the question of war or peace as an elected, constitutional monarch.

Structurally, that which made the Germanic kings of Western Europe nonabsolute monarchs in the first place was the existence of a domestic policy-making body, a "common counsel of the realm," that possessed the "power of the purse." It follows therefore that, in order to strip the presidents, prime ministers, and chancellors of the last vestiges of their monarchial war powers, one would have to create a foreign policy-making body possessed of Locke's fœderative powers, "the power of war and peace, leagues and alliances." As is suggested in Appendices D and E, it would be a small, *monofunction*, unicameral representative assembly of less than fifty operating under committee-of-the-whole rules. It would be "above" or superior to the president or prime minister as commander-in-chief, on the one hand, and, on the other hand, parallel to, but independent of the legislature. Schematically, this would mean transforming Figure 2 into Figure 3. Looking ahead, the contrasting speech act content found in each of the different boxes in Figures 2 and 3 will be spelt out in Figure 5 in Chapter 7. The elaboration there will be in the form of an authority-tracing schematic.

Expressed differently, the reality of constitutional monarchy is self-evident, once, that is, the capacity of the legislature to *exercise* its "power of the purse" in domestic affairs is contrasted with its incapacity to *decide* and *declare* war

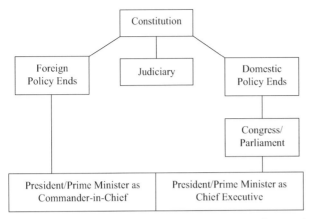

FIGURE 2   The asymmetric structure of a constitutional monarchy (hereditary or elected)

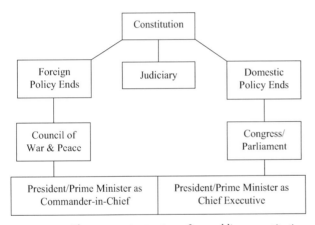

FIGURE 3   The symmetric structure of a republican constitution

in foreign affairs. As a result, the structural flaw in the three-branch structure is clear and obvious. The clear and obvious flaw is that institutionalized domestic policy-making in a common council of the realm has never been balanced by institutionalized foreign policy-making in a parallel, but separate, decision-making assembly. Both the asymmetric imbalance and the solution to that asymmetry are obvious for those who believe that monarchy—whether hereditary or elected, whether absolute or constitutional—is alien to a republican constitution.

CHAPTER 3

The Congressional Incapacity to Declare War
Legislative Sins of Omission vs. Executive Sins of Commission

Abstract

In an effort to better understand and explain the incapacity of legislatures to *decide* and *declare* war, executive decision-making is contrasted with collective decision-making. Both functional and organizational contrasts are explored.

The purpose of this chapter is to explore in greater detail the procedures for declaring war employed by a kingless, collective decision-making assembly with those used by an elected constitutional monarch. The chapter ends with the story of the War of 1812. The War of 1812 was the first international war of the new American Republic. Not insignificantly, it was also the war in which President James Madison demonstrated conclusively the incapacity of the United States Congress to *exercise* its power to *decide* and *declare* on its own initiative. In doing so, President Madison further demonstrated how this incapacity transformed the ostensibly republican structure of the Constitution into an elected constitutional monarchy. One hundred and sixty-one years later, Arthur Schlesinger would christen this transformation, the *Imperial Presidency*. Yet, the first Emperor was James Madison.

But, before telling the story, the stage is set by analyzing four contrasting examples: Two examples for an elected constitutional monarchy and two for a kingless assembly. For an elected constitutional monarchy, the first example is the 107th Congress and its "authorization" of President George W. Bush's invasion of Iraq in 2003. This case exemplifies *Scenario 3: An Unsolemn Functionally Equivalent Declarative Act by the Nation's Hereditary or Elected King that Involves a Legislature*. The second example highlights the 112th Congress and its "non-authorization" of President Barak Obama's participation in the "non-war" in Libya in 2011. This case exemplifies *Scenario 2: An Unsolemn Functionally Equivalent Speech Act by the Nation's War Leader*.

For a kingless assembly, the two examples are the Second Continental Congress and the Security Council of the United Nations. Like Periclean Athens and Republican Rome, both are kingless. They are collective decision-making assemblies that conduct foreign policy in the absence of permanent war leader who commands a standing army. And, finally, neither the Second Continental Congress nor the Security Council makes domestic policy. For the Second Continental Congress, the thirteen state governments made domestic policy. For the Security Council, the national governments of the member states make domestic policy. The Second Continental Congress and the United Nations Security Council will be used later on in future chapters to illustrate textual issues, but not here.

1   Two Examples of War Making Procedures in Kingless Assemblies

1.1   *The Second Continental Congress*

Organizationally, to repeat, the Second Continental Congress was a small, *monofunction*, majority-rule, unicameral, kingless assembly composed of fifty-five delegates operating under a committee-of-the whole rule. Functionally, the Second Continental Congress was a revolutionary assembly tasked with conducting the foreign affairs of Britain's thirteen rebellious colonies in North America. That is, it was tasked with what John Locke called the fœderative powers of the rebellious colonies, with the responsibility for domestic legislation remaining in the thirteen state legislatures. Hence, the functional distribution of responsibilities was exceptionally clear during the period 1774–1781. The State Legislatures took care of domestic policy and affairs; the Second Continental Congress took care of foreign policy and affairs.

Equally important, the Second Continental Congress was able to do that which the United States Congress has so conspicuously failed to do because it was a *small*, monofunction, revolutionary assembly. Consequently, its collective action problems were manageable, and no king existed to manipulate its work. Gilgamesh would not have approved.

In accordance with its committee-of-the-whole procedures, on Friday, 7 June 1776, Richard Henry Lee of Virginia took the floor to introduce the premises of three resolutions. The three premises are reproduced in Appendix A. Lee's motion was seconded by John Adams of Massachusetts. Notably, Lee's motion was the second step in a well-thought out political strategy leading to independence from Great Britain. The first step had been taken the month before on Friday, 10 May 1776, when John Adams introduced, and Richard Henry Lee had seconded, the premise that:

> Resolved, That it be recommended to the respective assemblies and conventions of the United Colonies, where no government sufficient to the exigencies of their affairs have been hitherto established, to adopt such

> government as shall, in the opinion of the representatives of the people, best conduce to the happiness and the safety of their constituents in particular, and America in general.
> *Journals of the Continental Congress* 1904-37, IV: 342

The establishment of thirteen state governments effectively cut the last political and legal ties with Britain and made the former colonies independent in fact, if not yet officially and explicitly. With this effective independence, the next step that had to be taken was the necessary performative enactment of the moral state of war against the crown, which was tantamount to a declaring of independence. Or, to say the same thing the other way around, a performative declaration of independence was tantamount to declaring war against the crown.

To achieve this second step, Lee's first premise of the three held:

> That these United Colonies are, and of Right ought to be, Free and Independent States, that they are absolved from all allegiance to the British Crown, and that all Political connection between them and the State of Great Britain is, and ought to be, totally dissolved.

The first premise of this member-led initiative was debated by the assembly for three days. It was then tabled for further thought and discussion. The interval provided time, however, for an *ad hoc* committee of five to draft a full, open and determined text based upon the resolution. The *ad hoc* committee reported back with its draft on Friday, 28 June 1776. On Monday, 1 July 1776, the premise of resolution was taken up again and debated by the entire assembly. It was approved the next day by the entire assembly. The committee's draft declaration was now taken from the table, and it was debated by the entire assembly, amended by the entire assembly, and voted on by the entire assembly on Saturday, 4 July 1776.

In sum, in 1776, a small, *monofunction*, unicameral, kingless majority-rule assembly organized as a committee-of-the-whole without responsibilities for domestic legislation conducted the foreign affairs of the rebellious colonies, on its own initiative, in such a manner as to enable it to *decide* and *declare* war simultaneously. The relevant contrast, of course, is with the large, *bifunction*, majority-rule, bicameral United States Congress organized into standing committees with its extensive—one might say overwhelming—domestic legislative responsibilities. Under these circumstances, the United States Congress has never successfully both *decided* and *declared* war simultaneously on its own initiative. Not only is the organizational contrast striking, but the functional differences are stark. To repeat, not for the last time, the Second Continental Congress was responsible for *all* fœderative powers and *no* domestic legislation. The United States Congress is responsible for *all* domestic legislation and only a limited number of fœderative matters—most notably, the *deciding* and *declaring* of war.

One may speculate that this functional intermingling of the two incompatible responsibilities was not initially debilitating. In 1789, the United States Congress might conceivably have declared war just as the Second Continental Congress had done thirteen years earlier. The First Congress counted sixty-five members in the House; it was organized under committee-of-the-whole rules, and its legislative workload was not overwhelming by modern standards. Had a member introduced the question of war or peace, the early Congresses would still have been small enough to have followed the committee-of-the-whole procedures used by the Second Continental Congress. Consequently, an early Congress might possibly have *decided* and *declared* war on its own initiative. But this is purely speculative since no member ever introduced such a proposition.

And, indeed, when Commander-in-Chief James Madison initiated the new republic's first international war in 1812, he employed *Scenario 3* to maneuver the Twelfth Congress into *declaring*, but not *deciding*, war against Great Britain. This first, precedent setting, exercise of the powers of the Imperial Presidency is briefly summarized in the section after the next section below. A more detailed retelling can be found in Chapter 2 of *Declaring War* (Hallett, 2012).

1.2   The Security Council

Organizationally, to repeat, the United Nations Security Council is a small, *monofunction*, majority-rule, unicameral, kingless assembly composed of fifteen delegates operating under a committee-of-the whole rules. The majority-rule element is, of course, qualified by the veto of the five permanent members. Functionally, the Security Council is an international assembly tasked with coordinating the foreign affairs of the five permanent members—China, Great Britain, France, Russia, and the United States. That is, with coordinating the fœderative powers of the five permanent members. Crucially, responsibility for domestic legislation remains in the nation-states, the members of the United Nations. Hence, the functional distribution of responsibilities is exceptionally clear. How, then, does the Security Council do that which the United States Congress has so conspicuously failed to do? In particular, how do its small size, its *monofunction,* and its committee-of-the-whole rules enable the Security Council to *decide* upon a functionally equivalent declaration of war without the Secretary General providing leadership and agenda setting?

Like the Second Continental Congress, the Security Council meets *in camera*. In the Council's private room, members introduce the premise of resolutions and debate these premises as a committee-of-the-whole. They then go on to draft, debate, and amend the texts of the final resolutions under committee-of-the-whole rules *in camera*, before adjourning to the Council's ceremonial chamber for public speeches and a public vote. For example, consider the timeline by which the no-fly zone was authorized over Libya in 2011. The authorization, need it be said, is a functionally equivalent declaration of war.

The Security Council first took note of large-scale protests against Mu'ammer Gaddafi and the subsequent fighting in Libya, on Saturday, 26 February 2011. On that day, it passed *Resolution 1970*, under its Chapter VII, Article 41 authority to call for "measures not involving the use of armed force." *Resolution 1970* demanded "an immediate end to the violence and calls for steps to fulfil (sic) the legitimate demands of the population." Needless to say, Mu'ammer Gaddafi ignored the resolution. The situation in Libya continued to deteriorate over the next three weeks.

To save the situation, the Arab League announced its support for a European sponsored, United Nations sanctioned no-fly zone over Libya, on Saturday, 12 March 2011 (Bronner and Sanger 2011, A1). Acting expeditiously, the Council passed *Resolution 1973* on Thursday, 17 March 2001, under its Chapter VII, Article 42 authority to act with armed force when "measures provided for in Article 41 would be inadequate or have proved to be inadequate." Again, the Council demanded, "the immediate establishment of a cease-fire and a complete end to violence and all attacks against, and abuses of, civilians." The demand this time however was backed up with a no-fly zone and other sanctions. The no-fly zone was immediately implemented by a NATO-lead multinational force. The insurrection continued until Thursday, 20 October 2011, when Gaddafi was captured and executed in his hometown, Sirte.

In sum, like the small, *monofunction*, majority-rule, unicameral, kingless committee-of-the-whole Second Continental Congress, the even smaller, *monofunction*, majority-rule, unicameral, kingless committee-of-the-whole United Nations Security Council represents the appropriate size and organization for a decision-making assembly charged with foederative functions, including the power to *decide* and *declare* war. All that is needed for such decision-making assemblies to emerge is the creation of a kingless, republican constitutional structure, as was illustrated in Figure 3. That is, all that is needed is the creation of a constitutional structure possessed of two characteristics: The first is the absence of a war leader possessed of a standing army and the "inherent," royal prerogative and divine right to conduct foreign affairs, including the *deciding* and *declaring* or war. The second is a purpose-built, *monofunction* assembly focused on foreign policy, leaving domestic policy to a parallel legislative assembly.

Consider next the very much more common monarchial institutions of modern constitutional monarchies, as exemplified by the conduct of the 107th and the 112th Congresses. The comparison draws out as clearly as is possible the total lack of legislative initiative and capacity to *decide* and *declare* war. The two stories, however, are unbalanced in length and complexity. The story of the 107th Congress in "authorizing" the 2003 invasion of Iraq is a simple and unexceptional example of *Scenario 3*. Gilgamesh would have been proud of how George W. Bush managed the 107th Congress. Inversely, the story of the 112th Congress in not "authorizing" *Operation Odyssey Dawn*, the 2011 no-fly zone over Libya, is a very convoluted example of *Scenario 2*. The upshot is that retelling the story of the 112th Congress demands the spilling of vastly more ink.

2   War and Non-War: Two Examples of Congressional Incapacity

2.1   *Non-Authorization by the 112th Congress*

The 2011 Arab Spring began with the overthrow of Presidents Zine El Abidine Ben Ali of Tunisia in January and Hosni Mubarak of Egypt in February. Within days of Mubarak's resignation, protests broke out in Benghazi, Libya. These protests soon escalated into a fully-fledged armed insurgency. By mid-March, Arab and international opinion had turned decisively against the Mu'ammer Gaddafi regime and for supporting the beleaguered insurgents. This led, on Thursday, 17 March 2011, to the passage by the United Nations Security Council of *Resolution 1973*, which established a no-fly zone over Libya. The next day, President Barak Obama committed American air forces to *Operation Odyssey Dawn*, the Pentagon's name for American participation to enforce the no-fly zone (Obama 2011).

Three days later, ever mindful that astute constitutional monarchs do not to keep their legislatures "unnecessarily in the dark," the president sent a letter to *The Speaker Of The House Of Representatives And The President Pro Tempore Of The Senate* dated 21 March 2011. In the letter, he explained that *Operation Odyssey Dawn* was humanitarian in nature, of very limited scope and duration, and that it had been authorized by Security Council *Resolution 1973*. He further justified his decision in terms of the usual monarchical authorities of the commander-in-chief and acknowledged that his letter was "consistent with the War Powers Resolution":

> For these purposes, I have directed these actions, which are in the national security and foreign policy interests of the United States, pursuant to my constitutional authority to conduct U.S. foreign relations and as Commander in Chief and Chief Executive.
>
> I am providing this report as part of my efforts to keep the Congress fully informed, consistent with the War Powers Resolution. I appreciate the support of the Congress in this action.
>
> OBAMA 2011a

The Libyan operation was arguably "in the national security and foreign policy interests of the United States," if not certainly so. Equally important, the president's letter of Monday, 21 March 2012 letter was arguably "consistent with the War Powers Resolution." "Consistent with," however, is not the same as "compliant with." As with similar letters since President Ronald Reagan, it failed to request a symbolic gesture of congressional support, as is called for in *Scenario 3*. The letter failed to request either a congressional declaration of war against Libya, which the Constitution requires, or an "authorization of force" resolution, which the *War Powers Resolution* recommends as an unconstitutional alternative to a declaration of war (Sidak 1991, 120–1). In sum, President Obama had clearly adopted *Scenario 2: An Unsolemn Functionally Equivalent Speech Act by the Nation's War Leader*.

The adoption of *Scenario 2* did not, of course, go unnoticed. Faced with well-placed public and congressional skepticism, the Department of Justice, Office of Legal Counsel, issued a lengthy legal memorandum on Friday, 1 April 2011 to argue more fully the president's case for "compliance." Entitled, "Authority to Use Military Force in Libya," the memorandum concluded:

> We conclude, therefore, that the use of military force in Libya was supported by sufficiently important national interests to fall within the President's constitutional power. At the same time, turning to the second element of the analysis, we do not believe that anticipated United States operations in Libya amounted to a "war" in the constitutional sense necessitating congressional *approval* under the Declaration of War Clause (12–3. Italic added.).

Again, while the first claim that the Libyan operation was in the national interest was at least plausible, the second claim that the operation did not "amount to war" provoked incredulous outrage (*e.g.*, Glennon 2011; Fisher 2012). This outrage was exacerbated when the White House claimed with a 15 June 2011 report, *United States Activities in Libya*, that the "non-war" was also a case of "non-hostilities":

President is of the view that the current U.S. military operations in Libya are consistent with the War Powers Resolution and do not under that law require further congressional *authorization*, because U.S. military operations are distinct from the kind of 'hostilities' contemplated by the Resolution's 60-day termination provision.

White House 2011, 25. See also KOH 2012. Italic added

What is one to make of the two claims? Can one truly claim that *Operation Odyssey Dawn* was simultaneously a "use of military force" that 1) does not amount "to a 'war' in the constitutional sense" and that 2) is also "distinct from the kind of 'hostilities' contemplated by the [War Powers] Resolution's 60-day termination provision?" First off, one must stand in awe at the audacity of the legalistic hair splitting. Second, the basic claim is that only the president can determine whether a quacking duck is a duck.

That said, notice how the two claims for *Operation Odyssey Dawn*, in effect, truncated Gilgamesh's three-step procedure. President Obama as commander-in-chief clearly exercised his "inherent power to commit our armed forces to battle." Planes were soon flying over Libya. Astutely, he also did not "keep Congress unnecessarily in the dark." He sent it a letter on Monday, 21 March 2011 "to keep the Congress fully informed." However, he did not take the third step. He did not seek a tangible symbol of congressional cooperation and support in the form of either an "*approval*" or an "*authorization*." This last step was unnecessary, or so it was said, because *Operation Odyssey Dawn* was neither a "war" nor "hostilities." On the Imperial Presidency side of the ledger, this is all well and good, par for the course. But where was the 112th Congress in all this? As expected, it was playing Keystone Cops chasing after the president's "non-war."

As might be expected, the initial reaction of the 112th Congress to the events in Libya was a suitably hortatory and precatory resolution of support for whatever policy President Obama might choose as the events unfolded over the next months. The vehicle for this initial obsequious expression of support was *Senate Resolution 85*, which was introduced by Senator Robert Menendez with ten co-sponsors on Tuesday, 1 March 2011, "Strongly condemning the gross and systematic violations of human rights in Libya, including violent attacks on protesters demanding democratic reforms, and for other purposes." "The other purposes," of course, is where the trouble began.

But before one gets to the "other purposes," the date and method of introduction is troubling. The first of March was at the very beginning of the crisis before the president had made his decision to participate in the "non-hostilities" of a "non-war." Indeed, the resolution was passed two weeks before passage of the Thursday, 17 March 2011 Security Council no-fly zone resolution.

The anticipatory character of the resolution did not bode well. More troubling still, *Senate Resolution 85* passed without a committee hearing by unanimous consent on the floor of the Senate in thirty-five seconds, with only Senator Chuck Schumer and the presiding officer present (Fisher 2012, 184–5).

While some may argue that thirty-five seconds of deliberation in an empty Senate chamber does not truly represent the sense of the full Congress, the Office of Legal Counsel, seeing its opportunity, took full advantage of this nonbinding resolution a month later. In its Friday, 1 April 2011 memorandum, it claimed *Senate Resolution 85* as evidence of congressional support for the president's decision to implement the Security Council's no-fly zone. It was able to do so because the resolution had, among other things, urged "the United Nations Security Council to take such further action as may be necessary to protect civilians in Libya from attack, including the possible imposition of a no-fly zone over Libyan territory" (Department of Justice 2011, 2). How perspicacious of the empty Senate chamber.

This hortatory and precatory resolution of support aside, the deleterious effects of the *War Powers Resolution of 1973* paralyzed the 112th Congress. Among the Resolution's initiative-killing provisions, the *War Powers Resolution* mandates a sixty-day grace period for the president before the Congress can react. This grace period forestalls any congressional initiative for sixty days, unless the president decides to activate the Congress sooner by making an explicit request for a congressional "authorization." Since President Obama made no such request, the 112th Congress was legally barred by the *War Powers Resolution* from initiating any action. On 23 May 2011, the sixty-day grace period ended. Like a dam bursting, the 112th Congress came to life. In addition to a number of proposals to cut funding (Hendrickson 2013, 5–8), the twelve inchoate resolutions listed below were introduced by two senators and six representatives (See also Grimmett 2012, 11–14). Of these twelve resolutions, eight died in committee, three were defeated on the House floor, and one passed in the House, but was immediately tabled for reconsideration. In essence, one saw scattered individual initiatives here and there, but no concerted or coordinated congressional effort anywhere.

The Founder's dream of a congressional initiative to *exercise* the power to *decide* and *declare* war was nowhere in sight. Instead, one saw the full impact of both the congressional incapacity to discharge its war powers function, its collective action problem, and the organizational limits of a large, *bifunction*, majority-rule, bicameral legislature operating under standing-committee rules. A better illustration of the meaning of "incapacity" is difficult to imagine. The rash of directionless activity in the 112th Congress may be tabulated as follows. Unless noted, all the resolutions died in committee:

I. Five Concurrent Resolutions without the force of law that were introduced but not passed.
Representative Dennis Kucinich
On 23 May 2011, House Concurrent Resolution 51: Directing the President, pursuant to Section 5(c) of the War Powers Resolution, to remove the United States Armed Forces from Libya. (11 cosponsors) (Defeated on 3 June 2011, 148 yeas to 265 nays)

Representative Scott Garrett
On 24 May 2011, House Concurrent Resolution 53: Declaring that the President has exceeded his authority under the War Powers Resolution as it pertains to the ongoing military engagement in Libya. (9 cosponsors)

Representative Thomas Rooney
On 31 May 2011, House Concurrent Resolution 32: Expressing the sense of Congress that the President should adhere to the War Powers Resolution and obtain specific statutory authorization for the use of United States Armed Forces in Libya. (1 cosponsor)
On 1 June 2011, House Concurrent Resolution 57: Expressing the sense of Congress that the President is in violation of the War Powers Resolution regarding the use of United States Armed Forces in Libya, and for other purposes. (16 cosponsors)
On 22 June 2011, House Resolution 2278: To limit the use of funds appropriated to the Department of Defense for United States Armed Forces in support of North Atlantic Treaty Organization *Operation Unified Protector* with respect to Libya, unless otherwise specifically authorized by law. (0 cosponsors)
(Defeated on 24 June 2011, 180 yeas to 238 nays)

II. Six Joint Resolutions with the force of law that were introduced but did not pass.
Senator Rand Paul
On 23 May 2011, Senate Joint Resolution 14: A joint resolution declaring that the President has exceeded his authority under the War Powers Resolution as it pertains to the ongoing military engagement in Libya. (0 cosponsors)
On 24 May 2011, Senate Joint Resolution 16: A joint resolution declaring that the President has exceeded his authority under the War

Powers Resolution as it pertains to the ongoing military engagement in Libya. (0 cosponsors)

Senator John Kerry
On 21 June 2011, Senate Joint Resolution 20: A joint resolution authorizing the limited use of the United States Armed Forces in support of the NATO mission in Libya. (11 cosponsors)

Representative Alcee Hastings
On 21 June 2011, House Joint Resolution 67: Authorizing the limited use of the United States Armed Forces in support of the NATO mission in Libya. (0 cosponsors)
On 21 June 2011, House Joint Resolution 68: Authorizing the limited use of the United States Armed Forces in support of the NATO mission in Libya. (0 cosponsors)
(Defeated on 24 June 2011, 123 yeas to 295 nays)

Representative Adam Smith
On 26 June 2011, House Joint Resolution 74: Authorizing the limited use of the United States Armed Forces in support of the NATO mission in Libya. (3 cosponsors)

III. A House Resolution without the force of law that were introduced and passed, but tabled.
Representative John Boehner (the Speaker of the House)
On 2 June 2011, House Resolution 292: Declaring that the President shall not deploy, establish, or maintain the presence of units and members of the United States Armed Forces on the ground in Libya, and for other purposes. (0 cosponsors)
(Passed on 3 June 2011, 268 Yeas to 145 nays, laid on the table for reconsideration)

The point that cannot be over emphasized is that the constitutional responsibility of the Congress is not to "direct" the president, nor to "express" the sense of the Congress, nor to "authorize" the limited use of the Armed Forces. Nor is it the constitutional responsibility of the Congress to "declare" that the president has exceeded his "authority." If the president has exceeded his "authority" as commander-in-chief, the responsibility of the Congress is to impeach him. More to the point, the constitutional responsibility of the Congress is plainly and clearly to *decide* and *declare* war, although it lacks the capacity to do so.

The befuddled and beflummoxed response of the 112th Congress in 2011 is, of course, not an aberration. It is the consistently repeated effect of its functional mismatch and the collective actions problems experienced by the large, *bifunction*, majority-rule, bicameral Congress operating under standing-committee rules. Without the leadership and agenda setting of the nation's war leader, the 112th Congress was both leaderless and without a political strategy, unlike the Second Continental Congress in 1776. Uncoordinated members proposed this, that, and the other resolution in a frantic burst of activity leading nowhere. The anti-climax of this dysfunctional activity occurred on Friday, 3 June 2011, with the passage of Speaker John Boehner's *House Resolution 292*. This triumph of congressional initiative was, nonetheless, short lived as the resolution was immediately tabled for reconsideration (*cf.* Hendrickson 2013, 13).

2.2 *Authorization by the 107th Congress*

Be the trials and tribulations of the leaderless 112th Congress as they may, before his 2003 invasion of Iraq, President George W. Bush provided decisive leadership for the 107th Congress to ensure its efficient and timely "authorization" for his invasion, as usually happens when *Scenario 3* is employed. The full story is told in a simple chronology of events:

At (t^1), President George W. Bush had made up his mind to invade Iraq by at least September 2002.
At (t^2), the text of a military order was *drafted*.

With the mid-term elections approaching in November, the time had come "to keep the Congress fully informed," to not "keep Congress unnecessarily in the dark." Consequently,

At (t^3), President George W. Bush ordered his White House staff to draft a Joint Resolution "To authorize the use of United States Armed Forces against Iraq."

This White House drafted resolution was sent to House of Representatives. It arrived on Thursday, 19 September 2002, and was introduced simultaneously into both chambers on Wednesday, 2 October 2002, a month before the mid-term elections.

At (t^4), the "authorization" passed nine days later on Friday, 11 October 2002. The president signed the now enacted White House drafted resolution on Wednesday, 16 October 2002 (White House 2002).

At (t^5), a public announcement of the execution of the military order was *drafted*.

At (t^6), military orders were issued.

At (t^7), 19 March 2003 at 10:16 P.M. EST, President George W. Bush addressed the Nation from the Oval Office, "My fellow citizens, at this hour, American and coalition forces are in the early stages of military operations to disarm Iraq, to free its people and to defend the world from grave danger. ... On my orders, coalition forces have begun striking selected targets of military importance to undermine Saddam Hussein's ability to wage war. ..."

The basics of Gilgamesh's three-steps had been followed without a hitch.

Nonetheless, the three-step procedure also demonstrated beyond cavil that the 107th Congress lacked all initiative and capacity. Among several other reasons, it was too busy campaigning for the mid-term elections. One of the secrets of Gilgamesh's three-steps method, after all, is to "consult" with one's "councils" only when circumstances make it politically impossible for the legislature to deny the request. For example, submit the request for an "authorization" just before mid-term elections. Or, in Tony Blair's case, his request for "support" was made on 19 March 2003, the day before the troops stepped off.

In sum, to fill the congressional vacuum, before his 2003 invasion of Iraq, a presidential decision led to a presidential request and efficient congressional compliance. Congressional efficiency was accomplished by creating a simple feedback loop: The White House staff wrote the resolution; the Congress passed the resolution, and the president signed the resolution written by his staff. The power and efficiency of this feedback loop is such as to make it impossible to speak of a congressional capacity to make a *decision* to go to war or to initiate the passage of a solemn, performative declaration of war.

But notice, the president sins by commission only because the Congress sins by omission. That is, the Imperial Presidency's sins of commission are possible only because the Founding Fathers imagined in 1787 that the soon to be created Congress of the United States could and would actually exercise the power to *decide* and *declare* war on its own initiative. After all, the Second Continental Congress had done exactly that thirteen years before. What impediment could possibly bar the new Congress for doing the same? At the time, therefore, it was not possible to think that the new Congress would not carry out its constitutional responsibility to *decide* and *declare* war on its own initiative? Yet, that was before the size and organization of the Congress changed dramatically over the two decades between 1789 and 1812.

3   James Madison and the Power to Declare War

As one might expect, James Madison is at the center of all this sinning. He is responsible for both the aspirational congressional power "to declare war" and the precedent setting reality of the president's "inherent power to commit our armed forces to battle," as kings have always done. An active and thoughtful politician, James Madison struggled to reconcile the conflicting demands of 1) constitutional theory, 2) partisan polemic, and 3) the practical political exigencies of managing congressional incapacity. To begin with constitutional theory, on Friday, 17 August 1787, Elbridge Gerry of Massachusetts and James Madison of Virginia moved in the Federal Convention to change the congressional power to "make" war into a congressional power to "declare" war. Gerry then noted that their amendment still gave "the Executive the power to repel sudden attacks" without the benefit of a procedurally perfect, solemn, performative declaration of war from the Congress (Madison 1966, 476). The unstated assumption of Gerry's remark was that, when the attack is not "sudden," a procedurally perfect, solemn congressional declaration was required, not an "approval," nor an "authorization," but, just as the Constitution says, a congressionally initiated decision and an solemn, procedurally perfect declaration of war.

As Madison and the Founding Fathers soon discovered, constitutional theory, naturally, leads to partisan politics and polemics over the "real" meaning of the theory. As happenstance would have it, the first polemical imbroglio over this congressional power "to declare war" occurred nineteen years before the War of 1812, in 1793. And, to be sure, the imbroglio had nothing to do with declaring war. Rather, it was about *not* declaring war. In 1793, revolutionary France was attacked by the First Coalition. To meet the attack the Committee of Public Safety decreed the *levée en masse* and looked to America for the aid promised in the *Franco-American Treaty of Amity and Commerce of 1778*. With Indian wars threatening on the western frontier, however, little enthusiasm existed in America for entering the European war. In response to the French request, President George Washington issued his *Proclamation of Neutrality of 22 April 1793*, which soon became controversial.

The largest part of the controversy resulted from the fact that Washington had acted with energy and dispatch in the face of a "sudden" crisis. This meant, in partisan terms, that he had acted without "consulting" with Congress. "Consultation," however would have been difficult. The Second Congress had adjourned *sine die* a month earlier, on Saturday, 2 March 1793, and the not-yet-elected Third Congress would not convene until Friday, 6 December 1793. In light of this and the difficulties of travel in 1793, Washington and his cabinet, with Thomas Jefferson concurring, decided to issue the *Proclamation* without "consultations."

As the controversy raged, Alexander Hamilton sprang to the president's defense in a series of newspaper articles under the name, *Pacificus*. Pressured by Jefferson to respond for the Republicans, not yet the Democrat-Republicans, Madison wrote as *Helvidius*. The subtle reference is to the Roman senator and stoic philosopher, Helvidius Priscus, who had opposed the tyranny of Emperor Nero during the first century of the Common Era.

As *Pacificus*, Hamilton penned a number of passages that have been interpreted to imply that he supported a strong executive, in general, and strong executive action in the conduct of foreign affairs, in particular. Interestingly, because the polemic was over the president's *decision not* to make war, Hamilton had little to say about executive war making. Instead, he observed hopefully that, like the executive and the courts, "The Legislature is free to perform its own duties according to its own sense of them" (1961–1987, XV: 42). In saying this, Hamilton was clearly an idealist, especially with regard to the congressional capacity to *decide* and *declare* war.

Still, in terms of constitutional theory, Hamilton's idealism is beyond reproach. As a practical matter, had Jefferson, Madison, and the Third Congress wanted to go to war against Britain in support of revolutionary France in accordance with the terms of the *Franco-American Treaty of Amity and Commerce of 1778*, they could have done so. All the Jeffersonian's in the Third Congress had to do was 1) to introduce a draft declaration of war on their own initiative, 2) debate and amend the draft declaration, and 3) vote and pass the draft declaration. Were President Washington to veto the enacted declaration of war, the Third Congress could have overridden his veto. Such a solemn and procedurally perfect congressional declaration would have rendered President Washington's *Proclamation of Neutrality* null and void without any fuss or muss. But, of course, no one wanted to enter a European war in 1793. The polemic was about the lack of "consultation" with the Congress and the possibility of a more pro-French policy, which the Jeffersonians favored.

As *Helvidius*, Madison penned a number of passages that have been interpreted to imply that he supported a weak executive, in general, and weak executive action in the conduct of foreign affairs, in particular. Not surprisingly, then, Madison had much to say about a hopeful legislative exercise of the power to decide and "to declare war" on its own initiative. Among the many such passages, one finds this excellent example, "Those who are to *conduct a war* cannot in the nature of things, be proper or sage judges, whether *a war ought to be commenced, continued, of concluded*" (Madison 1900–10, 6:148).

Yet, fatefully, Madison also went on to say that, in time of war, "The executive has no other discretion than to convene and give information to the legislature ..." (*ibid.*, 6:160). This second, seemingly innocuous observation was passed over unnoticed in 1793. After all, how could "convening and giving information to the legislature" compromise either a legislature's independence or its initiative to *decide* and *declare* war? But, as Gilgamesh would have explained if anyone were listening in the heat of the polemic, "convening and giving information" is the second step in the invariant three-step procedure by which astute war leaders take their nations into war. Unknowingly, Madison was describing *Scenario 3: An Unsolemn Functionally Equivalent Declarative Act by the Nation's Hereditary or Elected King that Involves a Legislature*. For, with certainty, no monarch—either absolute or constitutional—would convene his council until after he had made his *decision* to go to war. Then, after convening his council, no astute monarch would keep his council "unnecessarily in the dark." He would always "give it information." And, lastly, no astute monarch would "consult" with his councils unless he was certain that either new taxes or a symbolic "authorization" would result.

Partisan politics and pointless polemics are one thing, however; the practical politics of managing congressional incapacity is another. For, the inescapable practical political reality is—as Madison learned when he was elected president—that "Those who are to *conduct a war* [are] in the nature of [the complete congressional incapacity to *decide* and "to declare war"], the proper or sage judges, whether *a war ought* to be *commenced, continued*, of *concluded*"

3.1   *The War of 1812: Sins of Commission and Sins of Omission*

James Madison, as fate would have it, was Thomas Jefferson's Secretary of State from 1800 to 1808. He was then elected president to succeed Jefferson and served two terms, 1809 to 1817. He, consequently, was at the center of American foreign policy during the last of the Wars of the French Revolution and the entirety of the Wars of the French Empire. These last included a small peripheral action in North America, the War of 1812.

To Madison, therefore, fell the duty to *decide* upon and lead the nation during its first international war. As already noted, one can, of course, speculate that, had war come before 1812, the previous eleven congresses might have been able to exercise their constitutional responsibility to *decide* and *declare* war. However, the Twelfth Congress of 1811–1813 was no longer the Congress of the First Congress of 1789–1791, or even the Third Congress of 1793–1795. Twenty-two years of rapid expansion and growth had made a huge difference. The Louisiana Territory had been purchased; four new states had been admitted to the union, and the population had more than doubled. As a result, a fundamental transformation in the size, organization, and procedures of the Congress was well underway, a transformation that would not be complete until the end of the nineteenth century. In particular, by 1811, the House had grown to one hundred and forty-three members and its legislative workload had become, if not overwhelming, at least burdensome. In response, the modern standing-committee system was rapidly replacing the traditional committee-of the-whole system. Even in these earliest manifestations, the standing-committee system fragmented the members' attention, interests, and time, sapping member initiative. Collective action problems increased accordingly, which made the Congress ever more dependent upon presidential leadership and agenda setting (White 1951, 56; Cooper 1965; Hallett 2012, 184–96).

As a result of these changes in the size and organization of the House, if war with Great Britain were to be had in 1812, Commander-in-Chief James Madison had little choice but to abandon any sort of idealistic talk about a congressional capacity "to declare war." Like Gilgamesh and the war leaders of the nations of the world for over five thousand years, Madison would have to assume the role of an elected constitutional monarch and deal forthrightly with the practical political exigencies of managing congressional inertia and incapacity. He would have to make the *decision*, set the agenda, provide the leadership, and use his kingly discretion "to convene and give information to the legislature." "Convening and giving information," to repeat, is little more than another way of not "keeping the Congress unnecessarily in the dark."

For better or worse, this is precisely what happened with the able assistance of the War Hawks, who were led by freshman Representative Henry Clay, the newly elected Speaker of the House. Operating now as the nation's war leader, Commander-in-Chief Madison took the *decision* for war and against peace during August 1811. At the time, he was at his home, Montpelier, conferring with his new Secretary of State, James Monroe. As Monroe wrote to John Taylor in Saturday, 13 June 1812:

> Nothing would satisfy the present ministry in England, short of unconditional submission, which it was impossible to make. This fact being completely ascertained, the only remaining alternative, was to get ready for fighting, and to begin as soon as we were ready. This was the plan of the administration, when [the Twelfth] Congress met in November last; the President's message announced it; and every step taken by the administration since has led to it.
>
> MONROE 1960

Among the steps taken by the administration, one of the more effective was for Secretary Monroe to actually write the congressional declaration of war. John C. Calhoun of South Carolina, the very busy Chairman of the House Select Committee on Foreign Relations, was most appreciative to be relieved of this burden. The most effective step, however, was Secretary Monroe's frequent dinners at the "War Mess," the boarding house where Speaker Clay and most of the leading War Hawks stayed. This close executive "consultation" reached its climax on Sunday, 15 March 1812, when Secretary Monroe presented the president's legislative strategy to Speaker Clay. In an *aide-mémoire* of the meeting, Speaker Clay articulated the dictum that has ever since explained the loss of congressional independence and initiative, on the one hand, and, on the other hand, provide the rational for presidential control of the congressional power to *decide* and *declare* war:

> Altho' the power of declaring War belongs to Congress, I do not see that it less falls within the scope of the President's constitutional duty to recommend such measures as he shall judge necessary and expedient than any other which, being suggested by him, they alone can adopt.
> CLAY 1959–1984; 1:637. See also MONROE 1960

The power and force of five thousand years of history is not to be denied, not even by James Madison. Hamilton had said, "The Legislature is free to perform its own duties according to its own sense of them." But Speaker Clay knew differently. He was painfully cognizant of the partisan politics and organizational constraints that sapped congressional initiative to the point of incapacity. He, like Madison and Monroe, understood that the leadership and agenda setting of the nation's war leader was essential to setting the Congress in motion.

And what was Commander-in-Chief Madison's strategy for setting the Congress in motion toward war? The first step was taken two weeks after Speaker Clay's meeting with Secretary Monroe on Monday, 30 March 1812. On that day, the House Select Committee on Foreign Relations informed Monroe that the Committee would "be happy to be informed when, in the opinion of the Executive, the measures of preparation [for war] will be in such forwardness as to justify the step contemplated" (Cited in Brant 1941–61, 5:427). The second step was for Monroe to testify before the Select Committee on Foreign Relations, the next day, in a secret session. The burden of Monroe's testimony was that the president wanted to wait until the sloop-of-war, *Hornet*, returned from London in the late spring with the latest dispatches. If the government in London moved to meet the American demands, war would not be declared. If the government in London did not move to meet the American demands, war would be declared. This step condemned the members not to adjourn in March, as customary, but to stay in Washington through the rest of spring and perhaps into the summer.

Commander-in-Chief Madison's third step was to "gave information" to the Congress himself in a confidential message two days later, on Wednesday, 1 April 1812. Sitting behind closed doors, Madison's message was read. It requested a sixty-day embargo, which passed the House that same evening on a vote of seventy to forty-one. Unfortunately, the Senate was less forthcoming and amended the embargo bill to ninety days, which lessened the impact of the embargo.

The fourth step occurred on Monday, 18 May 1812 when the *Hornet* arrived in New York and forwarded its long-delayed dispatches to Washington. The dispatches arrived three days later (Madison 1900–10, 6:215). The government in London had not moved to meet the American demands; war would be declared. With this news, the fifth and final step in Commander-in-Chief Madison legislative strategy was put in motion. He sent his war message to the Twelfth Congress on Monday, 1 June 1812. The House passed the declaration—written by Secretary Monroe—in a secret session without debate by a seventy-nine to forty-nine vote on Thursday, 4 June 1812. On Wednesday, 17 June 1812, after much partisan wrangling, the Senate voted nineteen to thirteen for war.

Exceptionally, the Twelfth Congress did not "authorize" or "approve" Commander-in-Chief Madison's *decision* to go to war against Great Britain in 1812. Rather, it declared war solemnly, albeit not performatively, only lexically. This separation of the "*decision*" from the "*declaration*" created the appearance of compliance with the letter of the Declare War Clause. Yet, the Twelfth Congress was able to create this illusion only because Madison had followed the three-step procedures pioneered by Gilgamesh five thousand years before. First, Madison had *decided* the question of war or peace in August 1811. Second, he had "consulted" with the Congress to ensure cooperation and support by not keeping them "unnecessarily in the dark," by "convening the and giving them information." And, lastly, he had obtained their "approval" or "authorization." This time with a lexical declaration of war.

That is, to drive the point home, as with George W. Bush and the 107th Congress, James Madison supervised an efficient feedback loop. Secretary of State Monroe wrote the declaration; the Twelfth Congress passed the declaration, and the president as commander-in-chief signed the declaration written by Secretary Monroe. James Madison told the Twelfth Congress what to do, and the Twelfth Congress did what it was told to do. Thus, it has been for five thousand years.

4 Conclusion

To back up for a moment, and approach the story from a different angle. In a little noticed passage in his *Helvidius* paper, Madison suspended his polemical fire for a moment of reflection on constitutional theory:

> A declaration that there shall be war, is not an extension of laws: it does not suppose pre-existing laws to be executed: it is [also] not, in any respect, an act merely executive. It is, on the contrary, one of the most deliberate acts that can be performed: and when performed, has the effect of repealing all the laws operating in a state of peace, so far as they are inconsistent with a state of war; and of enacting, as a rule for an executive, as new code [the Laws of War] adapted to the relations between the society and its foreign enemy. In like manner, a conclusion of peace annuls all the laws peculiar to a state of war, and revives the general laws incident to a state of peace.
> *ibid.*, 6:145

As the passage demonstrates, Madison clearly understood that the power to *decide* and *declare* war was neither a legislative nor an executive power. It was something else; it was transformative. How then could Madison conclude on the next page, "that the powers of making war and treaties being substantially of a legislative, not an executive nature" (*ibid.*, 6:146)? How is it possible for a power that is indisputably non-legislative and non-executive to be "substantially" either legislative or executive? How is it possible for a *sui generis* power to be catalogued under either genus? It is possible because, in 1793, James Madison was upholding his half of a very partisan polemic.

CHAPTER 4

Defining War and the Declaring of War

Performative Speech Acts and Ontological Guillotines

Abstract

This chapter shifts from discussing the incapacity of legislatures to *intend/decide* and *draft/declare* war to defining the contested terms "armed conflict," war, and declarations of war. Disaster declarations and the 1931 Mukden Incident are employed as contrastive examples, among others.

1 Part 1: Declarations as Performative Speech Acts

For the international community, the *exercise* of the power to *intend/decide* and *draft/declare* war is governed by Article I of Hague Convention III of 1907, *Relative to the Opening of Hostilities*, "The contracting powers recognize that hostilities between themselves must not commence without previous and explicit warning, in the form either of a reasoned declaration of war or of an ultimatum with conditional declaration of war." For each nation individually, the *exercise* of the power to *intend/decide* and *draft/declare* war is governed by either a constitutional provision or a domestic law. The upshot is that, in each particular case, the *deciding* and *declaring* of war is governed by two different laws, the one international, the other domestic. The interaction of the two laws, need it be said, produces an interesting tension. This tension is uniquely observable in the case of the United States.

Consider, first, the internal domestic tensions found within the American Constitution: Article I, Section 8, Clause 11 stipulates that, "The Congress shall have power ... to declare war." Article II, Section 2, Clause 1 stipulates that, "The president shall be commander in chief of the army and navy of the United States, and of the militia of the several States, when called into the actual service of the United States."

As already noted, Alexander Hamilton did not think that this division of the sovereign's war powers should cause any controversy. After all, "The Legislature is free to perform its own duties according to its own sense of them" (1961–1987, XV: 42). But Hamilton was an idealist. In reality, this division was always going to be very controversial, first and foremost, because it violates five thousand years of state practice. Neither Agga nor Gilgamesh would understand such a violation. In reality, therefore, violating the royal prerogatives, the divine right, and the "inherent executive powers" of the elected constitutional monarch of the United States cannot be anything but controversial.

That said, the peculiar shape of the controversy derives from the fact that the American Declare War Clause is crisp and laconic to the point of impenetrable obscurity. Had the clause been more forthcoming, it would have explained how, when, and, perhaps, why the Congress should declare war. "Yet," as John Yoo has strikingly remarked, "the Constitution itself nowhere describes such a process [by which the Congress shall enact a declaration of war], nor does it explain how the Declare War Clause and the commander-in-chief power must interact. The Framers simply gave the former to Congress and the latter to the president, and left it at that" (2005, 152). The upshot is a system that Harold Koh has described as one of " 'executive initiative, congressional acquiescence, and judicial tolerance' " (*ibid.*, 12; 13).

Thus, according to John Yoo, Harold Koh, and many, many others, the domestic controversy will be settled once light is shed upon, first, the declaring "process" and, second, on "how the Declare War Clause and the commander-in-chief power must interact."

Consider, next, Hague Convention III, which is both less controversial and more informative. It is less controversial because all it does is to bind the contracting parties to *decide* and *declare* war. In doing this, Convention III simply codifies the ancient laws and customs of war as recognized by all nations throughout history. Invariant state practice is not usually controversial. Convention III is also more informative because it begins to answer not only John Yoo's procedural questions of *how*, but also his substantive questions of *why*. The procedural *how* is explained directly by stipulating that war must be declared "in the form either of a reasoned declaration of war or of an ultimatum with conditional declaration of war." The procedural *why* is explained indirectly by stipulating that either the "reasons" for commencing armed hostilities or the "conditions" for declaring armed hostilities conditionally must be declared.

Turning this coin over, however, the three principal shortcoming of Hague Convention III must be noted. The first shortcoming is that the Convention does not identify who is the competent or legitimate declarer of war: the nation's war leader or some other, collective body. This shortcoming has already been discussed in Chapter 1 and elsewhere. The next two shortcoming are contained in the clause "that hostilities between themselves must not commence without previous and explicit warning" (*les hostilités entre elles ne doivent pas commencer sans un advertissement préalable et non équivoque*).

In light of this clause, the second shortcoming is the Convention's emphasis on "fair play" and "good sportsmanship." To believe that "previous and explicit warning" is a significant function of declarations of war is only to demonstrate a near total lack of understanding. This waving of a red-flag, "Warning! Danger! I'm going to attack!" is grossly misleading, albeit very common, even traditional. A very much greater purpose of the text is to articulate the political purposes of the war, which political purposes are held not only to justify, but also to authorize the employment of military means. To achieve this much greater purpose, as the following clause states clearly, the "contracting powers" are required to write either "a reasoned declaration of war or an ultimatum with conditional declaration of war."

The second principal shortcoming of the Convention is that it fails to make clear that an "ultimatum" is not the only type of conditional declarations of war. For, conditional declarations of war come in two degrees—either with or without a time limit. Without a time limit, a conditional declaration of war is simply a negotiating document. It is a *rebus repetitis* demand that declares "conditionally" the grievances that have broken the peace and the remedies that will restore the peace. The hope is that, during the *rebus repetitis* negotiations, both the gravamina indicted and the remedies demanded will be accepted by the other party. If this happens, then war will be avoided. Either that, or the negotiations will lead to some other mutually agreeable compromise. Conditional declarations without a time limit are not found in modern history. Negotiations are no longer structured in this manner. One must go back to ancient Rome or medieval history to find examples. For example, the Roman conditional declaration without a fixed time limit against Perseus, son of Philip, King of Macedonia, in 168 BCE is cited below in Chapter 5.

With a time limit, conditional declarations become an ultimatum. Yet, they are still a negotiating document, but with a fixed time for the conclusion of the negotiations. At the end of the time limit, negotiations end, and, if not successful, armed hostilities begin. Conditional declarations with ultimata can be found in modern history. President William McKinley added a forty-eight-hour time limit to congressional conditional declaration of 20 April 1898 against Spain over Cuba, which is reproduced in Appendix A.

Speaking no longer in a hypothetical manner, but, rather, in a practical manner, one must recognize and acknowledge that neither Hague Convention III nor the Declare War Clause governs or has governed the actual exercise of the power to *intend/decide* and "to declare war" in either the modern world, generally, or in the United States, particularly. Instead, as elsewhere in the world, executive war making by the nation's war leader has been the norm for over two hundred years in the United States and for over five thousand years elsewhere in the world.

A further uninteresting detail of the Declare War Clause and Convention III is that both imply that an official, performative declaration of war is required for every war in order for that war to be considered legal and legitimate. Yet, before 1945, few were the wars anywhere in the world at any time in history that commenced with an official, performative declaration of war. Indeed, between 1700 and 1870, no more than ten wars had been declared officially, and no fewer than one hundred and seven had been declared unofficially with functionally equivalent speech acts (Maurice 1883, 4. *Cf.* Ward 1805; Eagleton 1938; Harbom and Wallensteen 2010, 501). Of greater consideration and weight, though, since World War II, no war anywhere in the world has been declared officially. Interpreted strictly, this means that most of the wars before 1945 and all of the wars since 1945 have been illegal and illegitimate in terms of the Declare War Clause and Hague Convention III.

But why have no wars been declared officially since 1945? For two reasons: 1) Everyone thinks official declarations of war are a waste of time, useless, if not dangerous. In the distant past, they may have added a certain element of seriousness and decorum, but, today, they add nothing and accomplish even less (*cf.* Fazal 2018). It's much more efficient just to start shooting. 2) The resort to war is considered by many to have been made illegal in the Charter of the United Nations, if not the Kellogg-Briand Pact. Since war is illegal, the declaring war is also illegal. Adding one and two together, the less said about the topic of declaring war or the two documents that govern the exercise of the power to *intend/decide* and "to declare war" the better.

1.1   *Defining the Indefinable*

Still, sometimes, not always, but sometimes, defining one's terms clearly is helpful, even useful. For example, if one wished to understand the raw power to *intend/decide* and "to declare war," one might find it both helpful and useful to define the two terms, "war" and the "declaring of war." Assuming so, two initial observations are essential: First, both "war" and the "declaring of war" had existed for thousands of years before either the Federal Convention met in Philadelphia in 1787 or the Hague Convention met in 1907. This means that the definitions were well understood and settled thousands of years before either 1787 or 1907. Consequently, none of the discussion or debate either at the Convention or thereafter is of much relevance to defining the two terms. Whatever the "inherent" executive or legislative powers might be, howsoever the Congress and the president might or might not "check and balance" each other, these and other fiercely debated topics are entirely irrelevant to defining "war" and the "declaring of war." Both "war" and the "declaring of war" have existed independently of all these constitutional dust ups for thousands and thousands of years.

Second, whereas defining these two terms appeared possible before World War II, since World War II, defining the two terms is no longer considered possible, at least for positivist legal scholars. The empirical reality of the post-World War II world has simply changed too radically, according to the conventional wisdom. As Rosara Joseph explains:

> States no longer [since World War II] make [procedurally perfect, performative] declarations of war or make [any other] formal recognition of a relationship of war. The term 'war' is now largely devoid of significance at international law, which now speaks of situations of 'armed conflict'. The demise of the declaration of war has obscured the boundary between peace and war and raises conceptual and practical uncertainty about when a situation of armed conflict exists.
> JOSEPH 2013, 201. *Cf.* FAZAL 2018

In sum, World War II was the last officially "declared" "war" in world history. But, to say this only means that, before World War II, when wars were still declared officially, albeit, in frequently, that:
1) the term "war" still possessed significance at international law,
2) international law did not speak only of situations of "armed conflict,"
3) the boundary between peace and war was not usually obscure, and
4) conceptual and practical uncertainty did not normally arise about when a situation of war existed.

However, this is a lost golden age. Since 1945, the tides of world history and human intellectual progress have swept all of this away and created a new terminological reality. Hence, one must conclude that even contemplating the effort to define "war" and the "declaring of war" is pointless. Still, with a detour around "armed conflict," the effort might possibly pay dividends.

1.1.1 Defining "Armed Conflict"?

Consider two aspects of the new empirical reality in turn: First, what is the point of studying or defining the term, "declaration of war," when states no longer *need* "to declare war?" This aspect is taken up in the next section. Second, what is the point of defining the term, "war," when states have changed the conversation and now speak of "armed conflict?" This aspect is taken up in this section.

In light of the new terminological convention, the sensible thing to do is to devote one's time and effort to defining "armed conflict." Thus, to be sensible, the 1958 Pictet commentary to the *Geneva Conventions of 1949* defined "armed conflict" as "any difference arising between States and leading to the intervention of members of the armed forces" (1958, 3:23), whereas, in 1996, the *International Criminal Tribunal for the former Yugoslavia* defined "armed conflict" as existing "whenever there is a resort to armed force between States or protracted armed violence between governmental authorities and organized groups within a State" (*Prosecutor v Tadic* (1996) 105 ILR 419, 488). Pictet believes that presence or absence of soldiers—members of a regular armed forces—are critical to the definition of "armed conflict." The *International Criminal Tribunal* believes that soldiers—members of a regular armed forces—are not critical. The perception of "armed force or violence" is the main point, whether perpetrated by soldiers or non-solders is irrelevant.

Still, the new post-World War II legal reality is not the only reality by which men live. One might mention, in passing, moral principles and values. For example, Article I, Section 8, Clause 11 of the Constitution of the United States has not been revoked. It is ignored in practice, but not yet revoked. Further, Article I of Hague Convention III of 1907, *Relative to the Opening of Hostilities* has also not been revoked. It is desuetude in practice, but not yet revoked. A tension, if not a contradiction, is thereby created. Yes, these two ancient and forgotten legal principles and moral values have been swept away on the tides of post-World War II positive conventions. "Armed conflicts" initiated without a solemn and official performative "declarations of war" are the new empirical reality. The new empirical reality is one in which unofficial, unsolemn, functionally equivalent speech acts initiate "armed conflicts."

Yet, might it still be conceivable that the old principles and values are not entirely irrelevant? For example, the Federal Convention of 1787 placed the power to *intend/decide* and "to declare war" in the Congress in order to achieve a certain value-driven goal of non-executive war making. Is this value no longer of any value? Arthur Schlesinger did not think so.

Perhaps, closer scrutiny of the *exercise* of "the power. ... to declare war" might yield useful insights. In particular, the value of non-executive war making has always been composed of two different and distinct propositions. The first and very much more important proposition was precisely "non-executive war making." Means had to be found, the Federal Convention believed, to keep "the branch of power most interested in war, & most prone to it" from *deciding* and *declaring* the question of war or peace. The second and very much less important proposition was that the legislative branch was chosen in 1787 as the new speaker of the declarative act to frustrate executive war-making.

More than two hundred years later, one must recognize and acknowledge that the less important proposition was impractical. The legislative has proven incapable of exercising this non-legislative power to *intend/decide* and "to declare war." But does this congressional incapacity negate the initial goal and value of non-executive war making? Is the incapacity of all legislatures a good reason to continue sustaining and supporting executive war making by the nation's war leader? Wherein lies the fault? Was the Federal Convention wrong in attempting to deny the president the power to *intend/decide* and "to declare war?" Or, was the Federal Convention wrong in relocating the power to *intend/decide* and "to declare war" into the legislative? Might some other non-legislative, non-executive locus of *intention, decision,* and "*declaration*" be found? Perhaps, the dilemma could be resolved if one made the effort to define the undefined terms, "war" and the "declaring of war."

1.2   *Codependency: the Speech Act Character of War*

As an initial step to define the undefined, one must recognize the codependent, causative relationship between "war" and the "declaring of war." A "declaration," to emphasize the obvious, is a speech act. It is a performative speech act as defined by John Austin (1975 (1962)). It, therefore, does what it says. Expressed schematically:

At (t^1), a presumably legitimate declarer of war opens its mouth or takes up its pen in accordance with the laws and customs of war and says words to the effect that, "We must, therefore, acquiesce in the Necessity, which denounces [the other party], and hold them, as we hold the rest of Mankind, Enemies in War, in Peace, Friends."

At (t^2), this socially sanctioned speech act:
  1) generates the moral state of war and
  2) transmits authorities to the commander-in-chief (Austin 1979, 100; 1975, 52).

At (t^3), once received, these transmitted authorities empower a hierarchy of subordinate speakers to "order" men and machines to maneuver over terrain.

At (t^4), the material maneuvers so "ordered" transform the material conditions of peace into the material conditions of "war."

Visualized more forcefully, a "declaration of war" acts like an ontological guillotine. It slams down and slices the continuum of time and the stream of world events, terminating peace and creating "war." Thud.

As should surprise no one, the performative speech act character of both "war" and the "declaring of war" were once widely recognized. This recognition also included the way in which official, performative declarations explicitly recognize the transmitted authorities that produced the material consequences of the declarative act. For example, consider the final paragraph of King William's *Declaration Against The French King* of Tuesday, 7 May 1689:

> [*the denunciation of war*] Being therefore thus necessitated to take up Arms, and Relying on the help of Almighty God in Our just undertaking, [*the declaration of war*] We have thought fit to Declare, and do hereby Declare War against the French King, and that We will in Conjunction with Our Allies, Vigorously Prosecute the same by Sea and Land (since he hath so unrighteously begun it) being assured of the hearty Concurrence and Assistance of Our Subjects in support of so good a Cause; [*the transmission of authorities*] Hereby Willing and Requiring Our General of Our Forces, Our Commissioners for Executing the Office of High Admiral, Our Lieutenants of Our several Counties, Governours of Our Forts and Garisons, and all other Officers and Soldiers under them, by Sea and Land, to do, and execute all acts of Hostility in the Prosecution of this War against the French King, his Vassals and Subjects, and to oppose their Attempts, Willing and Requiring all Our Subjects to take Notice of the same, whom We henceforth strictly forbid to hold any Correspondence or Communication with the said French King, or his Subjects; And because there are remaining in Our Kingdoms many of the Subjects of the French King; We do Declare and give Our Royal Word, that all such of the French Nation as shall demean themselves dutifully towards Us, and not Correspond with Our Enemies, shall be safe in their Persons and Estates, and free from all molestation and trouble of any Kind.
>
> BRIGHAM 1968 (1911), 147–50. The full text is reproduced in Appendix B

As can be read in Appendix D, before King William transmitted authorities to his subordinates "to do, and execute all acts of Hostility," he also indicted the gravamina that, in his estimation, had caused a breach of the peace. That is, like the *Declaration of Independence*, King William's absolute, performative declaration against Louis XIV is reasoned and, hence, Hague Convention III compliant. Unlike the *Declaration of Independence*, however, King William has also spoken to make explicit the transmitted authorities that follow naturally from his performance of this declarative act.

Yet, to reinforce the point, consider, first, an analogy, and, then, three thought experiments. The analogy is with "marriage" and the minister's "pronouncement" of marriage. "Marriage" is the term that designates the moral and material consequences of a minister's "pronouncement." No ministerial "pronouncement," no "marriage." When the minister says, "I now pronounce Arnold and Betty man and wife," this performative speech act generates transmissible authorities that empower the couple to assert a certain well-defined social status. Their previous moral state and material condition of bachelorhood and maidenhood is transformed instantaneously into the moral state and material condition of matrimony. Thud, falls the minister's ontological guillotine.

1.2.1 Three Thought Experiments

The three thought experiments begin by imagining a class in which the teacher wishes to demonstrate the codependent, causative power of "declarations of war." For the first experiment, the teacher selects two students, appointing one as the King and the other as the General in charge of the nation's armed forces. The General is told to commence military operations as soon as "war" is officially "declared" by the King, as any good soldier would. The King, then, is told to *intend/decide* on a country he wants to invade. Any country will do; San Merino is a good choice. However, the King is not allowed to speak; he is not allowed "to declare war." The King is told to perform the mental act of *intending/deciding* to go to war, but he is not allowed either to "declare" officially his *intention/decision* or to transmit authorities to his General to act. He is not allowed to let the ontological guillotine of his *intention/decision* to fall.

The point of course is that without this absolutely necessary performative speech act nothing will happen. Nothing will happen because "war" and the official "declaring of war" are codependent and causative. The absolutely necessary official declarative speech act generates the transmissible authorities that authorize the General "to do, and execute all acts of Hostility in the Prosecution of this War."

For the second experiment, the teacher reiterates the fact that no "war" was initiated in the first thought experiment. However, since most wars are not "declared" officially, how are they initiated? In response, the thought experiment is repeated, but the teacher changes the rules. The King is still forbidden "to declare war" officially. But, this time, he is allowed to speak. After he has chosen a country to invade, he can say anything he likes to his General. Not surprisingly, the student King finds this change in the rules bewildering. Silence fills the classroom. How can one possibly "intend to go to war" without "declaring" war officially? With some prompting, the student King eventually comes to understand the experiment and says something like, "Go invade Monaco; the gambling is great there." Or, "I order you to invade Monaco."

In other words, by uttering a functionally equivalent speech act, the student King trips the ontological guillotine and the bade falls. Thud. But the ontological blade does not cut cleanly. It wobbles as it falls impiously, without decorum. The point of course is that a procedurally perfect, solemn declarative speech acts have a doppelganger, like most, but not all, performative speech acts. They are doubled by functionally equivalent speech acts, such as a military "order" or some other functionally equivalent utterance. Thus, except for some random moral scruple, no need ever exists "to declare war" officially. Instead, all one has to do is to utter a functionally equivalent speech act. That is, to recall the analogy with "marriage," the minister's official "pronouncement" of "marriage" is doubled by "cohabitation." Thus, except for some random moral scruple, no need ever exists for a procedurally perfect, solemn "pronouncement" of "marriage." Instead, all a couple has to do is to utter a functionally equivalent speech act, such as "Let's move your stuff in next Saturday."

For the third experiment, the teacher organizes the class into a mock decision-making assembly. He, then, convenes the mock assembly and introduces a draft "declaration of war" against Andorra. The class debates and amends the draft declaration. When debate has concluded and agreement on the amended draft is reached, the teacher adjourns the mock decision-making assembly without calling the question and taking a vote. Again, the point is that without an absolutely necessary performative speech act—a "vote" enacting the draft "declaration of war," in this mock assembly—nothing will happen. "War" against Andorra will not come into being because it will not have been "declared." The ontological guillotine will not fall.

Three closely coordinated points of befuddlement now arise: The first is the affect of the outlawing of "war" since 1945, what Tanisha Fazal has call *Wars of Law* (2018). The second is the way in which the post-World War II term, "armed conflict," erases the codependent, causative relationship between "war" and the "declaring of war," thereby creating a new post-World War II reality. And, third is the way in which the erasure of the codependent, causative relationship leads to the misunderstanding of Hague Convention III compliant, fully reasoned declarations of war and the proliferation of functionally equivalent speech acts.

1.2.2   Rule of Law and the Outlawing of War

Outlawing vice is always popular. Yet, it is often counterproductive in terms of maintaining social discipline and respect for the rule of law. As examples, one might cite the outlawing of "the manufacture, sale, or transportation of intoxicating liquors," or drugs, or gambling, and so on. Mindful of this counterproductivity, "war" was first outlawed under Article 1 of the Kellogg-Briand Pact of 1928, "The High Contracting Parties ... condemn recourse to war for the solution of international controversies, and renounce it, as an instrument of national policy in their relations with one another." Unfortunately, though, this renunciation did not prevent World War II. In flagrant violation of the Kellogg-Briand Pact, the many belligerents in that "war" "declared war" officially, if only lexically. In doing so, the belligerents ensured that World War II was not an "armed conflict" under international law. Instead, they ensured that a procedurally perfect, declarative speech act would cause the ontological guillotine to fall. Thud.

After World War II, "war" was again outlawed and very much more successfully. This occurred under Article 2 (4) of the United Nations Charter of 1945, "All Members shall refrain in their international relations from the threat or use of force against the territorial integrity or political independence of any state, or in any other manner inconsistent with the Purposes of the United Nations." On the positive side, this post-World War II outlawing of "war" has, indeed, "save[ed] succeeding generations from the scourge of war, which twice in our lifetime has brought untold sorrow to mankind," to cite the preamble of the Charter. World War II was the last openly and officially "declared" "war" in human history.

On the negative side, this absence of openly and officially "declared war" since 1945 has only meant that "Members" have ignored Article 1 of Hague Convention III of 1907, *Relative to the Opening of Hostilities*, and commenced their armed hostilities with functionally equivalent speech acts. These functionally equivalent speech acts have naturally produced a simulacrum of procedurally perfect, solemn "war," now called "armed conflict," of which there have been over two hundred and fifty-two between 1946 and 2012 (Themner and Wallersteen 2013, 510). As Hanneke van Schooten has observed, perhaps ironically, "The fact that war is banished linguistically does not mean that it has vanished empirically" (2007, 376). Her excellent article is entitled pointedly, "The Legal Abolition Of War: Lip-Service To The Cause Of Peace?" Such irony, though, is the price one pays for outlawing "war," if not for outlawing intoxicating liquors, drugs, or gambling and the like vices.

1.2.3   Erasing the Codependent Relationship

The adoption of the term, "armed conflict," since World War II has also erased or obscured the codependent, causal relationship between the declarative speech act and its material consequences, "war." The philosophical reason for this erasure is the inability of international law scholars to think in other than positive terms. The rhetorical reason is that "armed conflict" is an euphemism for "war." The euphemistic quality of the term is symbolized by the fact that no one denies that the Korean *War*, the Vietnam *War*, the Persian Gulf *War*, the *Wars* in Afghanistan and Iraq, and the like are really and truly "wars." After all, a quacking duck is a duck, despite what either the Kellogg-Briand Pact of 1928 or Article 2 (4) of the United Nations Charter of 1945 may say.

The logical reason for the erasure is a category error. The error is observed most compellingly by recalling that, "The demise of the declaration of war has obscured the boundary between peace and war and raises conceptual and practical uncertainty about when a situation of armed conflict exists." Before the demise of official "declarations of war," no conceptual or practical uncertainty arose between peace and war whenever war was declared officially. To initiate its participation in World War II, the United States crossed the boundary between war and peace clearly and unambiguous at precisely 4:10 pm EST on Monday, 8 December 1941. That is the moment when President Franklin Roosevelt signed the official, if lexical, "declaration of war" against Imperial Japan that the Seventy-seventh Congress had passed at 1:10 pm EST, earlier in the afternoon. The text of this lexical declaration is reproduced in Appendix A.

In sum, all that is needed to de-obscurify "the boundary between peace and war" is "to declare war" performatively in a Hague Convention III compliant manner. Whensoever this is done, one complies with the laws and customs of war and explicitly, clearly and, unambiguous trips the ontological guillotine that is a declarative speech act. Thud.

Traditionally, of course, a technical language existed and was used that expressed and preserved the codependent, causative relationship between the absolutely necessary declarative speech act and its material consequences, "war." Naturally, these terms also preserved the adjective + noun, genus + specie structure one would expect. Thus, before World War II, officially and performatively "declared wars" were characterized as procedurally "perfect" or "solemn" wars. The point was that official, performative "declarations of wars" were normally made with due ceremony and reverence by a legitimate declarer of war in accordance with the laws and customs of war. They were, in a word, legally "perfect" and ceremonially "solemn." Inversely, unofficial, functionally equivalent "declarations of war" were characterized as procedurally "imperfect" or "unsolemn." The point, again, was that unofficial, functionally equivalent "declarations of wars" were normally made without due ceremony and reverence by an illegitimate declarer of war in violation of the laws and customs of war. They were, in a word, legally "imperfect" and ceremonially "unsolemn." Since World War II, the traditional vocabulary has not only been abandoned, but also misunderstood, to be replaced with the euphemism, "armed conflict."

1.2.4   An Imperfect "Perfect"

As an example of how the traditional terms are currently misunderstood, one can do no better than recall John Yoo's lexical defense of uninhibited presidential war making, aka, the Imperial Presidency. Yoo is a law professor and a former Deputy in the Office of Legal Counsel during George W. Bush's first term. In that position, Yoo put his war-power views to good use writing several of the legal memoranda that justified President Bush's "war on terrorism," including the use of torture. According Yoo, "declarations of war" are not absolutely necessary performative speech acts. They are neither codependent with nor causative of "war." Rather, an "original understanding" of the lexical definition of "declaration" demonstrates that:

> Declarations of war serve a purpose, albeit one that does not answer to the sole authority to initiate hostilities. Declarations do simply what they say they do: they declare. To use the eighteenth-century understanding [found in Samuel Johnson's *Dictionary of the English Language*], they make public, show openly, and make known the state of the international legal relationship between the United States and another country (2005, 15. *Cf.* 2002 1673, 1996, 242).

From an "original understanding" of Samuel Johnson's *Dictionary of the English Language*, Yoo then moves on to an "original understanding" of William Blackstone's *Commentaries*. There, Yoo rediscovers that, lexically, the declarer's job is no more than tying up the legal red tape so as "to 'perfect' a[n armed] conflict under international law":

> Instead of serving as an authorization to begin hostilities, a declaration of war was only necessary to "perfect" a[n armed] conflict under international law. A declaration served to fully transform the international legal relationship between two states from one of peace to one of war. *See* 1 William Blackstone, *Commentaries* *249–50. Given this context, it is clear that Congress's power to declare war does not constrain the President's independent and plenary constitutional authority over the use of military force.
>
>   United States Department of Justice 2001. See also YOO 2005, 42; 51

All well and good. If the lexical definition of "declaration" is as far as one is willing to go in understanding the *exercise* of the power "to declare war," then one must unquestionably agree with both Yoo and Blackstone. From this lexical perspective, tying up international-law red tape does in fact make an official, lexical "declaration" "perfect." Moreover, one should not fail to congratulate the

Congress of the United States for having tidied up the red tape in this way for four of America's many untidy wars.

Yet, notice the imperfection of this lexical understanding of "perfect." Notice the temporal problem in this lexical understanding of "declaration." The "[Imperial] President's independent and plenary constitutional authority over the use of military force," still requires him to *intend/decide* to go to war and, of the utmost importance, to communicate his *intention/decision* to others in an absolutely necessary declarative speech act. Without a functionally equivalent performative speech act, neither his *intentions* nor his *decision* as the "sole initiator of hostilities" will ever be known. Without at least a functionally equivalent performative speech act, the ontological guillotine will not fall. This, of course, was the point of the three thought experiments just above. Thud.

The absolutely necessary performative speech act does not have to be an official, lexical "declaration" of war; it can too easily be a functionally equivalent speech act. But, to repeat once again, the "sole initiator of hostilities" cannot remain silent. He must transform his subjective mental act into an external physical act, which must be, at a minimum, a functionally equivalent declarative act. To accomplish this absolutely essential functional task, he might issue a military "order," followed by a "televised address," for example.

Yet, truth be told, the explanation of the relationship between "war" and the "declaring of war" given so far is inadequate. To simply say that "war" and the "declaring of war" are performative speech acts and, thus, codependent and causative does not take one the distance. To go the distance, one must appreciate not only the full ontological import of a felicitous declarative act, but of much greater importance, the ontological import of their functionally equivalent doppelgangers. That is, one must appreciate the way in which official, felicitous, solemn, and procedurally perfect performative declarations are mimicked by functionally equivalent speech acts and how these doppelgangers authorize and produce simulacra of war, namely, "armed conflicts."

2   Part 2: Declarations as Ontological Guillotines: Transforming the Subjective into the Objective

And God said, Let there be light: and there was light. ...
Genesis 1:3

In the beginning was the Word, and the Word was with God, and the Word was God.
JOHN 1:1

To restart the argument, the boundary between peace and war need not raise any conceptual or practical uncertainty or obscurity, once one recognizes the absolutely necessary codependent and causative character of "war" and the "declaring war." Once recognized, this creative relationship reveals itself to be an ontological phenomenon: The declarer of war brings "war" into existence by "declaring war." Peace becomes war when a declarer says so. Thud.

To understand more fully the mechanics of this absolutely necessary ontological guillotine, a good contrastive place to start is to worry over disaster declarations before worrying over "declarations of war." Hurricane Katrina in 2005 provides a good example.

Hurricanes have torn through the coastal areas of the Gulf of Mexico for millions and millions of years. Well-known natural processes have mitigated the force of these storms whenever they have struck and facilitated recovery of the natural environment in each storm's aftermath, over these same millions and millions of years. In the context of these natural processes, one cannot truly speak of hurricanes as a "disaster." They are instead of the essence of the natural processes found in the cyclical meteorological environment of the Gulf coast. In terms of the natural environment, hurricanes just pass through on the way to somewhere else further north.

When Hurricane Katrina struck the Gulf coast in late August of 2005, its effects were, however, spoken of as a "disaster." Not principally because of the storm's material effects on the natural environment, but primarily because of its social effects on the human environment, in New Orleans, in particular. Further, and most critically, this accusation of "disaster" was an entirely subjective and intersubjective reaction. The reaction was subjective and intersubjective because no objective standard exists to measure natural "disasters." Like "war," natural "disasters" do not freeze at 0° C or boil at 100° C. The critical issue, therefore, is to understand how one transforms a subjective and intersubjective perception into an objective social fact. How is a subjective and intersubjective evaluation of rapid physical change to the built environment "manifested" or "declared" as an objective social fact; something called a "disaster" (or a "war")? For, until this transformation of the subjective into the objective is made, no social response to the "disaster" is possible. No succor is possible.

To conceptualize the problem, the perception of physical change can be imagined as a continuum that stretches from the glacial at one end to the explosive at the other end. Subjectively, physical changes at the glacial end tend not to be noticed, because their human impacts range from imperceptible to barely perceptible. Erosion is an example. In contrast, physical changes more toward the explosive end are noticed, because their human impacts are perceived both immediately and powerfully. The social effects of Category V hurricane winds appear somewhere closer to the easily perceived explosive end than to the less easily perceived glacial end of this imagined continuum. But where? Where on this imagined continuum of human perceptions is the threshold crossed that separates a "disaster" from a "non-disaster?" Without an objective standard, what is needed is an ontological guillotine, a heavy blade that falls at 9.7536 meters per second, cleaves the imagined continuum decisively, and separates a "disaster" neatly and cleanly from a "non-disaster." Thud.

For humans, this guillotine is a codependent, causative speech act. A performative speech act that brings a "disaster" into being, into existence. More precisely, spoken words transform the subjective and intersubjective into the objective: 1) A codependent, causative speech act takes an internal mental act and transforms it into an external physical act—speech. 2) Once spoken, the performative speech act is communicated to others, thereby creating our intention-filled social world. 3) Under favorable circumstances—what John Austin called "total speech situations"—the intentions communicated in the speech act generate the "transmissible authorities" that 4) motivate a consequential social and material response in the hearers of the performative speech act (1975, 52; 1979, 100). In the case of Hurricane Katrina, the "disaster" became a social reality by means of a "disaster" declaration. When spoken in a procedurally perfect, solemn manner, officially, the guillotine fell; the subjective and intersubjective became objective. Thud.

Thus, the guillotine is tripped and begins to fall decisively when public officials—mayors, governors, or presidents—speak with the authority of public law, in this case with the authority of the Stafford Act. For example, the blade was raised on-high on Sunday, 28 August 2005 when the Governor of Louisiana, Kathleen Babineaux Blanco, wrote:

> Dear Mr. President: Under the provisions of Section 401 of the Robert T. Stafford Disaster Relief and Emergency Assistance Act, 42 U.S.C. §§ 5121–5206 (Stafford Act), and implemented by 44 CFR § 206.36, I request that you declare: an expedited major disaster for the State of Louisiana as Hurricane Katrina, a Category V Hurricane approaches our coast south of New Orleans; beginning on August 28, 2005 and continuing.
> BLANCO 2005

The guillotine fell and slammed home when President George W. Bush responded on Monday, 29 August 2005:

> I have determined that the damage in certain areas of the State of Louisiana, resulting from Hurricane Katrina beginning on August 29, 2005, and

> continuing, is of sufficient severity and magnitude to warrant a major disaster declaration under the Robert T. Stafford Disaster Relief and Emergency Assistance Act, 42 U.S.C. §§ 5121–5206 (the Stafford Act). Therefore, I declare that such a major disaster exists in the State of Louisiana.
>
> Congressional Research Service 2005, 8

In sum, social phenomena, among them "disasters" and "wars," come into existence or are made manifest by means of declarative speech acts (*cf.* Searle 2010). A speech act functions like an ontological guillotine. It transforms the subjective and intersubjective into the objective, the internal into the external, the mental into the physical.

2.1 Functional Equivalent Ways to Declare War

The issue at this point is to understand and explain how and why legitimacy, when taken as a simple empirical event or fact, is completely irrelevant to the declarative speech act. How and why, one must ask, do the material conditions of war come into existence irrespective of the legitimacy or illegitimacy of the declarer?

More precisely, the issue at this point in the argument is no longer about understanding the ontological implications of *official, felicitous, perfect, solemn* performative declarative acts by *legitimate* declarers of war. Rather, the issue at this point is about understanding the ontological implications of *unofficial, infelicitous, imperfect, unsolemn* functionally equivalent acts by *illegitimate* declarers of war. To address the shadowy existence of these doppelgangers, one can do little better than examining the 1931 Mukden Incident and the bewildering definitional quandaries it posed for positive legal scholars.

2.1.1 Positively Missing the Point

In the wake of the Russo-Japanese War, from 1906 until the end of World War II, Imperial Japan deployed the Kwantung Army to Manchuria to protect its interests in the Manchuria and North China. At 10:00pm on Friday, 18 September 1931, a small explosive charge was detonated next to the Southern Manchurian Railway track just north of the Mukden railway station. The explosion caused no significant damage, but it did signal the commencement of the Mukden Incident. This incident led to the rapid conquest of all of Manchuria during the next five months. The "incident," however, was undertaken without the knowledge or authority of the Imperial government in Tokyo, which was powerless either to control or to oppose the Kwantung Army. Indeed, the illegal plot was undertaken without the knowledge of even the commanding officer of the Kwantung Army, Lieutenant General Honjo Shigeru. Rather, it was the work of a cabal of "patriotic" staff officers in the Kwantung Army's Special Services Agency (Yoshihashi 1963, 154).

Within hours of the explosion, Chinese officials informed Hayashi Hisajiro, the Japanese Consul General at Mukden, that "they would adhere strictly to the principle of non-resistance" to the attacks of the Kwantung Army (*ibid.*, 7–8). Hayashi immediately cabled this information to the Foreign Ministry in Tokyo. In an emergency Cabinet meeting the morning after the explosion, the Wakatsuki government *decided*, for its part, "on a non-aggression policy" (*ibid.*, 8). In short, both sides *intended/decided* not "to declare war." More, both sides went a step further and vigorously denied that the Japanese conquest of Manchuria by the Kwantung Army constituted in any sense the initiation of the state and condition of "war." This double denial of the existence of "war" in Manchuria created a very difficult problem for a positive legal philosophy: If neither of the responsible public authorities "declare war," if both deny that "war" exists, does a "war" exist? After all, if none of the responsible public officials "declares" Hurricane Katrina a "disaster," if they all deny that a "disaster" exists, then no "disaster" exists in terms of the Stafford Act, and succor will not be provided to the victims.

In an attempt to answer this perplexing question, Quincy Wright wrote a short comment in the *American Journal of International Law* in 1932, When Does War Exist? Intriguingly, Wright's comment provides a response without answering the question. He is unable to answer the question because the only terms and concepts he had at his disposal were the late nineteenth and early twentieth century positive distinctions "between war in the legal sense and war in the material sense" (*ibid.*, 362). Naturally, without the technical terms and concepts of a codependent, causative performative speech act, Wright struggled:

> War in the legal sense means a period of time during which the extraordinary laws of war and neutrality have suspended the laws of peace in the relations of states [as James Madison had also said over a hundred years before]. A state of war may exist without active hostilities, and active hostilities may exist without a state of war. ... It is clear, however, that an act of war starts a state of war only if there is a real intention to create a state of war. ... Suppose, however, that a state commits acts of war on a large scale [as with the Japanese invasion of Manchuria in 1931], but with repeated assertions that it is not intending to make war, is it possible for its acts to speak louder than its words? [Are quacking ducks, ducks?] It is believed that such a situation may become a state of war, but only if recognized as such by the victim or by third states. ... It is submitted that in

case a state using military force disclaims an intention to make war, and the victim cannot or does not recognize war [as China did not in 1931], a state of war does not exist until such time as third states recognize that it does.

ibid., 363, 365, 366

Like the material effects of a natural disaster, the fact of "war in the material sense" was incontestable, according to Wright. The joint Chinese-Japanese denial of this incontestable material fact, then, forced the responsibility to "declare" the existence of "war in the legal sense" onto third-party observers. In the event, this role was played mainly by the League of Nations. Secretary of State Henry Stimson also added his voice to the chorus when he declared, "it is clear beyond peradventure that a situation has developed [in Manchuria] which cannot under any circumstances be reconciled with [Japan's obligation to resolve her dispute with China pacifically]" (*ibid.*, 368). In other words, these third-party observers had to "declare" the existence of a Sino-Japanese "war" in the absence of the two belligerents making neither official "declarations" nor functionally equivalent "declarations."

Whereas third-party "declarations of war" may satisfy legal scholars of the positivist school, the only satisfaction achieved is to hide and obscure ontological guillotine that is a performative speech act. That is, the codependent and causative character of functionally equivalent speech acts. More to the point, the functionally equivalent speech acts that actually generated the "transmissible authorities" that brought a procedurally imperfect, unsolemn "war" into existence in Manchuria at 10:00pm on Friday, 18 October 1931 were known at the time, if not clearly so. They were two illegal military "orders," a false report, and, critically, Lieutenant General Honjo Shigeru's later endorsement of the two illegal "orders." Silence, after all, sometimes speaks louder than words.

What then was the initial functionally equivalent ontological guillotine that brought this procedurally imperfect and unsolemn "war in the material sense" into existence? The ontological trigger was the illegal "order" of the four principle conspirators who planned and executed the Mukden Incident—Colonel Itagaki Seishiro, Lieutenant Colonel Ishihara Kanji, Major Hanaya Tadashi, and Captain Imada Shintaro. It is believed that Captain Imada was the officer who supervised the planting of the explosive charge on the illegal "orders" of his superiors in the cabal (Yoshihashi 1963, 138).

Subsequently, as soon as the news of the explosion was received at headquarters, a long-standing operational plan was put into effect to respond to what was falsely reported as a Chinese attack on the Japanese forces in Mukden (*ibid.*, 161). This performative speech act, *i.e.*, the "order," to activate the operational plan, generated the "transmissible authorities" for the unsuspecting subordinate commanders to initiate the conquest of Manchuria.

The standing operational plan, however, was put into effect by Colonel Itagaki Seishiro without the knowledge of Lieutenant General Honjo Shigeru, who was absent from his headquarters at the time. When he learned of the incident at Mukden and the activation of the plan later the next day, he was too easily convinced not to countermand the second illegal "order" to implement the operational plan. Rather, Lieutenant General Honjo endorsed the illegal "order," saying, "Let the matter be carried out on my responsibility" (*ibid*., 167).

In sum, the chain of codependent, causative performative speech acts that generated the "transmissible authorities" that caused a procedurally imperfect, unsolemn "war in the material sense" in Manchuria in 1931 were:

At (t^1), the illegal "order" to Captain Imada to set an explosive charge next to the Southern Manchurian Railway track. This illegal "order," then,

At (t^2), triggered a false "report" of a Chinese attack, which led

At (t^3), to an apparently legal "order" that illegally activated the long-standing operation plan, which

At (t^4), was not countermanded by Lieutenant General Honjo, the commanding general.

General Honjo's silence gave color of legitimacy to the "transmissible authorities" generated by the illegal performative speech acts that activated the operations plan. The subordinate commands of the Kwantung Army, ignorant of the illegality of the initial "order" and the falsity of the initial report that triggered the operational plan, naturally, implemented the plan as "ordered." This led to the conquest of all of Manchuria over the following five months.

Therefore, instead of calling upon the non-codependent, non-causative "declarations" of the League of Nations, Secretary of State Henry Stimson, and other third-party observers, Wright should have noted that the ontological guillotine that brought the war in Manchuria into being was the material consequence was a series of illegal military "orders" and a false report. These ontological guillotines were the functionally equivalent performative speech acts that, in effect, "declared war" unofficially, imperfectly, unsolemnly, and illegitimately.

Further, and interestingly, the series of illegal, functionally equivalent speech acts exemplified by Mukden Incident also answers John Yoo's unasked question as to how an Imperial President "declares war" unofficially. For example, sometime before 1:00pm on Sunday, 7 October 2001, President George W. Bush issued a military "order" to commence armed hostilities against Afghanistan. This "order" was necessarily given in secret. The secrecy of his "order," naturally required that his "the sole authority to initiate hostilities" be "perfected," because "... under international law. A declaration served to fully transform the international legal relationship between two states from one of peace to one of war." This "perfecting" address was televised at 1:00pm on Sunday, 7 October 2001. It announced publicly the beginning of military operations in Afghanistan, *Operation Enduring Freedom*:

> Good afternoon. On my orders, the United States military has begun strikes against Al Qaida terrorist training camps and military installations of the Taliban regime in Afghanistan. These carefully targeted actions are designed to disrupt the use of Afghanistan as a terrorist base of operations and to attack the military capability of the Taliban regime.
> BUSH 2001

To further illustrate the "perfecting" quality of these types modern, procedurally imperfect, functionally equivalent declarative speech acts, compare President George W. Bush's televised address with Prime Minister Tony Blair's televised address for the 2003 invasion of Iraq. The full texts of these two functionally equivalent declarations of war are reproduced in Appendix E.

Exercising his "the sole authority to initiate hostilities" as an Imperial President, George W. Bush "perfected" his secret military order with a public address to the nation at 10:16pm on Wednesday, 19 March 2003:

> My fellow citizens, at this hour, American and coalition forces are in the early stages of military operations to disarm Iraq, to free its people and to defend the world from grave danger. On my orders, coalition forces have begun striking selected targets of military importance to undermine Saddam Hussein's ability to wage war.
> BUSH 2003

On the other side of the international dateline, exercising his "the sole authority to initiate hostilities" as an Imperial Prime Minister, Tony Blair likewise "perfected" his secret military order with an address to the nation on Thursday, 20 March 2003:

> On Tuesday night I gave the order for British forces to take part in military action in Iraq. Tonight, British servicemen and women are engaged from air, land and sea. Their mission: to remove Saddam Hussein from power, and disarm Iraq of its weapons of mass destruction
> BLAIR 2003

Military "orders" are, thus, the first half of the normal, functionally equivalent declarative act that substitute for Hague Convention III compliant, official, open, performative "declarations of war." These "orders" generate the illegal "transmissible authorities" that activate subordinate military commanders. The commander-in-chef's "orders" are then "perfected" either with 1) a public announcement of the commencement of armed hostilities or with 2) some sort of an "authorization," "approval," or "support" from a legislative assembly, or, alternatively, with 3) a lexical declaration by a legislative assembly.

CHAPTER 5

The Declaring of War as a Conflict Resolution Strategy

Abstract

The chapter discusses the conflict resolution potential of conditional declarations of war. This potential is unlocked by a strict adherence to procedural justice. Unlocking procedural justice, however, implies a strict adherence to the decorous solemnity that the Romans called *pium* ("piety"). In the case of war, *pium* is achieved most effectively through parliamentary procedures in a decision-making assembly. Parliamentary procedures are both procedurally just and *pium* because the *intention/decision* is not made privately before the text is *drafted* in private and, subsequently, *declared* publicly. Rather, the text is *drafted* in a public process before a public vote brings into existence the collective *intention/decision* simultaneously with the *declaration*.

The chapter concludes with a brief discussion of the Roman conception and practice of war: Conceptually, the purpose of war for the Romans was not to compel victory through an act of force, but to agree upon a renewed association through a treaty of alliance, often in the form of a peace treaty. Practically, a strict adherence to the solemn decorum of the *jus fetiale* facilitated a substantively just declarative act, the Romans believed. Namely, an act that sought an agreed upon a renewal of association through a treaty of alliance with the conflict partner.

...

> A journey of a thousand *li* begins with the first step.
> *Dao De Jing* 64

...

> We do not punish a nation until We have sent forth a messenger to forewarn them.
> *Qur'an* at 17:15

> Therefore the only justification for war is that peace and justice should afterwards prevail.
>
> CICERO (*De officiis* I, xi, 35)

What, if any, might be the conflict resolution potential of a procedurally perfect, solemn Hague Convention III compliant declaration of war? In pursuit of such a stray thought, Louis Kriesberg's *Constructive Conflicts: From Escalation to Resolution* (1998) provides a good path to follow. According to Kriesberg, conflicts spiral through time in a cycle of escalation and de-escalation until they terminate. In summary outline, the spiraling cycle begins with a set of circumstances that form the *Basis* of the conflict. The conflict remains latent until something happens to make it *Manifest*. Once *Manifest*, the conflict spirals through an indefinite number of complex escalations and de-escalations until these cycles *Terminate*. Depending upon the quality of the *Termination*, the resolution is only temporary, and the ill-formed *Termination* renews the *Basis* for another round of the same conflict. Or, the resolution is permanent, and the well-formed *Termination* resolves the conflict, but sets up the conditions for another, different conflict. Life without conflict, after all, is called the afterlife.

Kriesberg's account is insightful and helpful. In particular, the critical moment in his model is the ontological moment of conflict "manifestation," when a latent conflict is transformed into an open and public dispute. Thus, for Kriesberg too, the moment in which the conflict is "made public" is the moment that trips the ontological guillotine. Thud. And, with this "thud," the spiral of conflict escalation and de-escalation is launched and visibly unwinds towards termination. Needless to say, the character and qualities of the absolutely necessary ontological or manifestive act will strongly influence the subsequent escalatory and de-escalatory course of the conflict. This observation leads, then, to a grid of well or poorly made *intentions/decisions*, on the one hand, and well or poorly made *declarations*, on the other hand. From this grid, one is able to visualize the range of manifestive acts, as is illustrated in Figure 4. In short, the ontological guillotine can fall in a productive manner so as to facilitate conflict resolution; or the ontological guillotine can fall in a counterproductively manner so as to facilitate conflict exacerbation. With regard to war, then, how can conflict exacerbation be avoided in the ontological moment of manifestation?

Conflict Resolution Potential	The Decision	The Declaration
MAXIMAL	Well Made	Well Written
AMBIGUOUS	Poorly Made	Well Written
AMBIGUOUS	Well Made	Poorly Written
MINIMAL	Poorly Made	Poorly Written

FIGURE 4 Conflict resolution potential of the manifestive moment

1 The Shortcomings of Hague Convention III

At the beginning of Chapter 4, the Declare War Clause of the Constitution of the United States, was presented as both more controversial and less informative than Article 1 of Hague Convention III of 1907, *Relative to the Opening of Hostilities*. The principal reason for this was that Convention III not only identified the two types of open and determined declarative speech acts—absolute or conditional—but also stipulated the criteria for determining the moral and legal character of each type:

1) Absolute declarations of war require, at a minimum, a fully "reasoned" indictment of the gravamina that have provoked the enmity and the remedies that would restore amity, and
2) Conditional declarations of war required, at a minimum, reasonable "conditions."

Needless to say, the Hague criteria also define the meanings of "well" and "poorly" in Figure 4, and, hence, the conflict resolution potential of any given declarative act. This being the case, one must further observe that the four lexical declarations made by the United States Congress between 1812 and 1941 would have tended to exacerbate their respective conflicts, and not to have facilitated resolution. In contrast, the well-reasoned, absolute *Declaration of Independence* would have tended to facilitate the resolution of the conflict with Great Britain. To repeat, these declarations are reproduced in Appendix A.

In Chapter 4, the comment was also made in passing that examples of conditional declarations without time limits could be found only with the greatest difficulty in modern history. One had to go back to medieval history or to ancient Greece and the Roman or to Sumer in order to find examples. This absence of modern examples was explained as resulting from the fact that negotiations no longer begin as in former times. Namely, that negotiations are no longer governed by either by the Sumerian code outlined in *Agga and*

Gilgamesh or the Roman *jus fetiale*, which is discussed in the final section of this chapter. Negotiations no longer begin with a *rebus repetitis*, i.e., a conditional declaration of war without a time limit, which, if unsuccessful, then progresses to either a conditional declaration with a time limit or an absolute declaration. This particular spiral of escalation and de-escalation is no longer employed since roughly the seventeenth century.

The unexplored assumption in Chapter 4, therefore, was that modern negotiations *could*, once again, be so structured in this ancient manner. And, if so structured, modern negotiations *would* better "manifest" a conflict and, thereby better facilitate its resolution. For, what well-drafted conditional declarations can and should do is to declare clearly and precisely the gravamina that have generated the conflict and the peace terms that will end it.

Speaking pragmatically, in order to restructure international negotiations in the ancient manner, the nations of the world would, first, have to revive and adhere to Hague Convention III of 1907, *Relative to the Opening of Hostilities*. Second, they would have eschew bombast, cynicism, and bad faith in the texts of their conditional declarations of wars. For, one of the most striking differences between Roman and medieval conditional declarations is the bombast, cynicism, and bad faith of the latter and the absence of bombast, cynicism, and bad faith in the former. That is, to jump to the conclusion, one of the most striking differences between Roman and medieval conditional declarations is medieval conditional declarations were *decided* and drafted by monarchs, whereas the conditional declarations of the early Roman Republic were drafted by an assembly, the Senate, vetted by *collegium fetialis*, and, finally, voted on by the people of Rome in their tribes.

2   Unconditional Cynicism and Bad Faith

Consider a Roman example, before considering a medieval example: According to Livy, in 171 BCE, the minds of the kings of Europe and Asia were concerned about a looming third war between the city of Rome and Perseus, King of Macedonia. At the inauguration of Publius Licinius and Gaius Cassius as the consuls for that year, the Senate decreed that the new consuls would make the appropriate sacrifices to the gods and consult the *haruspices* diviners. This was done without sign of foreboding from either the gods or the *haruspices*. Thereupon, the new consuls went to the Senate and introduced a draft conditional declaration of war without a time limit. After debate, the draft was voted and approved. After the fetial priests of the *collegium fetialis* had vetted the draft text, legates were dispatched to Macedonia to open negotiations with Perseus in the hope of avoiding war. The text of their negotiating instructions, the enacted conditional declaration of war, read:

> ... whereas Perseus, son of Philip, King of Macedonia, contrary to the treaty made with his father Philip and renewed with himself after the death of his father, had invaded allies of the Roman people, had devastated their land and seized their cities, and whereas he had entered on plans for preparing war against the Roman people, and had assembled arms, soldiers and fleet for the said purpose, resolved that, unless he offered satisfaction in these matters, war against him be undertaken.
> LIVY 1919, XLII, XXX, 10–11

In this case, the negotiations failed to restore amity. The legates returned to Rome and denounced Perseus before the Senate. The same procedures were now employed to declare war absolutely. But, this time, after the *fetiales* had vetted the text, the Senate then instructed the consuls to present the draft to the *comitia centuriata*, the assembly of all men eligible for military service. The Assembly of the Hundreds also debated and voted on the now fetial vetted draft declaration. Once enacted by the Hundreds, the Third Macedonian War commenced. It ended in 168 BCE at the Battle of Pydna, the capture of Perseus and his family, and the division of his kingdom into four new republics. Two decades later, in 146 BCE, the republics were dissolved, unruly Macedonia became a Roman province, and Roman hegemony was firmly established over the rest of Greece.

But what of the ontological guillotine? What of manifestive moment? The deliberate pace of the solemn parliamentary procedures, the serious indictment of the gravamina charged against Perseus, and a simple plea for redress certainly betoken a desire to resolve the conflict short of armed hostilities. Of perhaps greater importance, though, is the way in which the parliamentary procedures produced a text characterized 1) by a serious analysis of the root causes of the conflict and 2) an equally serious proposal to resolve or remedy the conflict—observance of the treaty signed by his father and ratified by himself. To be sure, cynicism and bad faith cannot be ruled out absolutely. Still, the likelihood is minimal on the evidence of the text and the deliberate pace of the solemn parliamentary procedures, their decorum, solemnity, and "piety." Conflict resolution, not conflict exacerbation, motivated the Romans of the Republic in 171 BCE.

In American history, the only comparable texts produced by means of comparable parliamentary procedures are the several petitions to the King from the Second Continental Congress during 1775 and early 1776 (Maier 1997). The

Declaration on Taking Arms of Thursday, 6 July 1775 is of particular note. The only difference between the two is that, unlike the solemn, conditional declaration to Perseus, the 1775 *Declaration* was not an official conditional declaration of war. Rather, it was a functionally equivalent conditional declaration of war. When the negotiations called for in the 1775 *Declaration* failed, an absolute declaration of war was made a year later in 1776, the *Declaration of Independence*.

To jump to the conclusion again, the contrast between collective decision-making and executive decision-making is stark when looked at in detail. In particular, none of the solemn parliamentary procedures constrain a nation's war leader or his mental processes. With energy and dispatch, he makes his *decision*, consults with his council or councils as he pleases, and *declares* war either officially or with a functionally equivalent speech act, again as he pleases. Operating in this executive mode, which is outside of the constraints of parliamentary deliberation and decision-making, no need exists for the text to possess a serious analysis of the root causes of the conflict or an equally serious proposal to resolve or remedy the conflict. The only need is for the text to please the nation's war leader. For example, consider the conditional declaration delivered to Venice from the Ottoman Sultan, Selim II, on Tuesday, 28 March 1570.

> Selim, Ottoman Sultan, Emperor of the Turks, Lord of Lords, King of Kings, Shadow of God, Lord of the Earthly Paradise and of Jerusalem, to the Signory of Venice: We demand of you Cyprus, which you shall give us willingly or perforce; and do you not irritate our horrible sword, for we shall wage most cruel war against you everywhere; nor let you trust in your treasure, for we shall cause it suddenly to run away from you like torrent; beware to irritate us.
>
> HILL 1940-8, 3:888

Formally, the document is a conditional declaration of war without a time limit. And, as a matter of fact, time for additional negotiations was available. Selim did not begin his siege of Cyprus until three months later, landing his force on the island on Monday, 3 July 1570. Negotiations could conceivably have continued. Formally, the document also leaves open the possibility of settlement short of armed hostilities. The Signory of Venice may meet the sultan's demand "willingly." Realizing that Venice was overextended and unable to defend Cyprus any longer, the Signory might conceivably have negotiated an advantageous withdrawal. In addition, Selim's warning to the Signory of Venice not to "trust in your treasure" points directly to the bribery and corruption that had worked so well for Venice in the past and might just work again in this case.

Still, formalities aside, the document reads less like a conditional declaration without a time limit and more like an ultimatum. And, indeed, that is the way the Signory of Venice read it, immediately declaring war absolutely on Selim II. In the event, the last fort on Cyprus fell to Selim II on Wednesday, 1 August 1571. Venice was, indeed, overextended and unable to defend Cyprus any longer.

The bombast and braggadocio, if not cynicism and bad faith, of Selim's conditional declaration is a natural consequence of the process by which the *decision* was made. Selim did not have to suffer the constraints of parliamentary procedures. One can easily imagine how flattered Selim was when his viziers presented him with the draft text. Further, this tone of cynicism and bad faith is found in royal declarations generally. For example, the same tone of bombast and braggadocio, if in a lower register, is found in King William's absolute declaration against France reproduced in Appendix B.

In text-based parliamentary procedures, the relative absence of cynicism and braggadocio would appear to arise from two factors: First, the minimal requirement for all parliamentary deliberation is that the text of that which is to be *decided* must be settled and fixed before a vote. Once this minimal requirement is met, a larger or smaller minority of the participants in a decision-making assembly will oppose the measure, whatever it is. Such is human nature. Ten percent of any group will reliably and regularly oppose any and every proposal. This natural and foreseen "collective action problem" imposes a certain deliberate pace to allow for persuasion and a certain seriousness of text so as to sway the undecided. Oxymoronically, conflict resolution, not war, is normally the initial, manifestive moment of parliamentary decision-making.

3 Parliamentary vs. Executive Decision-Making: the Decision Is the Declaration vs. the Decision Is Not the Declaration

Yet, at a deeper, more fundamental, more important level, a critical temporal difference separates parliamentary from executive decision-making. That is, between collective and individual decision-making. This temporal difference was also addressed in Chapter 1, although not explicitly. There, the explicit focus was on the form of the declarative speech act, on the empirical logic of the ceremony, on the solemnity of the declarative act, whether uttered in due form or not uttered in due form. Here, the focus is explicitly on the temporal logic of the ceremony, on whether or not the *intention/decision/declaration* come into existence simultaneously or sequentially. This change in focus can be illustrated by reproducing the schematic summary found in Chapter 1:

I. Unsolemn Functionally Equivalent Declarations by an Individual, not in due form: *Scenarios 1* to 3:
   At (t^1), an individual does the mental act of *intending/deciding*.
   At (t^2), an individual does the physical act of *drafting*.
   At (t^3), an individual does the physical act of *declaring*.
II. Solemn Declarations by a Collectivity, in due form: *Scenario 4*
   At (t^1), a decision-making assembly *drafts* a well-reasoned text that justifies the moral imperative of the *decision* to go to war.
   At (t^2), a decision-making assembly votes on the amended draft declaration, therewith simultaneously enacting the *intention/ decision/ declaration*.

The critical difference between the collective and the individual speech acts, as already noted, is that, when the ontological guillotine falls, the former is a public, enacting performance, whereas the latter is a private mental act. More fully, before the vote, no collective *intention* or *decision* or *declaration* exists and the *draft* remains unsettled, a new amendment may still be offered and the debate continued. Then, in the instant of the vote, the decision-making assembly speaks and settles the moral heart of the matter. Moreover, this moral heart was spoken, not with the authority of a private mental act, but with the authority of a collective public act. Consequently, in the instant of the vote, a collective *intention/ decision/ declaration* comes into existence all at once. A certain sensible legitimacy flows from the simultaneity of this collectively made, transparently public *intention/ decision/ declaration*.

In contrast, before the drafting of the functionally equivalent *public announcement*, a private *intention* and *decision* already exists in executive decision-making. Ominously, this means that the moral heart of the matter—the *intention/decision*—has already been settled. Consequently, in the time lag between the private *intention* and *decision* and the functionally equivalent *public announcement*, a certain sensible illegitimacy flows from this privately made functionally equivalent private speech act.

More precisely and consequently, when spoken by an individual, the *intention/decision* is not contingent on the text of the *declaration*. The text of the functionally equivalent *public announcement* depends solely on the political needs and desires of the individual, who has already *decided* to go to war. That is, in the words of President George W. Bush speaking in full executive mode, "But I'm the decider, and I decide what is best" (2006). As examples of two executive "deciders" "deciding," reconsider the televised addresses of President George W. Bush and Prime Minister Tony Blair announcing the onset of military operations against Iraq in 2003. The full texts are reproduced in Appendix C. As George W. Bush said:

> My fellow citizens, at this hour, American and coalition forces are in the early stages of military operations to disarm Iraq, to free its people and to defend the world from grave danger. ...

As Tony Blair said:

> On Tuesday night I gave the order for British forces to take part in military action in Iraq. Tonight, British servicemen and women are engaged from air, land and sea. Their mission: to remove Saddam Hussein from power, and disarm Iraq of its weapons of mass destruction. I know this course of action has produced deep divisions of opinion in our country. But I know also the British people will now be united in sending our armed forces our thoughts and prayers. ...

Technically, the two texts may be characterized as procedurally imperfect, unsolemn and unreasoned, absolute, functionally equivalent declaratives acts. Not unexpectedly, they lack the clear four-part structure of a Hague Convention III compliant declaration of war. They exhibit no clear indictment of the gravamina, no clear denunciation of both the enemy and of the war, no clear declaration of peace terms (although the military objective of "liberation" is clear), and no clear declaration of war. Basically, the two statements are the (t^7) public announcements of the president and the prime minister's previous military order at (t^6) in *Scenario 3*. The texts also address a number of the domestic political controversies sparked by the war and call for support both for "our troops" and for the general war effort. The information value and the conflict resolution potential of the two statements is nil, unlike the *Declaration of Independence*.

The nil value of the two functionally equivalent declarative acts results in at least two ramifications or consequences: First, an absence of the power to persuade and, second, a deeper insight into the reasons for "executive proneness to war." With regard to the first ramification, a parliamentary text that will persuade the reluctant members of a decision-making assembly will—to some indefinite marginal degree—persuade the opposing belligerent. Communicating with the opposing belligerent persuasively in well-reasoned, Hague Convention III compliant language is one of the *sine qua non* for conflict resolution and reconciliation.

"Some indefinite marginal degree," however, is an important, if minor, step toward conflict resolution and reconciliation. Of very much greater importance, a text that will persuade the reluctant members of a decision-making assembly will—to a much greater degree—persuade third parties. This is a much larger step towards resolving a conflict. Third parties often take sides. For example, the French might sign a Treaty of Amity and Commerce in 1778. They might also extend war loans and send an army and a fleet. Allies, even if neutral, are usually a decisive factor in war, if not in other disputes.

Consider a negative example first: Slobodan Milosevic, President of the Former Yugoslavia, loudly proclaimed his self-satisfying reasons for a Serbian domination of Bosnia and Kosovo during the 1990's. Crucially, these functionally equivalent declarations of war failed to persuade third parties that he had any good reasons. This lack of third-party support in the international community eventually forced Milosevic to accept the *Dayton-Paris Agreement* on Thursday, 14 December 1995 for Bosnia and the *Kumanovo Agreement* on Wednesday, 9 June 1999 for Kosovo. Third party pressure and armed assistance to the Bosnians and the Kosovars decided the outcome.

Consider next a positive example: Nelson Mandela delivered a statement from the dock during his trial at Rivonia on Monday, 20 April 1964. This statement has long served as a functionally equivalent declaration of war for the African National Congress (Mandela 1964). Needless to say, it was persuasive. So persuasive, that most of the international community eventually took sides and applied diplomatic, economic, and sports pressure on the apartheid Government of South Africa. Eventually, this international pressure, combined with great internal pressures, led to the release of Mandela from prison on Sunday, 11 February 1990. Negotiations for a new constitution soon followed and were successfully concluded. In sum, the ability to gain the support of third parties is usually critical to the success of any enterprise, especially war. In American history, this principle was demonstrated most effectively by the way in which the persuasive power of the *Declaration of Independence* facilitated French support for the revolution.

In short, when the ontological guillotine falls synchronically in a parliamentary vote, the declarative act is usually procedurally solemn and, hence, productively manifested. Under these circumstances, the conflict resolution potential of the manifestive moment will normally be maximal. In sharp contrast, when the ontological guillotine falls asynchronously in a private mental act, the time-lagged executive process is always procedurally unsolemn and, hence, counterproductively manifested. Under these circumstances, the conflict resolution potential of the moment will normally be minimal to nil.

With regard to the second ramification, recall James Madison's letter to Thomas Jefferson of Monday, 2 April 1798, "The constitution supposes, what the History of all Govts demonstrates, that the Ex. is the branch of power most interested in war, & most prone to it. It has accordingly with studied care vested the question of war in the Legisl" (Cited in Schlesinger 1973, 5) . History, most certainly, does demonstrate the interest and proneness of the "Ex." for war. Yet, the fundamental driver of executive war making is not the war leader's psychological disposition. It is not the "Ex.'s" interest in or proneness to war *per se*. Rather, this "proneness" is the clear result of the "Legisl's" incapacity to *exercise* "the power. ... to declare war," in the first place. And, in the second place, of the absences of an alternative assembly to utter the declarative speech act collectively. Naturally then, the default alternative is for the nation's war leader *exercise* "the power . ... to declare war." And, consequently, *faute de mieux* is the full and complete explanation of executive war-making, in general, and of the Imperial Presidency, in particular.

Still, to observe more concretely the temporal differences between collective and executive declarative acts, compare two open and determined, absolute declarations of war: The *Declaration of Independence* and the 1917 declaration against Imperial Germany for World War I. The *Declaration of Independence* is a fully determined, Hague Convention III compliant, solemn performative declaration, as one would expect of a text produced by a decision-making assembly. The declaration of 1917 is an open, but not an determined, lexical declaration. It is therefore not Hague Convention III compliant because it is not a "reasoned" text. An undetermined, "unreasoned" text is, of course, what one would expect of a text produced by a politically astute, elected constitutional monarch. Namely, a war leader who wisely employs *Scenario 3: An Unsolemn Functionally Equivalent Declarative Act by the Nation's Hereditary or Elected King that Involves a Legislature*.

Compare, first, the length and persuasive quality of the two texts, before comparing the deliberative, synchronic parliamentary procedures and asynchronic executive processes by which the respective texts were created. Again, both texts are reproduced in Appendix A.

> WHEN in the Course of human Events,. ... To prove this [tyranny], let Facts be submitted to a candid World. ... He has dissolved Representative Houses repeatedly, for opposing with manly Firmness his Invasions on the Rights of the People. ... For depriving us, in many Cases, of the Benefits of Trial by Jury:. ... He has plundered our Seas, ravaged our Coasts, burnt our Towns, and destroyed the Lives of our People. ... We have appealed to their native Justice and Magnanimity, and we have conjured them by the Ties of our common Kindred to disavow these Usurpations,. ... We must, therefore, acquiesce in the Necessity, which denounces our Separation, and hold them, as we hold the rest of Mankind, Enemies in War, in Peace, Friends. ... in the Name, and by Authority of the good People of these Colonies, solemnly Publish and Declare, That these United

Colonies are, and of Right out (sic) to be, Free and Independent States;. ... with a firm Reliance on the Protection of divine Providence, we mutually pledge to each other our Lives, our Fortunes, and our sacred Honor.

In contrast, consider the length and persuasive quality of the text drafted by President Wilson's State Department:

> Joint Resolution: Declaring that a state of war exists between the Imperial German Government and the Government and the People of the United States and making provision to prosecute the same.
> *Whereas* the Imperial German Government has committed repeated acts of war against the Government and people of the United States of America: Therefore, be it
> *Resolved by the Senate and House of Representatives of the United States of America in Congress assembled*, That the state of war between the United States and the Imperial German Government which has thus been thrust upon the United States is hereby formally declared; and that the President be, and he is hereby, authorized and directed to employ the entire naval and military forces of the United States and the resources of the Government to carry on war against the Imperial German Government; and to bring the conflict to a successful termination all the resources of the country are hereby pledged by the Congress of the United States (Approved, April 6, 1917. Pub. Res. No. 65-1, 40 Stat. 1).

Textually, both declarations are absolute and open. However, the *Declaration of Independence* possesses a certain sensible legitimacy because it is determined, and fully so. It is Hague Convention III compliant. It explains fully and elegantly the reasons for the war, namely, the twenty-seven grievances that have provoked it and the remedy that will end it. The initial negotiating position of the colonial peace commissioners in Paris is fully stated and elegantly reasoned. Inversely, the 1917 declaration possesses a certain sensible illegitimacy because it is determined, but only minimally so. It is not Hague Convention III compliant. It states that, "the Imperial German Government has committed repeated acts of war." But which "acts of war?" How many? Where? When? Wilson's initial negotiating position at the Versailles Conference is neither stated nor reasoned in this manifestive moment. Tripping the ontological guillotine and getting the United States into war officially is the only purpose of the 1917, lexical declaration, not negotiating peace, not resolving the conflict.

Yet, the contrast in textual legitimacy and illegitimacy is not the main point here. Textual legitimacy is the main point of the next chapter, but not here. Here, the main point turns on what can only be called the legitimating parliamentary procedures by which the *Declaration of Independence* was produced. These legitimating procedures are, then, contrasted with the very much less legitimating personal decision-making of President Woodrow Wilson, the "decider," employing *Scenario 3*.

In an effort to draw this contrast out, the synchronic, deliberative procedures used by the Second Continental Congress will not be repeated here because they have already been outlined in an authority-tracing schematic in Chapter 3. But, clearly, those procedures color the *Declaration of Independence* with an indisputable glow of legitimacy. No *one* decided the question. No *one* imposed his will upon the world. A collective phenomenon—war—was *decided* collectively. In the simultaneity of the vote, war was *intended/ decided/ declared*, collectively. Monarchy—either absolute or constitutional—was nowhere in sight. Gilgamesh would have been appalled.

With the legitimating parliamentary half of the comparison in hand, the illegitimating executive half needs, initially, to highlight the continuity from Gilgamesh to Selim, Ottoman Sultan, Emperor of the Turks, Lord of Lords, King of Kings, Shadow of God, etc. to Charles v, the Wise, and on to Commander-in-Chief Wilson. Namely, as Gilgamesh was the national war leader of Erech, and Selim was the national war leader of the Ottoman, and Charles v was the national war leader of the Franks, so Wilson was national war leader of the Americans. All three employed virtually the same asynchronic process to produce a text that expressed their personal sentiments and desires for war. And, finally, one must also take note that what is true of Commander-in-Chief Wilson as the nation's elected, constitutional monarch and war leader—the "decider"—is also true of every other president.

President Wilson was reelected in November 1916 on the catchphrase, "He kept us out of war." Inaugurated on Saturday, 3 March 1917, Wilson informed his Cabinet at (t^1), on Tuesday, 20 March 1917, that he had *decided* to enter the Great War because Imperial Germany had resumed unrestricted submarine warfare. To make his *decision* officially public, Wilson astutely chose to employ *Scenario 3: An Unsolemn Functionally Equivalent Declarative Act by the Nation's Hereditary or Elected King that Involves a Legislature*. To this end, at (t^2), Wilson convened a special session of the Sixty-fifth Congress for Monday, 2 April 1917. At (t^3), on April Fool's Day, Sunday, 1 April 1917, Wilson spent the whole day at his typewriter composing his address to Monday's Joint Session (Wilson 1966–1993, 41:vii-viii). At (t^4), about 10:00pm, he sent a note to Secretary of State Robert Lansing requesting him to draw up a congressional resolution "in the sense of these words":

> ... I advise that the Congress declare the recent course of the Imperial German Government to be in fact nothing less than war against the

government and people of the United States; that it formally accept the status of belligerent which has thus been thrust upon it; and that it take immediate steps not only to put the country in a more thorough state of defense but also to exert all its power and employ all its resources to bring the Government of the German Empire to terms and end the war.

ibid., 41:516

At (t^5), the next day, Wilson approved the State Department's draft, which was then delivered to the House leadership just before Wilson addressed the joint session at 8:32pm. In a burst of congressional initiative, the Senate made several amendments to the State Department draft during the following days. For example, the State Department's original draft reads, "*Whereas.* The recent acts of the Imperial German Government are acts of war against the Government and people of the United States." The Senate's amended version reads, "*Whereas* the Imperial German Government has committed repeated acts of war against the Government and people of the United States of America." With this display of congressional independence and initiative, the draft passed at (t^6), on Good Friday, 6 April 1917. At (t^7), that same night at 12:14am, President Wilson approved the Sixty-fifth Congress's approval of the State Department's draft of the president's *intention/decision* of 20 March 1917 (*ibid.*, 41:ix). The asynchronic executive feedback loop was now buckled. Gilgamesh, Selim, and Charles V would have approved. Louis Kriesberg would not have approved. The manifestive moment did little or nothing to resolve the conflict.

4 The *Jus Fetiale*: Procedural Justice Sustains Substantive Justice

In conclusion, a further discussion of the conflict resolution bias of the ancient Roman conception and practice of war may be appropriate. The Roman's viewed war as a quasi-judicial process. Not as a judicial process, because no courts existed in *inter*-national relations, as they do in *intra*-national relations, but as a quasi-judicial process. Morally, the foundations of this quasi-judicial process were built on the fact that the Romans were not moral relativists. They did not believe that either *intra*- or *inter*-national relations were anarchic. Neither Thucydides nor Thomas Hobbes determined their thinking. Neither Carl Schmitt nor Hans Morgenthau taught in their schools. Instead, the Romans were moral realists. They believed that both *intra*- and *inter*-national relations were undergirded by what they called, the natural law (*jus naturale*), on the one hand, and by socially constructed customs and laws (*lex*), on the other hand. In addition, for war, they believed in a special law, the *jus gentium*, "the rules of nations," most particularly in the sanctity of treaties. *Inter*-national peace depended, not on enforcement, but on keeping one's promises, one's agreed upon treaties.

But, if neither *intra*- nor *inter*-national social orders were anarchic, the "rules" of those two orders were sometimes violated. These violations sometimes created the appearance of anarchy. Whether a question of appearance or actuality, violations of either the natural law or of the socially constructed legal order may be addressed in either one of two different ways: Violators may be punished (corrected?) with an act of force to compel compliance and redress, or offenders can be hailed into court for judgment and redress. Both options are available, but, were one to impose a conflict resolution bias, as the Romans did, one would try the judicial option before the blunt force option.

As just noted, however, when resolving *intra*-national violations, a bias towards the judicial option is not only praiseworthy, but also practical. Practical, because either customary or statutory, third-party adjudicating institutions—courts—normally exist. When resolving *inter*-national violations, in contrast, a bias towards the judicial option was impractical because no courts existed. Yet, if a fully "judicial" option is impractical, might a quasi-judicial option exist? If so, what would such a quasi-judicial option look like?

What a quasi-judicial option would not look like is like a third-party court. Nor would a quasi-judicial option look like a one-party act of force to compel compliance and redress. As already noted in Chapter 1, John Stuart Mill has observed that, "it is as little justifiable to force our ideas on other people, as to compel them to submit to our will in any other respect" (Mill 1867, III: 166–7). What a quasi-judicial option must look like is like a two-party negotiations. But not just any two-party negotiation. A quasi-judicial negotiation must look like the offender has been hailed into negotiations so that, in the fullness of time, the conflict partners may settle upon an agreed judgment and redress. So that the conflict partners may renew their relationship on a more solid foundation as friends, as allies, as *socii*.

The quasi-judicial negotiations, therefore, must not only look *pium*; they must actually possess the slow, solemn, step-by-step, decorum that is the hallmark of procedurally just human interactions. Thus, quasi-judicial negotiating procedures must not only address the substantive justice of the dispute, but the means and methods of procedural justice as well. Denouncing the enemy's substantive injustice, and ignoring the required, solemnly decorous, procedural justice, the Romans believed, was grossly *impium*.

Substantively, then, the negotiations must engage the specificities of the alleged violations. This means that the offender must be indicted with specific violations of the natural law, on the one hand, and with equally specific violations of the *jus gentium*, on the other hand. In particular, the charges under the *jus gentium* should specify treaty violations, as is exemplified by the 171 BCE conditional declaration against Perseus above.

Procedurally, the negotiations must conform to the decorous solemnity of all judicial procedures, which is what the "rules" of the *jus fetiale* do. For, to repeat, without the decorous solemnity of *pium*, procedural justice is sacrificed to expediency. But expediency beclouds, when it does not traduce, substantive justice. That is, to speak in the more modern language of conflict resolution, decorous quasi-judicial negotiators think and talk, not in terms of enemies to be chastised, but in terms of "conflict partners," allies, or *socii*. As Hannah Arendt has summarized the Roman conception and practice of war:

> ... that unique and great notion of a war whose peace is predetermined not by victory or defeat but by an alliance of the warring parties, who now become [conflict] partners, *socii* or allies, by virtue of the new relationship established in the fight itself and confirmed through the instrument of *lex*, the Roman law. Since Rome was founded on this treaty-law between two different and naturally hostile people, it could become Rome's mission eventually "to lay all the world beneath laws"—*totum sub leges mitret orbem*. The genius of Roman politics—not only according to Virgil but, generally, according to Roman self-interpretation—lay in the very principles which attended the legendary foundation of the city (1963, 211. For the Roman sources of *pium* and the *jus fetiale*, see Watson 1993. Conveniently, Watson cites Dionysius of Halicarnassus on pages 2–3 and Livy on pages 10–12 for the *jus fetiale*).

Arendt's summary of the Roman conception and practice of war is of interest for two reasons: First, because the roots of both international law, in general, and Hague Convention III, in particular, are located in those conceptions and practices, specifically, in the *jus fetiale*. Second, because the institutions and laws of the Roman Republic were, in part, the models to which the members of the Federal Convention looked when drafting the Constitution in 1787. This was especially the case with regard to taking the power to *decide* and *declare* war from the executive, the nation's war leader.

Whereas the complex republican institutions of Rome are clearly not dispositive to govern a modern society, three of the foundational attitudes that supported Rome's republican institutions are: The first was a profound antipathy toward monarchy. The second, and more significant, was a nexus that understood both war and the declaring of war as a quasi-judicial process governed by law. But, third, and the most significant, was the Roman belief in the critical importance of procedural justice in order to achieve substantive justice. What they called *pium* or a decorous "piety." For, they believed that all social interactions *ought to* be govern by the strictest adherence to solemn decorum in the *exercise* of the laws, protocols, rites, rituals, and rules.

The antipathy of the Romans toward monarchy is well known and seen, first, their ability to sustain their kingless republican institutions for almost five hundred years, from the revolt against the last king, Tarquinius Superbus, in 509 BCE until the indefinite dictatorship of Julius Caesar in 48 BCE. Then, even after the founding of the Roman Empire by Caesar and Octavian, every possible title except "king" was used—dictator for life, *Princeps*, Caesar, Augustus, Emperor—any title but "*rex*."

With respect to *pium*, the relevant contrast is with the modern attitude of war as compellence. For example, Thomas Schelling speaks highly of "compellence" in his *Arms and Influence* (1966, 70–1), while Carl von Clausewitz's first definition of war is that, "*War is thus an act of force to compel our enemy to do our will*" (1976, 75). War for the Romans, however, was one of two conflict resolution alternatives. As Cicero explains in *De Officiis*:

> ... there are two ways of contending [*decertandi*] an issue—one is by force [*vim*], and the other is by reason[ed debate, discussion, or controversy (*disceptationem*)]. The former is the prerogative of beasts, the latter of men, so that we should only have recourse to the former when the latter is no avail (1928, I, xi, 34).

More specifically, Cicero identifies the three objective stages that add up to the elements of a procedurally "lawful" or "pious" declaring of war:

> The only excuse, therefore, for going to war is that we may live in peace unharmed. ... As for war, humane [*sanctissime* = most holy or solemn] laws touching it [war] are drawn up in the fetial code of the Roman People under all the guarantees of religion [*i.e.*, decorous rites]; and from this it may be gathered that no war is just, unless it is entered upon after an official demand for satisfaction [*rebus repetitis* = the request for restitution] or reparation has been submitted [to the conflict partner] or warning [*denuntiatum* = denunciation] has been given [by the fetial priests] and a formal declaration made [*indictum* = indictment].
>
>   *ibid.*, I. xi. 35, 36. See also *De Re Publica* 1928, II, xvii 31

From "the fetial code of the Roman People" (*i.e.*, the *jus fetiale*), the passage identifies three of the sufficient conditions for a procedurally "lawful" or "pious" declaration of war. Still, one must notice that Cicero has not spoken of the indispensable necessary condition for procedurally "lawful" or "pious" declarations of war. Namely, the existence of a decision-making assembly possessed of the capacity to *draft*, debate, amend, and vote on the synchronic *intention/ decision/ declaration*. The very definition of tyranny for Cicero and the Romans of the Republic was to have a king, emperor, president, prime minister, chancellor, or any other permanent war leader *intend/decide* and, then later, *draft* the text and *declare* war on his own subjective whim, asynchronically. Tragically, if not inevitably, a few years after Cicero wrote *De Officiis* to his son, then studying in Athens, the *jus fetiale* would be abrogated by the *imperium* of Caesar and Octavian. And, with that, the five-hundred-year-old republican insistence on procedurally just, solemn, "pious," synchronic declarative speech acts by collective assemblies died and passed away.

In sum, whereas armed hostilities might well become the final arbiter of a dispute, the obligatory rites and rituals of the *jus fetiale* were designed to promote the resolution of conflicts with neighboring tribes before the disputes cycled into armed hostilities (Watson 1993, 62). In a word, without *pium*, "piety" in the Roman sense of decorum, both procedural justice and substantive justice would be lost, the Romans believed. And, finally, whereas Cicero's "peace and justice" is a higher standard than the "fair, durable, and mutually agreeable" standard found in modern conflict resolution, the foundational attitudes of both Cicero and Roger Fisher and William L. Ury differ little (1991). For, is it not the case that, when one approaches opponents as conflict partners and war as an objective, fact-based, quasi-judicial process, the object is no longer Clausewitz or Schelling's "compellence?" Rather, the objective, now, is to unlock the conflict resolution potential of the manifestive moment with a solemn and "pious" conditional declaration of war. But this potential is unlocked most easily when a decision-making assembly using legitimating parliamentary procedures to simultaneously *intend/ decide/ declare* the question of war or peace on the basis of an objective, textually legitimate, open and determined declaration. Functionally equivalent *public announcements* decided asynchronically by the nation's war leader possess little or no conflict resolution potential.

CHAPTER 6

The United Nation's Security Council
An "Original Understanding" vs. "Original Intentions"

Abstract

Several structural issues in modern constitutional monarchies are raised, including the power of the "power of the purse." To illustrate these issues, Security Council *Resolutions 82* and *83* of June 1950, which "authorized" the Korean War, are analyzed. Beyond the structural issues, the two resolutions are significant because that they are, first, Hague Convention III compliant and, second, demonstrate the conflict resolution potential of procedural justice, the *jus fetiale*, and conditional declarations of war.

The difference between two different types of decision-making assemblies was spoken of in Chapter 3. The one type possessed a demonstrated capacity to *intend/ decide/ declare* war simultaneously; the other type did not. The collective speaker of the former type, it was argued, was organized as a small, *monofunction*, majority-rule, unicameral assembly, employing committee-of-the-whole rules; whereas the collective speaker of the latter was organized as large, *bifunction*, majority-rule, bicameral assembly, employing standing committees rules. As examples of the former, the Second Continental Congress was mentioned repeatedly. Discussed also were the procedures used by the United Nations Security Council and the 107th Congress to authorize the 2011 no-fly zone over Libya.

Here, in this chapter, attention returns to Security Council. But this time the purpose is to focus on the texts of *Resolutions 82* and *83* of June 1950. These two resolutions were the Security Council's initial responses to the North Korean invasion of South Korea. A mild irony infects the example because of President Harry Truman's recourse to the Security Council in 1950. This move is said by many to be the event that marks the beginning of the post-World War II usurpation of the congressional war powers by the Imperial Presidency (*e.g.*, Schlesinger's Chapter 6, The Presidency Ascendant: Korea (1973)).

Be the degree of irony as it may, Security Council *Resolutions 82* and *83* of June 1950 are of considerable interest because they represent one of the very few modern examples of the employment of Hague Convention III compliant procedures. *Resolution 82* is, in effect, a functionally equivalent, conditional declaration of war without time limit, whereas *Resolution 83* is, in effect, a functionally equivalent, absolute declaration of war. In other words, the Security Council maximized the conflict resolution potential of the manifestive moment. That the conflict had already lurched forward beyond resolution into armed hostilities does not diminish the fact that the traditional ceremonies and formalities found in both the *jus fetiale* and Hague Convention III were observed by the Security Council, if not by the North Koreans.

1 Original Irrelevance: Perceiving a Separation of Powers

An examination of the texts of *Resolutions 82* and *83* is also useful because they highlight several structural issues found in modern constitutional monarchies, and most strikingly in the Constitution of the United States. These structural issues concern 1) the existence or non-existence of "inherent" legislative and executive powers, 2) the possible separation of those two powers, and 3) the failings of a system in which one of the powers is supposed to "check" and "balance" the other. This endless constitutional debate over a perceived "separation of powers" is possible only because one has forgotten to ask the normative, rule-of-law questions concerning the decorously "pious" procedures for producing legitimate texts. This forgetfulness is remedied most directly by looking at examples where proper procedures produce legitimate texts. Namely, texts that are Hague Convention III compliant, such as *Resolutions 82* and *83*. But, before doing so, one can no longer delay confronting the endlessly speculation on the "original intentions" of the Framer's of the Constitution, as commentators have been doing since 1793, or, alternatively, on the Framer's "original understanding" of the Constitution, as has become the fashion more recently.

1.1 *John Yoo's "Original Understanding"*

John Yoo has already been introduced in Chapters 1, 2, and 3. He is reintroduced here for his critical views on those who seek refuge in a doctrine of "original understanding." These refugees believe—reasonably enough—that it is difficult, if not impossible, to parse the "original intent" of men dead over two hundred years. A better approach, John Yoo argues, is to "reconstruct the historical [or "original"] understanding of the constitutional text and structure ..." (Yoo 2005, viii). This change from speculative psychology to an "historical understanding" has the two additional values, according to John Yoo. First off, it conforms to the actual practice of presidential war making. Second, it validates the theory of a "unitary executive" and encourages the further development of "enhanced executive powers," which, if not imperial, are at least royal. Taken all together, this means that a doctrine of "original understanding" allows Yoo to propose " ... a constitutional theory of the foreign affairs power that differs, at times sharply, from the conventional [*i.e.*, "original intent"] academic wisdom but that describes more accurately the actual practice of the three branches" (*ibid.*, 2005, viii; see also ix, x, 7–8, 19).

Mindful therefore of history and practice, John Yoo finds a functioning model for "a constitutional theory of the foreign affairs power" in ancient British law and its constitutional monarchy. Beyond cavil, the Constitution of the United States is deeply influenced by British law and experience. British law and experience is, therefore, a natural source for interpretative guidance. As a hereditary constitutional monarchy, the power to *decide* and to *declare* war in both British law and experience is a royal prerogative, if no longer a divine right. As already cited in Chapter 2, John Locke located this royal prerogative among the king's fœderative powers in Chapter XII, *Of the Legislative, Executive, and Federative Power of the Common-wealth* of his 1690 *Second Treatise* (1764). Likewise, William Blackstone (1769) held most categorically that, "[T]he king has also the sole prerogative of making war and peace" (Cited in Yoo 2005, 41.).

In sum, Yoo has found a way to realize his first value: to align his "original understanding" with actual practice. He has accomplished this by re-branding Britain's hereditary constitutional monarchy for the American market as a "unitary executive" with "enhanced executive powers." This "rebranding," however, is just another way of saying that the American presidency is an elected, constitutional monarchy. Yoo could have cited Gilgamesh at this point, but does not.

Further, Yoo's first value also means that any congressional power to *decide* and *declare* war must be a power without power. And, again, this is precisely the case, as British law and experience confirm. According to John Yoo, "British practice also underscored the irrelevance of the declaration of war to the balance of war powers between Crown and Parliament," because "A declaration only perfected or made 'completely effective' hostilities between two nations, which otherwise could take the form of an 'incomplete state of hostilities'" (*ibid.*, 51; 42). To further confirm his conclusion, Yoo cites Alexander Hamilton's observation in *Federalist No. 25* that, "the ceremony of a formal denunciation of war has of late fallen into disuse" (*ibid.*, 123).

As was done in Chapter 4, one must comment on Yoo's (and Blackstone's) imperfect understanding of "perfected" hostilities. But the much more important point is that, if the congressional power to *decide* and *declare* war is "irrelevant," and, hence, not a "check" to "balance" the president's royal prerogative to "make" war, than the Constitution contains a significant imbalance, if not a debilitating defect. Yoo's response to this dilemma is to suggest that, "Thus, the appropriations power and the power to raise the military give Congress sufficient check on presidential war making" (*ibid.*, 22; see also 2, 54, 159.). Emphasizing current practice once again, "My argument is that the Constitution, in particular the dynamic manner in which it balances the executive against the legislative branches, can be read to permit existing practices" (*ibid.*, 17). And, what are the existing permitted practices? "[T]he branches of government have established a stable, working system of war powers. ... Put less charitably, we have a system that Harold Koh describes as one of 'executive initiative, congressional acquiescence, and judicial tolerance'" (*ibid.*, 12; 13).

In sum, rebranded British law and experience as an hereditary constitutional monarchy combined with actual American practice as an elected monarchy since 1789, the two factors together, force one to conclude, according to Yoo, that the congressional power to *decide* and *declare* war is a nugatory power of no weight or value. This is the case because the power to *decide* to go to war belongs exclusively to the president as commander-in-chief, the nation's war leader. In its place, as in all constitutional monarchies, one must turn to the congressional "power of the purse" to find a truly powerful check upon the president's "proneness" to war. The moment the Congress stops raising troops or stops appropriating funds; the war stops, "*nervos belli, pecuniam infinitam*," "the sinews of war, infinite treasure" (Cicero 1969, *Philippics* v, ii, 5).

The hopeful conclusion of John Yoo's "original understanding" doctrine is, therefore, that salvation is possible. But, first, one must abandon an "original intent" interpretation and recognize the actual practice of presidential war making. The abandonment of an "original intent" interpretation, then, allows one to adopt an "original [British] understanding" of the power to *decide* and to *declare* war, which, then, allows one to grasp hold of the "power of the purse" as the final arbiter of power in both hereditary and elected constitutional monarchies. King John's bishops and barons on the field at Runnymede in 1215 had come to the same conclusion, eight hundred years earlier.

Comforting as this conclusion may well be, one might still ask whether the "power of the purse" actually gets the job done in a constitutional monarchy? Is the power of the purse truly an effective constraint on monarchical war making? Yoo is a little short on actual, practical evidence, but he does point out that, "We should not, however, mistake a failure of political will for a violation of the Constitution" (Yoo 2005, 159). The point is well taken and fair, but a modicum of actual evidence would be reassuring. In searching for this evidence one discovers a less than reassuring plethora. Indeed, one discovers only three lonely examples, one British, the two American.

The British case concerns Charles I and his difficulties with his stiff-necked Scots subjects. To deal with their stiff-neckedness, Charles I *decided* to wage the disastrous Bishop's War, 1639–1640. His first campaign in 1639 consisted of much inconclusive maneuvering that exhausted his finances before it exhausted the Scots. To repair his finances, Charles I recalled Parliament for the first time since 1629. This, the Short Parliament, sat on Monday, 13 April 1640. Charles I immediately requested new taxes to renew the war against the recalcitrant Scots. When his request was not only refused, but demands for extensive reforms made as well, Charles I dissolved Parliament on Tuesday, 5 May 1640. Notwithstanding the state of his depleted finances, Charles I cobbled together a second army, which was no more successful than the first. Badly outmaneuvered once again during the 1640 campaign, Charles I was forced to sign the humiliating Treaty of Ripon on Monday, 26 October 1640. His finances now in even worse shape, Charles I recalled Parliament on Tuesday, 3 November 1640. Still in no mood to raise taxes without needed reforms, Parliament again refused supply. This led to the English Civil War. Charles I lost the war, and, as a result, his head to the executioner's ax. From the perspective of constitutional theory, this British case is a less than inspiring example. Igniting a civil war and beheading the president is not the optimal design for a system of checks and balance.

Yoo does mention this case (2005, 47–8). However, he does not mention that this is the only case of Parliament refusing supply for a war in a thousand years of British history. Given the number of wars Britain has fought in the last thousand years, the paucity of other examples suggests that the "power of the purse" is a less powerful check than Yoo might have hoped. In addition, this paucity also suggests that something other than a loss of political will as the reason that the "power of the purse" fails to restrain the propensity of either hereditary or elected constitutional monarchs to war. Internal institutional organization, procedures, and functions, perhaps, matter.

The two American cases concern the war in Vietnam. During January 1971, the Ninety-first Congress exercised its "power of the purse" to "end" further incursions into Cambodia:

> SEC. 7. (a) In line with the expressed intention of the President of the United States, none of the funds authorized or appropriated pursuant to this or any other Act may be used to finance the introduction of United

States ground combat troops into Cambodia, or to provide United States advisers to or for Cambodian military forces in Cambodia.

Pub. L. No. 91-652, 84 Stat. 1942

One might suggest that an exercise of the congressional "power of the purse" that is "In line with the expressed intention of the President the United States," does not actually count as a "check" to "balance" an Imperial President's propensity to war. Instead, the legislation is better understood as another example of an Imperial President "not keeping the Congress unnecessarily in the dark." In effect, President Nixon has informed the Ninety-first Congress that he has no future plans to invade Cambodia. For, the 1971 Cambodian restriction was permitted only after all American troops had left Cambodia and only after extensive negotiations with President Richard Nixon (Kriner 2010, 40). This hardly sounds like an independent and forceful exercise of the congressional "power of the purse." Indeed, it illustrates how a politically astute war leader maintains control of his councils in a difficult situation. Gilgamesh would have approved.

Two years later, during July 1973, the Ninety-third Congress exercised its power of the purse to "end" the war in Vietnam, if one may use the term. It forbade " ... support directly or indirectly [for] combat activities in or over Cambodia, Laos, North Vietnam and South Vietnam or off the shores of Cambodia, Laos, North Vietnam and South Vietnam by United States forces" (*e.g.*, Pub. L. No. 93-50, 87 Stat. 129). Yet, again, was this actually an independent and forceful exercise of the congressional "power of the purse?" The 1973 Vietnam restriction came six months after the *Paris Peace Accords* were signed on Saturday, 27 January 1973, and three months after President Richard Nixon had completed the withdrawal of American combat troops from South Vietnam. As he said in his address to the nation on Thursday, 29 March 1973, "For the first time in 12 years, no American military forces are in Vietnam" (Nixon 1973). Many "advisors" remained, but no combat troops. This example raises two nagging questions: Does cutting funding for direct or indirect "combat activities" that are no longer occurring represent a robust display of either the "power of the purse" or of political will? Does cutting funding eight years after sustained combat operations began and after 58,109 American in-theater deaths represent a case of congressional restraint on presidential war making?

In a search for additional examples, one might want to consider the generally ineffective congressional efforts to end funding for covert operations, such as the 1982 Boland amendment (Pub. L. 98–473, 98 Stat. 1935–1937. For other unsuccessful or partially successful cases, see Johnson 2012, 28–31; 39–41 and Grimmett 2007.). But to do so only reinforces the conclusion that the "power of the purse" is basically ineffective. A power that is actually exercised once or twice in five hundred years is not a power upon which one can rely. In addition, once again, the paucity of examples demonstrates that something other than a loss of political will accounts for the impotence of both the congressional power to *decide* and *declare* war and the congressional "power of the purse" to restrain presidential war making. Might the absence of recognized procedural and textual models be a large part of the problem?

1.2   Arthur Schlesinger, "Original Intent," and "Collective Judgment"

Those who seek refuge in a doctrine of "original intent" believe—reasonably enough—that it is beyond obvious that the Founding Fathers envisioned that the Congress would *decide* and *declare* war, and not the president. This claim is obvious, it is held, from the "original intent" of the text of Article 1, Section 8, Clause 11, "The Congress shall have the power ... to declare war." Clearly, Congress was intended "to declare war." However, according to this very orthodox view, as John Yoo has pointed out, the minute one begins to imagine the procedures by which the Congress will *exercise* this power, it becomes equally obvious that any actual *exercise* of the congressional power "*to declare war*" depends absolutely upon the president's power as commander-in-chief *to decide* to go to war. As argued in Chapter 3, James Madison was the first to recognize this absolute dependency, but Speaker Henry Clay soon concurred: As he wrote in his *aide-mémoire* to Secretary of State James Monroe of Sunday, 15 March 1812:

> Altho' the power of declaring War belongs to Congress, I do not see that it less falls within the scope of the President's constitutional duty to recommend such measures as he shall judge necessary and expedient than any other which, being suggested by him, they alone can adopt.
>
> CLAY 1959–1984; 1:637.   See also MONROE 1960

And indeed, so obvious is the absolute dependency of the Congress on the commander-in-chief's decision that the Ninety-third Congress enacted it into law under the *Purposes and Policy* section of the *War Powers Resolution of 1973*:

> Sec. 2. (a) It is the purpose of this joint resolution to fulfill the intent of the framers of the Constitution of the United States and insure that the collective judgment of both the Congress and the President will apply to the introduction of United States Armed Forces into hostilities, or into situations where imminent involvement in hostilities is clearly indicated

by the circumstances, and to the continued use of such forces in hostilities or in such situations.

<blockquote>Pub. L. 93-148; 87 Stat. 555</blockquote>

Yet, this most obvious of "original intentions" suffers greatly from its being entirely too obvious. To focus on the obvious, as Sherlock Holmes often warned Doctor Watson, is to overlook the critical clue.

The critical clue, as John Yoo has noted, is not located the "original intentions" of the Framers of the Constitution, but in the actual practice of America's British derived constitutional monarchy (Nelson 2014). Even more obscure than the critical clue, however, is the following dilemma: Are the obvious institutional and technological changes that have occurred since World War II the source of the flaw? Or, is some other less obvious factor the source of the flaw, such as organization and procedure?

In response, virtually all agree with Arthur Schlesinger that institutional and technological changes since World War II have greatly strengthened the presidency at the expense of the Congress. These post-World War II changes, it is held, have made the creation of *The Imperial Presidency* all but inevitable (1973; Fisher 1995. See Andrew Rudalevige 2005 for an update of Schlesinger and Scarry 2014, who identifies nuclear technological as the cause.). Certainly, Schlesinger's title is striking. His thesis also appears obvious, as does everything connected with an "original intent" interpretation of the Declare War Clause. Beyond question, institutional and technological changes have taken place since World War II. Equally beyond question, the presidency has become stronger and stronger since World War II, at the expense of the Congress. Case closed.

Still, like the Hounds at Baskerville that did not bark, a non-obvious response does exist: That non-obvious response does not point so much to the "collective action problem" of all modern legislatures, but to a confusion of functions. As long as large, majority-rule, bicameral legislatures organized into standing committees concentrate on their primary lawmaking duties, they function reasonably well. Only when a legislature struggles to discharge a second, largely unrelated function, does dysfunction arise. In the presence of this dysfunction, how much presidential strength does it take to fill the legislative void?

In a word, as John Yoo has correctly pointed out, the actual practice of the United States since 1789 has exhibited very little evidence of the "original intentions" of the Framers of the constitutional text, but much evidence of a British-style constitutional monarchy, albeit an elected monarchy, and not hereditary monarchy. More, a constitutional monarchy was undoubtedly the "original understanding" of the Framers before they met in Philadelphia and created their revolutionary new constitution. They too had studied Locke and Blackstone.

Or, to say the same thing in different words, the actual practice of the United States since 1789 has exhibited very little evidence of the Madison of 1787, or even the Madison of 1793, but much evidence of the Madison of 1812, as argued in Chapter 3. Hence, the actual practice has been for the president to take the *decision* for war or peace in the manner of a constitutional monarch, as his royal prerogative, if not his divine right. Then, once *decided*, the president frequently, but not always, employs *Scenario 3: An Unsolemn Functionally Equivalent Declarative Act by the Nation's Hereditary or Elected King that Involves a Legislature.* He "convenes and gives information" to the large, *bifunction*, majority-rule, bicameral Congress, which faithfully provides him with either a *pro forma*, lexical declaration or some sort of a precatory and hortatory, not to say unconstitutional, "authorization."

2 Searching for Suitable Textual Models

As already noted in Chapter 3, the procedures and texts of the small, *monofunction*, unicameral Second Continental Congress are most relevant to the procedural and collective action problems that beset the large, *bifunction*, majority-rule, bicameral Congress. But, because the Second Continental Congress is well known, the lesser-known Security Council will be highlighted here to illustrate the importance of the texts.

Before exploring the matter further, three caveats are in order: First, one must remember that President Harry Truman's use of the Security Council sprang from the silence and inactivity of the Eighty-first Congress. The Eighty-first Congress showed no interest "to fulfill the intent of the framers of the Constitution of the United States and insure that the collective judgment of both the Congress and the President" would apply to the Korean War. Missing in action must be the verdict. Indeed, the Eighty-first Congress was so anxious for President Truman not to "convene and give it information," that the Democratic leadership expressly advised President Truman against requesting a congressional vote on Korea. Such a vote might give the Republicans a political advantage in the November mid-term elections (Auerswald and Campbell 2012, 8, n3).

Second, the Soviet delegation had boycotted all Security Council meetings since January 1950 to protest the continued presence of Nationalist China on the Council. Since Mao Tse-tung's victory over Chang Kai-shek in October

1949, the Soviets had demanded that the defeated Nationalist be replaced by the triumphant Communist on the Council. Unable to force the issue, the Soviet delegation had walked out and refused to participate in any of the small, *monofunction*, unicameral Security Council's business. The absence of the Soviet delegation on the Council clearly reduced to a minimum the collective action problems in the Security Council, which greatly facilitated the passage of the two initial resolutions on Korea. Needless to say, this was the last time the Soviets boycotted the Council.

Third, and finally, the small, *monofunction*, unicameral Security Council cannot declare war officially. Nor has it ever done so. As an alliance coordinating committee, it lacks both the sovereign right to *decide* and *declare* war and the armed forces to wage war. Only the member states possess these sovereign rights and military powers. That being said, the Council's Chapter VI and VII coordinating resolutions are nonetheless functionally equivalent declarations of war. More to the point, the issues in hand are those of solemn procedures and reasoned texts, and, on both counts, the small, *monofunction*, unicameral Council provides an illuminating example, most notably, because it employs committee-of-the-whole procedures and produces Hague Convention III compliant texts.

2.1 *The Security Council and the Exercise of a Functionally Equivalent Power to Declare War*

The United Nations and its Security Council came into existence in San Francisco on Tuesday, 26 June 1945. By coincidence, five years later, on Monday, 26 June 1950, North Korean forces crossed the Thirty-eighth parallel and invaded South Korea. In response, President Harry Truman immediately deployed American forces from Japan to meet the crisis. But instead of turning to the Eighty-first Congress for a declaration of war, President Truman turned to the new and untested United Nations Security Council.

In terms of its functions, the Security Council has one primary function. In accordance with Article 24, "the Security Council [has] primary responsibility for the maintenance of international peace and security." Crucially, it has no responsibilities for the domestic policies of the member states. Also of crucial importance, the Security Council is a fifteen-member, small, *monofunction*, unicameral assembly that operates with committee-of-the-whole procedures. It does not employ standing-committee rules.

The war in Korea began during the rainy season. The main North Korean attack crossed the Thirty-eighth parallel in the rain at 4:00am Korean time on Monday, 26 June 1950 or 2:00pm Eastern Daylight Time (EDT) on Sunday, 25 June 1950. But, of course, movement to the line of departure and the initial probing began earlier. By Saturday midnight, officials in the Departments of

Defense and State were aware of an impending large-scale attack. This led to a call at 3:00am Sunday morning to Earnest A. Gross in Lake Success, New York, the temporary home of the United Nations. Gross was the acting chief of the US delegation to the United Nations in the absence of Ambassador Austin R. Warren, who was at his home in Vermont for the weekend. Mr. Gross immediately phoned Secretary General Trygve Lie to inform him of the impending attack and to request an emergency meeting of the Security Council later in the day. The Secretary General contacted Sir Benegal N. Rau of India, the Council's chairman, who agreed to call a meeting pending verification from the UN Temporary Commission on Korea in Seoul. At the same time calls were made to the UN guards and staff to report for work in the morning. By 8:00am, the guards and staff were arriving at the UN's offices. At 10:30am, Secretary General Lie received "a brief dispatch" from the Temporary Commission on Korea in Seoul confirming the attack (Text at *NY Times*, June 26, 1950, p5:3). This dispatch, not the American request, provided the legal basis for the Security Council to meet and consider the situation in Korea.

As in 1776 at the Second Continental Congress, so in 1950 at the Security Council, the procedures of this small, *monofunction*, unicameral body began when the delegates gathered in their lounge for informal talks among themselves. This occurred at 1:00pm Sunday afternoon. At 2:32pm, Sir Benegal officially called the Council to order under committee-of-the-whole procedures and immediately gave the floor to Secretary General Lie, who reported on the situation in Korea. Mr. Gross then spoke a few words and presented a draft resolution. Sir Benegal next called Dr John M. Chang, the Korean Ambassador, to speak. Ambassador Chang words were followed by short speeches of support for South Korea by the other delegates. After the public speeches, the Council recessed for an hour to allow the delegates to withdraw to a private office provided by the Secretary General. During this hour, the American resolution was amended to soften its tone by calling on both North and South to institute an immediate ceasefire. The original draft had called on only the North to cease hostilities. The amended draft having been agreed to, the Council reconvened at 5:30pm. Norway, followed by the other delegates, spoke again in support of the resolution. At the conclusion of these speeches, the alternate delegate from Yugoslavia, Djuro Nincitch, voiced his dissent and offered an alternative resolution that proposed an investigation of the situation instead of condemnation and a ceasefire. Without the presence of the Soviet ambassador, the Yugoslav proposal found no support and was soundly defeated. At the end of the public speeches, the vote was taken, and *Security Council Resolution 82* passed nine to none—Britain, China, Cuba, Ecuador, Egypt, France, India, Norway, and the US, with Yugoslavia abstaining (*NY Times*, June 26, 1950, p1:8, 6:5).

As in 1776, so in 1950, the committee-of-the-whole procedures of this small, *monofunction*, unicameral body were simple—convening the Council or Congress, introducing the resolution; debating until "the sense of the meeting had been made manifest," as Thomas Jefferson expressed the thought; amending it in a closed meeting; further debate; and a final public vote (Malone 1948–81, 3:457). These simple, straightforward, and legitimating parliamentary procedures for the *intending, deciding*, and *declaring* simultaneously work in a small, *monofunction*, unicameral body because the transaction costs are manageable; the difficulties in coordinating shared interests are minimal (as long as the Soviet delegation boycotted); hence, the collective action problems are tractable. In a large, *bifunction*, majority-rule, bicameral body, like the United States Congress, these simplifying conditions simply do not exist. Hence, the disparity in size, organizational complexity, and procedures explain both the incapacity of the large, *bifunction*, majority-rule, bicameral legislatures to *decide* and *declare* war and the capacity of the small, *monofunction*, unicameral Security Council to produce a functionally equivalent document. Next consider the text of *Resolution 82*:

> *The Security Council,*
> *Recalling* the finding of the General Assembly in its resolution 293 (IV) of 21 October 1949 that the Government of the Republic of Korea is a lawfully established government having effective control and jurisdiction over that part of Korea where the United Nations Temporary Commission on Korea was able to observe and consult and in which the great majority of the people of Korea reside; that this Government is based on elections which were a valid expression of the free will of the electorate of that part of Korea and which were observed by the Temporary Commission; and that this is the only such Government in Korea,
> *Mindful* of the concern expressed by the General Assembly in its resolutions 195 (III) of 12 December 1948 and 293 (IV) of 21 October 1949 about the consequences which might follow unless Member States refrained from acts derogatory to the results sought to be achieved by the United Nations in bringing about the complete independence and unity of Korea; and the concern expressed that the situation described by the United Nations Commission on Korea in its report 9 menaces the safety and well-being of the Republic of Korea and of the people of Korea and might lead to open military conflict there,
> *Noting* with grave concern the armed attack on the Republic of Korea by forces from North Korea,

I

Determines that this action constitutes a breach of the peace; and
    Calls for the immediate cessation of hostilities;
    Calls upon the authorities in North Korea to withdraw forthwith their armed forces to the 38th parallel;

II

Requests the United Nations Commission on Korea:
(*a*) To communicate its fully considered recommendations on the situation with the least possible delay;
(*b*) To observe the withdrawal of North Korean forces to the 38th parallel;
(*c*) To keep the Security Council informed on the execution of this resolution:

III

Calls upon all Member States to render every assistance to the United Nations in the execution of this resolution and to refrain from giving assistance to the North Korean authorities.
    Adopted at the 473rd meeting by 9 votes to none, with 1 abstention (Yugoslavia).

The most important feature of the text is that the small, *monofunction*, unicameral Security Council spoke. It discharged its responsibilities under Chapter VII (39 and 41) to "determine the existence of any threat to the peace, breach of the peace, or act of aggression and shall make recommendations." The Council did not become taciturn and leave it to the Secretary General to decide what to do, as the large, *bifunction*, majority-rule, bicameral Eighty-first Congress left it to President Truman.

    Equally important, *Resolution 82* is Hague Convention III compliant and similar in structure to the D*eclaration of Independence*, although it lacks the elegant style and philosophical depth. In a simplified outline, both documents indict the gravamina and propose a remedy. King George's tyranny and independence in 1776; the North Korean attack and a cessation of hostilities in 1950. In its preambular recital, *Resolution 82* indicts the gravamina by explaining both the legal background and the specific warrant for the resolution, "the armed attack on the Republic of Korea by forces from North Korea." In its operational portion, the resolution proposes three moderate and sensible remedies for the indicted gravamina. In addition, the Council has also denounced the aggressor, the North, which is a critical, but often forgotten, element of a declaration of war.

    In sum, *Resolution 82* not only addressed the *ad bellum* criteria of the traditional just-war criteria but also accomplished step one of any good conflict resolution strategy: the articulation of the grievances and the desired peace terms/war aims in a conditional declaration. As a functional equivalent of a solemn, conditional declaration of war, it set the stage for more intensive negotiations, without yet expanding the armed hostilities to involve the United Nations. But, of course, passing resolutions is one thing; enforcing them is another. The prospects for North Korean compliance were not good, as the *New York Times* headline reported the next day, "U.N. TOLD ITS ORDER MAY BE 'ACADEMIC'" (June 27, 1950, p1:6).

When North Korea neither ceased hostilities nor withdrew to the Thirty-eighth parallel, the same committee-of-the-whole procedures with their reduced collective action problems were used again to pass *Resolution 83*. Sir Benegal received a copy of an American draft resolution in the morning of Tuesday, 27 June 1950 at 11:30am. The other delegates soon received their copies. After informal discussions among the delegates and consultation with their governments, Sir Benegal convened the Council before an overflow crowd of five thousand spectators at 3:16pm that afternoon.

Speaking first, Ambassador Austin, now returned from Vermont, introduced the American draft. With the Soviet delegate, Jacob A. Malik, absent, the other delegates all spoke in support of the draft without amendment, except for Dr. Ales Bebler, the delegate from Yugoslavia, who had also returned to Lake Success. By 5:12pm, the speeches had concluded, and the Council was ready to vote. However, Sir Benegal of India and Mahmoud Bey Fawzi of Egypt had not yet received instructions from their governments. A recess was called to allow the two delegates more time to receive instructions. Unable to receive instructions, Sir Benegal and Ambassador Fawzi were unable to vote when the Council reconvened at 10:45pm. As expected, *Resolution 83* passed seven to one—Britain, China, Cuba, Ecuador, France, Norway, and the US voting yes, with Yugoslavia voting no (*ibid.*, June 28, 1950, p1:2, 7:1).

> *The Security Council,*
> *Having determined* that the armed attack upon the Republic of Korea by forces from North Korea constitutes a breach of the peace,
> *Having called for* an immediate cessation of hostilities,
> *Having called upon* the authorities in North Korea to withdraw forthwith their armed forces to the 38th parallel,
> *Having noted* from the report of the United Nations Commission on Korea that the authorities in North Korea have neither ceased hostilities nor withdrawn their armed forces to the 38th parallel, and that urgent military measures are required to restore international peace and security,

> *Having noted* the appeal from the Republic of Korea to the United Nations for immediate and effective steps to secure peace and security,
> *Recommends* that the Members of the United Nations furnish such assistance to the Republic of Korea as may be necessary to repel the armed attack and to restore international peace and security in the area.
> *Adopted at the 474th meeting by 7 votes to 1 (Yugoslavia).*

Again, as in 1776, so in 1950, the simple committee-of-the-whole procedures of a small, *monofunction*, unicameral body enabled the Security Council to produce a second functionally equivalent declaration of war, now, an absolute declaration. Rebuffed in its call for the ceasefire and withdrawal of *Resolution 82*, the Council spoke again. It discharged its responsibilities under Chapter VII (43), "Should the Security Council consider that measures provided for in Article 41 would be inadequate or have proved to be inadequate, it may take such action by air, sea, or land forces as may be necessary to maintain or restore international peace and security." Likewise, the text of *Resolution 83* possessed the two-part structure of a well-crafted declaration of war, a functionally equivalent, absolute declaration this time. It indicted the gravamina and proposed suitable remedies, clearly articulated peace terms/war aims—the *status quo ante bellum*. In doing so, the small, *monofunction*, unicameral UN Security Council provided President Truman with the functional equivalent of an official congressional declaration of war. And, indeed, in the absence of the capacity of the large, *bifunction*, majority-rule, bicameral Eighty-first Congress to discharge its constitutional responsibility to *decide* and *declare* war, who could object to President Truman's claim that *Resolutions 82* and *83* authorized the use of the American armed forces to serve under the United Nations Command Korea? Certainly, not the members of the Eighty-first Congress.

3 Conclusion

For over five thousand years, national war leaders—be they styled as kings, emperors, presidents, prime ministers, and chancellors—have both *decided* on and *declared* war. As the nation's war leaders, these absolute and constitutional monarchs were all said to possess an inherent, often, a divine right to *decide* the question of war or peace for the nation and, then, to publish and declare their decision. In 1787, a group of radicals meeting in Philadelphia possessed the audacity to repudiate this ancient and hoary royal prerogative. Violating the settled practice of millennia, these radicals attempted to create a modern republic and, hence, to transfer the power to *decide* and *declare* war from a single individual—the nation's war leader—to a decision-making assembly.

Audacity, however, is one thing; foresight is another. For, in the event, the radicals had no appropriate model to follow. Indeed, the only national model with which they were familiar was Great Britain's constitutional monarchy, as John Yoo insistently points out. In the absence of any other model, they chose to transfer the power to *decide* and *declare* war to a new, untried and untested "Congress." Most pointedly, in 1789, this Congress was still small enough to employ committee-of-the-whole rules, but, ominously, it was also both *bifunctional* and bicameral. Yet, time does not stand still. Within two decades, the *small* Congress that employed committee-of-the-whole rules had transformed itself into a *large* Congress that employed standing-committee rules. This transformation created a number of troubling, but unasked, questions: For, if the decision for war or peace is not to be made by a single individual, but by a decision-making assembly, then what are the institutional characteristics of that body? What is its optimal size? What are the optimal procedures? What is the optimal form and content of the text it is charged with drafting, debating, amending, and voting?

Once these pragmatic, normative questions are asked and answered by learning from the appropriate models, might it not then be possible during the course of the twenty-first century to fulfill the promise of 1787? Might it not be possible during the course of the twenty-first century to constitute and establish a small, *monofunction*, unicameral body organized under committee-of-the-whole rules to usurp the Imperial President's five-thousand-year-old divine right, royal prerogative, or "inherent executive power" to *decide* and *declare* war? Might it not be possible, as suggested in Appendices D and E, to transform the current elected, constitutional monarchy into a truly republican government?

CHAPTER 7

A Monarchial vs. a Republican Constitution
Misplacing Ends and Means

Abstract

Both war- and lawmaking are collective social interactions. Therefore, should the absolutely necessary, performative speech act that bring both wars and laws into existence not be uttered collectively? Responding affirmatively, this chapter investigates some of the issues surrounding the aspiration of replacing modern, elected constitutional monarchies with truly republican forms of government. The chapter builds upon insights from the previous chapters.

∴

> He [Pierce Butler of South Carolina] was for vesting the power [to make war] in the President, who will have all the requisite qualities, and will not make war but when the Nation will support it.
>
> [I (Elbridge Gerry)] never expected to hear in a republic a motion to empower the Executive alone to declare war
> > The Federal Convention, Philadelphia
> > Friday, 17 August 1787

∴

Most modern constitutions are not thoroughgoing, absolute monarchies. They are instead mixed constitutions. These mixed, asymmetrical constitutions are monarchical with respect to the nation's foreign affairs, parliamentary with respect to the nation's domestic affairs. This curious asymmetry is explained by one of the many accidents of history: Up until roughly the sixteenth century, the nations of world were organized for war, not peace. Peasants tilled the soil; priests prayed, and warriors ruled. Among the warriors, the strongest was the nation's war leader. As the strongest, he ruled as king, combining in his person all governmental powers and functions, for peace as for war, domestic as well as foreign.

From roughly the sixteenth century, however, several west European counties struggled to empower their Common Councils of the Realm vis-á-vis the king. Critically, though, the struggle was conducted without questioning the king's monopoly on foreign affairs and war. Thus, as already noted in Chapter 2, John Locke assigned the conduct of foreign affairs and war, what he called the fœderative powers, to the king exclusively (Locke 1764 [1690], XII). Montesquieu concurred with Locke on this point. (Montesquieu 1914, XI, 6). Consequently, the struggle from the beginning was about who should control domestic affairs. And, in turn, the control of domestic affairs boiled down to who controlled "the power of the purse," as has been discussed in Chapters 2 and 6. Consequently, who controlled foreign affairs and war were never in dispute. That question had been settled five thousand year ago by Agga and Gilgamesh.

This west European struggle to control domestic affairs had two elements: power and reason. As a practical matter, raw power was going to decide who controlled domestic affairs through its control of the "power of the purse." Could the slowly emerging parliaments and estates general rebel and organize an army and navy that was stronger than the king's? The Dutch Eighty-Years War (1568–1648), the English Civil War (1642–1649), the American War of Revolution (1775–1783), and the Wars of the French Revolution (1789–1799) demonstrated that, yes, indeed, rebellious parliamentary armies and navies could defeat royal armies and navies.

Yet, raw power is never enough. A reason and rationale was also needed to explain and justify the overthrow of ancient traditions, divine rights, and royal prerogatives, on the one hand, and, on the other hand, to motivate a large proportion of the population to support the revolution. This ideological need was filled by an appeal to two different doctrines—one for the first step in a revolution, the other for the second step. For the second step, one could justify the revolution by and appeal to the soon-to-be-told mystical myth of a "social contract" to which a "sovereign people" could not only abjure, but adjure, as well. For the first step, one could justify the revolution by employing the very down-to-earth theological, practical, and moral doctrine of the Lesser Magistrate. This latter doctrine found an early expression in the preamble of the *Dutch Act of Abjuration* of 1581:

> As it is apparent to all that a prince is constituted by God to be ruler of a people, to defend them from oppression and violence as the shepherd his

sheep; and whereas God did not create the people slaves to their prince, to obey his commands, whether right or wrong, but rather the prince for the sake of the subjects (without which he could be no prince), to govern them according to equity, to love and support them as a father his children or a shepherd his flock, and even at the hazard of life to defend and preserve them. And when he does not behave thus, but, on the contrary, oppresses them, seeking opportunities to infringe their ancient customs and privileges, exacting from them slavish compliance, then he is no longer a prince, but a tyrant, and the subjects are to consider him in no other view. And particularly when this is done deliberately, unauthorized by the states [i.e., the Estates General or the legislature], they may not only disallow his authority, but legally proceed to the choice of another prince for their defense.

THATCHER 1907, 189

Uninterested in the prince's conduct of foreign affairs, the Dutch Estates General was interested only in defending its "ancient customs and privileges." However, to do even that, it had to overcome Philip II's claim of a divine right to obedience. To do this, the Dutch Estates General invoked, as can be read, the Lesser Magistrate Doctrine in the late sixteenth century. The doctrine had been developed in the early sixteenth century by Protestant theologians in response to then on-going persecution by Catholic princes in Germany and elsewhere, especially, in France. Martin Luther, Jean Calvin, and others justified resistance to tyranny by melding together subtle theological, practical, and moral observations to conclude that private persons should not resist tyranny, but that certain well-established social institution not only could, but should.

Theologically, as Jean Calvin wrote, the lot of private individuals was to suffer persecution and tyranny because individuals have a duty to obey "the venerable and majestic authority of rulers, an authority which God has sanctioned by the surest edicts." Yet, if individuals could only suffer, a Lesser Magistrate not only could, but had a positive duty to resist:

"For when popular magistrates [*i.e.*, magistrates elected by the people] have been appointed to curb the tyranny of kings ... So far am I from forbidding these officially to check the undue license of kings, that if they connive at kings when they tyrannise and insult over the humbler of the people, I affirm that their dissimulation is not free from nefarious perfidy, because they fradulently betray the liberty of the people, while knowing that, by the ordinance of God, they are its appointed guardians (1845 (1553), IV.XX.31).

Practically, Calvin's unstated point was that private individuals lacked both the material resources and the organizational capacity "to curb the tyranny of kings," whose police and military resources are abundant. In order to avoid violating the probability of success criterion in a hopeless rebellion, only a relatively well-established social institution could muster both the material resources and the organizational capacity to resist with any hope of success. In making this practical point, Calvin, first, alluded to the Ephori of the Spartans, the Tribunes of the Romans, and the Demarchs of the Athenians as examples of "popular magistrates [who] have been appointed to curb the tyranny of kings" in the ancient world. Then, turning his attention to more recent times, where none of the ancient antidotes to tyranny existed, he suggested tentatively that "perhaps there is something similar to this in the power exercised in each kingdom by the three orders, when they hold their primary diets." And, indeed, "the three orders" of the Dutch Estates General took this suggestion to heart and rebelled in 1581 "to curb the tyranny of" Philip II.

In short order, the Dutch example was taken up and followed by the other "primary diets" listed just above. All of the English, American, and French revolutionary assemblies listed, needless to say, proved to possess both the material resources and the organizational capacity not only "to curb the tyranny of kings," but, then, to take control of the "power of the purse" and, hence, of the nation's domestic affairs. In the twentieth century, the principle was expanded to encompass social institutions beyond "the three orders, when they hold their primary diets." In effect, these other social institutions now claimed the status of "Lesser Magistrate" empowered to "to curb the tyranny of kings." A partial list would include the Indian National Congress, the Chinese Communist Party, the Mau Mau Movement, the Southern Christian Leadership Conference, the Vietnamese Workers Party, the African National Congress, and many more revolutionary organizations.

Morally, though, the Lesser Magistrate Doctrine is the Nuremburg Principle writ large. Both doctrines interrogate the relationship between superiors and subordinates in a hierarchy. Empirically, all relationships in an hierarchy are determine by power and authority. Superiors possess power and authority; subordinates do not. Therefore, superiors command, and subordinates obey. Morally, however, the relationship is a rather more complicated one of cooperation and non-cooperation. At the level of the individual, the Nuremburg Principle holds that subordinates must not cooperated when the orders are illegal.

"I was only obeying orders" is not a defense when the command is criminal. At the level of a society, the Lesser Magistrate Doctrine holds that subordinate officials must not cooperated with tyranny. In the case of tyranny, they "may not only disallow his authority, but legally proceed to the choice of another prince for their defense." Consequently, empirical power and authority are, ultimately, not dispositive. Ultimately, morality—right or wrong—*ought to* determine cooperation or non-cooperation in a hierarchy.

But, if the Lesser Magistrate Doctrine did provide solid theological, practical, and moral reasons and rationales for resisting tyranny, it did not provide firm grounds for going the next step. It did not provide firm grounds for instituting an entirely new form of government, in general, and a modern constitutional monarchy, in particular. The point is critical because, at the end of the sixteenth century, the Dutch Estates General demanded only to "legally proceed to the choice of another prince for their defense." It did not want a new form of government. All it wanted was a prince who would no longer "infringe their ancient customs and privileges." However, by the end of the next century, in the aftermath of the English Civil War, the demand was for much more than swapping out one prince for another.

The conceptual crux of the second step, therefore, was explaining how mere mortals could radically alter "the venerable and majestic authority of rulers, an authority which God has sanctioned by the surest edicts." The response, of course, was to replace the divine origins of the ancient, hereditary monarchies with a new mystical myth. Beginning with the English Civil War, Thomas Hobbes, John Locke, Jean-Jacque Rousseau, and others developed various versions of a "social contract" adjured to by "consent" of the "sovereign people" while living in a "state of nature" at some long ago time out of memory.

Helpfully, the two new theories displaced god: The Lesser Magistrate Doctrine replaced god with the collective speech acts of the members of the revolutionary assemblies as the font of and alternative political legitimacy and authority within an ancient hierarchy. The "social contract" theory replaced god with the "consent" of the "sovereign people" as the font of political legitimacy and authority to justify a new hierarchy. The combination of the two theories explained, to the satisfaction of most people, the right of the Lesser Magistrates, first, to abjure the old, divinely instituted monarchies and, then, in the wake of the revolution, to institute the new, constitutional monarchies through the mystical "consent" of the "sovereign people." But, of course, the "sovereign people" never gave their "consent." What actually happened was a collective speech act. A decision-making assembly *intended*, *decided*, and *declared* the new revolutionary order synchronically by means of a vote on a well-debated and amended *draft* text.

Less abstractly, at the end of the eighteenth century, the rebellious American colonialist began to take the mystical metaphor literally. After the Second Continental Congress had abjured allegiance to George III, the revolutionary Lesser Magistrates became Founding Fathers. They began writing explicit "social contracts," not in a "state of nature," but in "state houses." They met in special constitutional conventions of elected representatives held at well-known locations to write and ratify very well documented "social contracts." This movement from myth to collective speech acts is illustrated most cogently in the three paragraphs of the preamble to the 1780 *Constitution of the Commonwealth of Massachusetts*, which was written by John Adam. Echoing both the *Dutch Act of Abjuration* and the American *Declaration of Independence*, Adam's first paragraph is an elegant period that reaffirms:

> The end of the institution, maintenance, and administration of government, is to secure the existence of the body politic, to protect it, and to furnish the individuals who compose it with the power of enjoying in safety and tranquillity (sic) their natural rights, and the blessings of life: and whenever these great objects are not obtained, the people have a right to alter the government, and to take measures necessary for their safety, prosperity and happiness.
> ADAMS 1850-56, 4:219

But notice the difference between 1581 and 1780. In 1581, the Lesser Magistrates of the Dutch Estates General were engaged in an essentially conservative project. To their reckoning, their form of government was not "altered" when they disallowed the authority of a tyrannical prince and they then proceeded "to the choice of another prince for their defense." Rather, their abjuration conserved and defended "their ancient customs and privileges." In fact, of course, their abjuration did "alter" not only their form of government, but also that of many other governments in the centuries that followed. Nonetheless, their original intention was restorative, and not revolutionary. From their perspective, swapping out the tyrannical Philip II of Spain for a new prince would change little. It would only restore "their ancient customs and privileges."

By 1780, however, much more was afoot than swapping out a tyrannical king. Indeed, the "social contract" myth was being pressed into service to create a *Novus Ordo Seclorum*, a New Order of the Ages. Rebellion would no longer restore a traditional political society that had come into being through a slow accretive process of custom building, what Judith Butler calls performativity (1999). Instead, the revolutionary Lesser Magistrates of Massachusetts become Founding Fathers uttered the clearly performative speech acts of "agreement," "ordination," and "establishment" that would bring the *Novus Ordo Seclorum* into existence. Collective speech acts would now replace myths. Thus, in the elegant eighteenth-century period of his third paragraph, Adams eschews the accretive performativity of 1581 for a clearly performative ontological guillotine in 1780:

> We, therefore, the people of Massachusetts, acknowledging, with grateful hearts, the goodness of the great Legislator of the universe, in affording us, in the course of His providence, an opportunity, deliberately and peaceably, without fraud, violence or surprise, of entering into an original, explicit, and solemn compact with each other; and of forming a new constitution of civil government, for ourselves and posterity; and devoutly imploring His direction in so interesting a design, do agree upon, ordain and establish the following Declaration of Rights, and Frame of Government, as the Constitution of the Commonwealth of Massachusetts.
> *ibid.*, 4:220

Between his restatement of the Lesser Magistrates Doctrine in his first paragraph of the preamble and the performative declaration and enactment of the new political order in his third paragraph, Adams summarizes the anti-Aristotelian "social contract" myth in his middle paragraph in two short periods:

> The body politic is formed by a voluntary association of individuals: it is a social compact, by which the whole people covenants with each citizen, and each citizen with the whole people, that all shall be governed by certain laws for the common good. It is the duty of the people, therefore, in framing a constitution of government, to provide for an equitable mode of making laws, as well as for an impartial interpretation, and a faithful execution of them; that every man may, at all times, find his security in them.
> *ibid.*, 4:219–20

The elegance periods of the first and third paragraphs notwithstanding, what is most remarkable about this middle paragraph of the preamble is that its two sentences are *non sequitur*. The second sentence does not follow from the first. Whereas the first sentence extols the wonders of the anti-Aristotelian "social contract" myth, the second sentence launches one in an entirely new direction toward a modern, asymmetrical, elected, constitutional monarchy composed of three branches.

Reconsider the myth's misleading emotional power, which is on full display in the first short period. Misleading, because, as Aristotle would be the first to point out, "The body politic [cannot possibly be] formed by a voluntary association of individuals." The body politic can most certainly be altered and reformed by a collective speech act, as the Massachusetts Convention was doing. But no human every lived in an ungoverned "state of nature" and formed "a voluntary association of individuals." The hard, cold, cruel fact is that the libertarian paradise of radical individualism never existed. As Aristotle was at pains to point out, individuals are born into families not of their choosing; these families live in societies not of their choosing, and these societies are already governed with pre-existing customs, if not pre-existing statutes and written constitutions.

Thus, the body politic is most certainly not formed by individuals "consenting" to join a "voluntary association." After reaching their majority, citizens may assent to or dissent from the customs and laws of their society and government. They may even rebel against the tyrannous political order of their societies, as the Dutch did in 1581, the English did in 1640, the Americans did in 1776, and the French did in 1789–1793, and so on. But they can never "consent" to a "social compact," except metaphorically. In point of fact, then, the body politic is always governed by a pre-existing government of long-established constitution, until altered. To repeat, no human has ever lived in a "state of nature." This simple fact is recounted in the first three chapters of Genesis, if not by legions of anthropologists. Something stronger and more solid than "consent" to a mystical "social contract" by a "sovereign people" is surely needed.

For something stronger, consider, next, the *non sequitur* of the second sentence. Consider especially its new direction and the way in which that new direction leads to a modern, asymmetrical, elected constitutional monarchy. Adams most correctly points out that the "duty" of the revolutionary Lesser Magistrates turned Founding Fathers is not to restore or recover the "ancient customs and privileges" that have accreted from the past through performativity, as the Dutch Estates General held. Rather, the "duty" of the Lesser Magistrates of Massachusetts is, first, to speak performatively in the here and now and declare both the ends and the means of their *Novus Ordo Seclorum*. They discharge this declarative "duty" by uttering the constitutive speech act that is Adams' third paragraph, "We, therefore, the people of Massachusetts, ... do agree upon, ordain and establish the following Declaration of Rights, and Frame of Government, as the Constitution of the Commonwealth of Massachusetts."

The "duty" of the Lesser Magistrates of Massachusetts is, second, to articulate the practical organization of a government. Initially, this means agreeing upon, ordaining, and establishing the purposes or ends of the government;

namely, "to take measures necessary for their [the people's] safety, prosperity and happiness." With those ultimate ends in mind, the next step is to organize the governmental means. This very practical step is accomplished by Adams in the text of the rest of the *Constitution of the Commonwealth of Massachusetts*. In the most practical manner possible, such a government consists of one branch "to provide for an equitable mode of making laws," another branch "for an impartial interpretation [of those laws]," and, finally, a third branch for "a faithful execution of them [the laws]."

But notice the asymmetry of Adams' standard three-branch structure. It explains how the ends of domestic, peacetime legislation will be enacted, how domestic, peacetime legislation will be interpreted, and how domestic, peacetime legislation will be faithfully executed. To have a three-branch government for peacetime is completely unobjectionable, even inestimable. But what about wartime? Where is the three-branch government for wartime? As in peace, so in war, the ends of war must be *determined*, *decided*, and *declared*; the laws of war must be adjudicated in courts-martial, and the nation's military means must be commanded. What about wartime?

As one might expect, wartime was not fully addressed by John Adams in the Commonwealth's *Constitution*. As has been the case for over five thousand years, the governor's command of the Commonwealth's military and naval forces was secured in Article VII. Everyone understood that foreign affairs and war, Locke's fœderative power, had to be handled by the executive, as it always had been. In 1780, this meant by the governor of Massachusetts. Critically, though, seven years later, at the 1787 Federal Convention, the delegates there chose to fineness the absence of a symmetrical "wartime branch" by distributing the many foreign affairs and war powers of the sovereign here and there between the legislative and the executive branches (For a list, see Hallett 2012, 172–73.). Most consequentially, the delegates assigned the power to *decide* and *declare* war to the Congress and the power of commander-in-chief to the president. The dispensation, need it be said, has not worked as hoped. Despite the best of intentions to constitute a fully republican, symmetrical government, a republican government in times of war as well as in times of peace, all this dispensation has actually accomplished is to institute a modern, elected, constitutional monarchy.

1   Constitutional Symmetry: the Road Not Taken

The ideological path by which the modern world evolved the asymmetric, elected constitutional monarchies of today is explained by the combination of the Lesser Magistrates Doctrine and the emotional and rhetorical power of the "social contract." That said, how might constitutional asymmetry be transformed into a constitutional symmetry? How might the mixed, neither-fish-nor-fowl, modern, asymmetrical, elected constitutional monarchy championed by Pierce Butler be transformed into the fully symmetrical republican constitution hoped for by Elbridge Gerry? For, to repeat, that which shocked Gerry in Butler's remarks was the maldistribution of ends and means as between the two political branches of government.

Two detailed responses to this maldistribution are reproduced in Appendix D and E. But what is needed here is a more general response. Specifically, one needs to recognize that a philosophically sound distribution of ends and means is naturally grounded in the ontological-guillotine character of speech act theory. This is the case owning to the fact that a performative speech act is the absolutely necessary condition for *deciding* and *declaring* policy ends, in the first instance, and for *deciding* and *ordering* the means required to achieve policy ends, in the second instance. To demonstrate this absolutely necessary speech act nexus, the judicial branch is neglected because it is neither controversial nor problematic.

The analysis is summarized in Figure 5: Performative Structures: Time, Agent/Speaker, and Quality. The two "Symmetrical Constitutions" columns on the left of Figure 5 are basically an authority-tracing schematic of Figure 3, while the two "Asymmetrical Constitutions" columns on the right of Figure 5 are basically an authority-tracing schematic of Figure 2. The far righthand column, Monarchy, is self-explanatory.

With that summary in mind, four levels of foundational assumptions are relevant: First, at the level of means, no one can object to the nation's war leader/chief executive executing both foreign and domestic policy means. The energy and dispatch needed for the successful execution of policy means in both domains can come only from an individual officer wearing two hats at the culminating point of a well-established governmental hierarchies. Combining the two executive functions in one individual is common sense in terms of executing policy means.

Second, at the level of ends, no one can object to a decision-making assembly determining foreign and domestic policy ends. The foundational principle here is that social ends should be determined socially; collective ends should be determined collectively. The decorum and deliberation needed for the solemn and thoughtful determination of any and all policy ends can come only from a purpose-built decision-making assembly. Separating two distinct and different policy-making functions into two distinct and different, purpose-built assemblies is common sense in terms of determining policy ends.

Symmetrical Constitution		
	Asymmetrical Constitution	
		Monarchy
assembly for foreign policy	**assembly for domestic policy**	**conventionally "legitimate" war leader**
t_1: introduce ends PUBLIC SPEECH ACT	t_1: introduce ends PUBLIC SPEECH ACT	t_1: determine ends PRIVATE MENTAL ACT
t_2: debate ends PUBLIC SPEECH ACT	t_2: debate ends PUBLIC SPEECH ACT	t_2: decide ends PRIVATE MENTAL ACT
t_3: vote/announce ends PUBLIC SPEECH ACT	t_3: vote/announce ends PUBLIC SPEECH ACT	t_3: announces ends PRIVATE SPEECH ACT
commander of military means	**head of civil administration**	**conventionally "legitimate" chief executive**
t_1: determine means PRIVATE MENTAL ACT	t_1: determine means PRIVATE MENTAL ACT	t_4: determine means PRIVATE MENTAL ACT
t_2: decide means PRIVATE MENTAL ACT	t_2: decide means PRIVATE MENTAL ACT	t_5: decide means PRIVATE MENTAL ACT
t_3: prepare order PRIVATE SPEECH ACT	t_3: prepare order PRIVATE SPEECH ACT	t_6: prepare order PRIVATE SPEECH ACT
t_4: sign order PUBLIC SPEECH ACT	t_4: sign order PUBLIC SPEECH ACT	t_7: sign order PRIVATE SPEECH ACT
t_5: publish & declare means PUBLIC SPEECH ACT	t_5: publish & declare means PUBLIC SPEECH ACT	t_8: publish & declare ends and means PUBLIC SPEECH ACT

Asymmetric Constitution

FIGURE 5   Performative structures: time, agent/speaker, and quality

Third, as a consequence of the first two foundational assumptions, everyone must object to a *bifunctional* legislature. Everyone must object to a legislature that exceeds its functional capacities by attempting to *determine, decide*, and *declare* not only the ends of domestic policy, but of foreign policy as well. In a complex and globalizing world, the knowledge and skills needed to make domestic policy are simply not the same as the knowledge and skills needed to make foreign policy. In a complex and globalizing world, the knowledge and skills needed to make foreign policy are simply not the same as the knowledge and skills needed to make domestic policy. This experiment in *bifunctional dysfunction* has been tried for over two hundred years in the United States Congress. It has not worked; it need not continue.

Fourth, and finally, once the *raison d'être* for purpose-built, *monofunctional* assemblies is acknowledged, one must, next, search for their mode of operation. The search begins with the recognition of the absolutely necessary role that performative speech acts play as the ontological guillotine that brings both policy ends and policy means into existence. In general, this calls for tracing of the transmission of the moral and legal authorities for any and all human interactions. In particular, this calls for a schematization for the synchronic quality of parliamentary decision-making, as opposed to the asynchronic quality of executive decision-making.

To be sure, other, supporting explanations are also needed. For example, the geometric explanation is that parliamentary decision-making occurs as public discussions, debates, and votes within a space, within a crowded room. This spatial configuration is significantly different from executive decision-making, which occurs as mental acts within the head of the executive. Other explanations emphasize the differing "processual standards" of executive and legislative acts, as Mariah Zeisberg writes (2013, 36–7). Or, other explanations emphasize the assembly's "exercise of public reason," as Maxwell Cameron writes. Such exercises of public reason are necessary, he continues, because "[administrative or executive] actions that are not preceded by public deliberations and followed by review cannot meet the test of legitimacy" (2013, 39–43, 140. See also Grynaviski 2013.). But, however differently one expresses the superior character of *monofunctional*, majority-rule, decision-making assemblies for determining policy ends, no one denies their superiority. Not means, but ends.

2   Procedural Legitimacy and the Ontology of Policy Ends and Means

Mindful of these four foundational assumptions, Figure 5 illustrates two claims about the three different governmental structures: A symmetrical, republican constitution in the two left-hand columns, an asymmetrical hereditary or elected constitutional monarchy in the two righthand columns, and an absolute monarchy in the far righthand column. An absolute monarchy falls out of the analysis at this point as irrelevant conceptually to the construction of a modern, hereditary or elected constitutional monarchy. The first claim concerns the ontology of the manifestive moment and asks how performative procedures declare and bring into existence the moral ends desired. The second claim concerns the complexity of transmissible authorities. This second claim asks how the manifestive enactment of the ends endows legitimacy or illegitimacy on the chain of transmitted authorities required to execute and implement the material means.

2.1   *The Ontology of a Procedurally Legitimate Declaration of Policy Ends in a Republic*

Ontologically, when a decision-making assembly speaks performatively to declare and, thereby, to enact a policy end, an absolutely necessary, but not sufficient, condition has been met. The synchronicity of this absolutely necessary, but not sufficient, manifestive speech act, therewith generates and transmits authority to an executive agent/speaker who is, thereby, authorized to determine the sufficient material means. The executive speaker's speech act, in turn, transmits moral authorities to a myriad of subordinate speakers who implement the sufficient means by which the material consequence of the desired ends are achieved or not achieved. Such procedurally legitimate transmissible authorities are found in symmetrical, republican constitutions as is outlined in the left-hand and middle columns of Figure 5 for both foreign and domestic policies, respectively.

Concerning a decision to go to war, consider once again the Second Continental Congress and its *Declaration of Independence*, as the paradigmatic example, The Second Continental Congress was not a conventionally legitimate declarer of war, as any king will explain. Nonetheless, as a legitimate Lesser Magistrate, the Second Continental Congress spoke with procedural legitimacy during June and July 1776. In doing so, it transformed a procedurally imperfect war against Great Britain into a procedurally perfect war. It *determined*, *decided*, and *declared* the political ends of the war. This performative act then transmitted legitimate authorities to Commander-in-Chief, General George Washington, who *determined*, *decided*, and *ordered* the military means.

Schematically, the *monofunction*, committee-of-the-whole procedures of the Second Continental Congress are outlined in the upper, "Ends" portion of the middle column of Figure 5:

At (t^1), Friday, 7 June 1776, Richard Henry Lee of Virginia *introduced* the premises of three resolutions. The premises were seconded by John Adams of Massachusetts. Both acts were PUBLIC SPEECH ACT:
  1. That these United Colonies are, and of Right ought to be, Free and Independent States, that they are absolved from all allegiance to the British Crown, and that all Political connection between them and the State of Great Britain is, and ought to be, totally dissolved.
  2. That it is expedient forthwith to take the most effectual measures for forming foreign Alliances.

3. That a plan of confederation be prepared and transmitted to the respective Colonies for their consideration and approbation (Maier 1997, 41).

Pressing business delayed discussion of the resolutions until the next morning.

At (t^2), Saturday, 8 June 1776, initial debates by the delegates of the premises began. They lasted three days in a second PUBLIC SPEECH ACT.

The three resolutions were tabled on Tuesday, 11 June 1776 while the delegates considered the matter further. Yet, in anticipation of eventual passage, three *ad hoc* committees were appointed—one "to prepare the declaration," one "to prepare and digest the form of a confederation to be entered into between these colonies," and one "to prepare a plan of treaties to be proposed to foreign powers" (*Journals of the Continental Congress* 1904–37, V:431). To prepare the draft declaration, a Committee of Five was appointed, composed of Benjamin Franklin, John Adams, Roger Sherman, Robert R. Livingston, and Thomas Jefferson. As the junior member, Jefferson was given the task of actually composing the draft. The *ad hoc* Committee of Five reported back with its draft declaration on Friday, 28 June 1776.

At (t^3), Monday, 1 July 1776, the first Virginia resolution for independence was taken from the table and the debate begun at (t^2) was taken up again for further *debate* in a third public speech act.

At (t^4), the premise was *approved* by a vote the next day in a fourth public speech act.

At (t^5), The Committee's draft declaration was now taken from the table, *debated*, and *amended* in a fifth PUBLIC SPEECH ACT.

The purpose of this debate was to amend the *ad interactionem* justificatory and prudential criteria argued in the draft declaration. For a decision-making assembly to act without justification and prudence would be the height of irresponsibility. Then, finally:

At (t^6), Saturday, 4 July 1776, after the end of the extended debate at (t^5), the question was called, and a *vote* is taken by the members, based on the assembly's justificatory and prudential determination in a sixth public speech act.

Critically and importantly, with the vote, the question was both *intended, decided*, and *declared* simultaneously in an open and solemn PUBLIC SPEECH ACT. A collective interaction, war, was *decided* and *declared* both simultaneously and collectively in a procedurally perfect manner.

Four observations are of interest: In the first place and most importantly, the Second Continental Congress was not "checking and balancing" an executive officer. Rather, it was hammering out a Hague Convention III compliant text. It was *determining* and *declaring* the policy ends, which ends would guide General George Washington in his execution of the military means. In short, "checking and balancing" an executive officer is seldom a good reason to enact any policy. Analyzing institutional roles and functions in terms of "checks and balances" explains little, except that political power games are being played.

In the second place, one must, again, underscore, highlight, and emphasize the critical importance of the simultaneity of *decision* and *declaration* in the act of voting. Which is to say more precisely, in terms of performance, the main temporal difference between an executive and a collective "enactment" is the synchronicity or asynchronicity of the immaterial, mental act of *intension/decision* and the culminating physical act, the *declaration*.

In the third place, despite the unfathomable complexity of the PRIVATE MENTAL ACTS of the individual members, the parliamentary procedures are largely a sequence of PUBLIC SPEECH ACTS. That is, because the decision-maker is a collective body, the procedures are of necessity PUBLIC, and not PRIVATE. The procedures may not always be public in the sense of "open to all." For certainly, occasions occur when this larger "public" must be excluded, as in July 1776. However, the procedures are always "public" in the sense that they are both witnessed and challenged by the other members of the decision-making assembly, who can later testify to what was said and done. The contrast here is with an executive who can easily shut the door of his office, mull his options over, and emerge to announce is *decision*.

In the fourth place, because the procedures of a decision-making assembly are both public and collective, no *one*—no single, lone individual—can impose his will upon others or on the world. Rather, a *decision* has been taken socially, the mental anguish and biases of the individual members notwithstanding. A manageable, *monofunctional*, decision-making assembly acts in the stead of and for the benefit of a larger, unmanageable collective body. This manageable, *monofunctional*, collective body has taken a social issue under advisement, and, in response, it has articulated what it considers collectively to be the most desirable policy ends. The contrast with executive decision-making is both stunning and vitally important.

With the declaration and enactment of the necessary policy ends, however, the power and authority of the decision-making assembly terminates, and the power and authority of the executive speaker/agent begins. Optimally, the executive's enactment of the sufficient material means is based, not upon his own personal power and authority, as in a monarchy, but, instead, upon an authority transmitted to him by the decision-making assembly in its collectively *declared* articulation of the ends sought.

2.2 The Ontology of a Procedurally Legitimate Ordering of Policy Means in a Republic

Ontologically, the faithful execution of policy ends requires an executive, first, to receive legitimating authority to speak performatively. Then, armed with this legitimating authority, the executive speaker transmits his legitimating authority on to a myriad of subordinate speakers/agents to implement the sufficient material means by which the ends sought can be accomplished. This procedurally legitimating transmission of authority is that which makes a symmetrical constitution a republican constitution. Schematically, as illustrated in the two left hand columns of Figure 5, the procedures for bringing into being both foreign and domestic policy means are the same:

At (t^1), based on the legitimating authorities transmitted to him, an executive must *decide* on the prudence of acting or not to acting in a first PRIVATE MENTAL ACT.

At (t^2), if he *decides* to act, an executive next *determines* the appropriate material means sufficient to achieve the ends sought in a PRIVATE MENTAL ACT.
These two initial PRIVATE MENTAL ACTS are the critical hinge upon which all turns.
The *determination* and *decision* are often made only after considerable mental anguish, as an executive weighs the pros and cons of acting or not acting, of this option versus that option.

At (t^3), after an interval of time, an executive must speak and transmit authority to his immediate staff, in a PRIVATE SPEECH ACT, *ordering* them to prepare the appropriate executive order, national security directive, proclamation, executive agreement, or the like.

At (t^4), he must *sign* the document prepared by his staff in a PUBLIC SPEECH ACT. The signing may be either a fully public ceremony or, at a minimum, it must take place in front of either witnesses or an attesting authority. The legitimacy of the document signed is vouchsafed, first, by the attesting witnesses, and, second, by the authority transmitted to the executive by the decision-making assembly.

At (t^5), the chief executive officer normally *publishes and declares* his act officially in a fully PUBLIC SPEECH ACT, such as publication in an official gazette.

With this final, fully PUBLIC SPEECH ACT, the downhill transmission of authority from its point of origin in a decision-making assembly to the very last implementing speakers/agents in the administrative chain of command rolls on.

These subordinate officials are now lieutenants or stadholders, namely, those who stand, speak, and command in the place of and with the authority of their superiors. For, they have now been authorized to speak performatively by the authorities transmitted to them by the executive, who, in turn, had been authorized to speak performatively by the decision-making assembly.

Four observations are of interest: In the first place, the executive procedures are largely a sequence of private acts, only emerging into a truly public light at the very end, at (t^5). In the second place, the complexity of the procedures is found in two different locations: In small part, the complexity is located in the temporal lags, in the way in which mental and material acts, private and public acts occur at different times in the process. In large part, the complexity is located in the aforementioned mental anguish of at (t^1) and (t^2) *determination* and *decision*. Although snap judgments based upon "gut feelings" are frequent enough, *decisions* normally incur significant anxiety as options, consequences, and values are weighed and measured, reweighed and remeasured by the executive decision-maker, his staff, and other influences. In the end, though, despite any complexity, when all has been considered and reconsidered, the executive procedure is usually, and a *decision* is made with "energy and dispatch," at least when compared to the leisurely pace of decision-making assemblies.

To repeat, the contrast between individual and collective decision-making must be noted again: On the one hand, the executive officer is a single speaker—a some*one*—a single, lone individual with the power to impose his will upon others, his staff and the executive bureaucracy, immediately, upon the nation and world, ultimately. On the other hand, the moral criteria implicit in the faithful execution of the collectively determined policy ends severely limits his power. Legitimately, he cannot do anything he desires. He *ought to* order only those prudent policy means that fall within the authorities transmitted to him by the collective assembly.

In the fourth place, and exceptionally critical, the scope of the chief executive's agency is not so much "checked" or "balanced" by the decision-making assembly as "guided" and "directed" by the collectively declared policy end his executive *decisions* are meant to execute. At least, this is the case when the rule of law prevails.

3   Conclusion

Pierce Butler spoke prophetically on Friday, 17 August 1787 in favor of a modern, asymmetric, elected, constitutional monarchy. Still, little doubt exists that the other members of the Federal Convention hoped for something different. They hoped for a true republic, and not an asymmetric, elected constitutional monarchy, as Elbridge Gerry reminded Butler. Unfortunately, though, two complementary design flaws frustrated this hope: A mal-distribution of the sovereign's fœderative powers, to recall Locke's term, was exacerbated by the failure to establish an independent, *monofunction*, decision-making assembly to *determine* and *decide* the ends of the nation's foreign policy. The obvious sign of this exacerbating mal-distribution has always been the incapacity of the *bifunctional* Congress to *decide* and *declare* war. To fill the vacuum, President James Madison took, as it were, Butler's advice and assumed all the duties and responsibilities of an elected constitutional monarch with regard to foreign affairs. The natural result was to transform the hoped-for republic into a modern, elected, asymmetric, constitutional monarchy. On the positive side, this transformation saved the United States from being an abnormality. It saved the United States from being different than all the other modern states of the world. On the negative side, this transformation traduced the hopes of the Federal Convention for a republic.

The net effect of the traduced hopes has been and continues to be at least two different confounding confusions. More pointedly, a closer look at the speech act foundations of the modern, elected, constitutional monarchies reveals not the "consent" of a "sovereign people" to a "social contract," but a cascade of transmissible authorities that were generated by procedurally legitimate performative speech acts uttered by revolutionary Lesser Magistrates turned Founding Fathers. These cascading transmissible authorities, to repeat, were enacted initially in Philadelphia during the summer of 1778 and, later, ratified in thirteen especially elected decision-making assemblies during the course of 1788—the ratifying conventions. To best understand this cascade, one must turn to John Austin's theory of performative speech acts, as has been done here, and not to Thomas Hobbes, John Locke, Jean-Jacque Rousseau, or

John Adams. Behind the mystical myths, then, the actuality is much simpler, if less emotionally impactful. The actuality is collective decision-making by means of synchronic performative speech acts uttered collectively.

The second confounding confusion regards the relationship between the executive and legislature in a republic. The empirical actuality of this relationship is best explained and understood in terms of "ends and means," and not in terms of "checks and balances." In his book, Arthur Schlesinger speaks of the dwindling "away [of] checks, both written and unwritten, that had long held the Presidency under control." Yet, the undwindling of either written or unwritten "checks" is not the remedy to restore "balance." In point of fact, the republican remedy is to distinguish between two different decision-making assemblies. The one assembly should determine domestic policy ends; the other assembly should determine foreign policy ends. The collective *decisions* of the first assembly would, thereby, transmit legitimating authorities to the president as chief executive officer to execute the laws of the land. The collective *decisions* of the second assembly would, thereby, transmit legitimating authorities to the president as commander-in-chief to execute the military means. The model relationship is that between the Second Continental Congress and General Washington or between the United Nations Security Council and the commander of a United Nations force. A fuller exploration of constitutional import of "ends and means" as an explanatory concept is the burden of the next chapter.

CHAPTER 8

Ends and Means or Checks and Balance?

Obscuring Agency by Authorizing War in the Unites States and Europe

Abstract

The chapter employs Clausewitz and a generalized version of the traditional just-war criteria—the just interaction criteria—to argue that no republican constitution can be based upon a theory of "checks and balance." Rather, a republican constitution must be based on a structural and functional distinction between ends and means. Namely, between a collective speaker who *decides* and *declares* policy ends and an executive speaker who *decides* on and *orders* the material means chosen to accomplish the political end. In this regard, the shortcomings of recent legislative veto laws, in France, Germany and elsewhere are compared to the 1973 *War Powers Resolution*.

If presidential war making is unacceptable because it transforms a theoretically republican Constitution into an asymmetric, elected, constitutional monarchy, what is to be done about it? The simplest response is to amend the Constitution to repair the defect. But how? As noted in Chapter 4, John Yoo has correctly identified one of the textual sources of the problem in the American Constitution by observing that, "Yet the Constitution itself nowhere describes such a process [by which the Congress shall enact a declaration of war], nor does it explain how the Declare War Clause and the commander-in-chief power must interact. The Framers simply gave the former to Congress and the latter to the president, and left it at that" (2005, 152). His seemingly logical response to this textual ambiguity is to amend Article II to read, "the president 'shall have Power, by and with the advice and consent of Congress, to engage in War'" (*ibid.*, 153). The simplicity of the proposed amendment is enchanting. So, enchanting that its spirit has been adopted by most European countries since the fall of the Berlin Wall in 1989. Unfortunately, Yoo's suggestion will not work because it has not worked either at the level of theory or at the level of practice.

At the level of theory, Yoo's proposal has not worked because an explicit statement that any legislature shall "advise and consent" changes nothing. It still leaves the *decision* to go to war fully in the hands of the nation's war leader as commander-in-chief, as has always been the case. As has always been the case, the war leader *decides* the question of war or peace on his own authority in the executive manner. He then employs either *Scenario 3* to "consult" with the legislature, or he employs either *Scenario 1* or *2* and does not consult. At the level of theory, the effect of Yoo's suggestion is only to make explicit that which is now implicit, namely, that modern constitutions are not republican in character, but asymmetric, elected, constitutional monarchies in character.

At the level of practice, Yoo's proposal has already been tried and failed in two incarnations. The first incarnation was James Madison's use of his kingly discretion "to convene and give information to the legislature" in 1812. This procedure has already been discussed in Chapter 3 and has resulted in four technically minimal, lexical declarations of war over two hundred years, two per century. Namely, those of 1812, 1898, 1917, and 1941. After World War II, when both war and the declaring of war were outlawed in the Charter of the United Nations, something different obviously had to be found. President Harry Truman initiated the search in June 1950 by avoiding both the Constitution and the Eighty-first Congress altogether. Instead, he called upon the "advice and consent" of the new United Nations Security Council. After consideration, the Security Council approved his requested "authorization," and American and other allied forces were soon engaged in the Korean War. This story was told in Chapter 6.

Initially, for the first three month of the Korean War, President Truman's venue shopping did look like the solution. No one objected—strongly. However, the surprise entry of large numbers of Chinese "Volunteers" into the fighting during October and November of 1950 changed this initial absence of objections. With the Chinese entry, the United Nation's forces in Korea suffered a sever defeat and a costly retreat. Once the front stabilized along the Thirty-eighth parallel, the war turned into the unpleasant stalemate of trench warfare during 1951–1953. Combat finally ended on Monday, 27 July 1953 when an armistice was signed. With the dramatic retreat and the seemingly endless grind of trench warfare during 1951–1953, public support for the war declined rapidly. Taking advantage of the situation, the Republicans in the Congress began criticizing President Truman for his mismanagement of the war, in general, and, in particular, for bypassing the Congress initially. The president should not have gone to the Security Council when the war first broke out in June 1950.

To avoid such controversies, the politically astute President Dwight Eisenhower came up with a solution that has pleased many. Basically, his solution is a variation on *Scenario 3: An Unsolemn Functionally Equivalent Declarative Act by the Nation's Hereditary or Elected King that Involves a Legislature*. President Eisenhower requested, not a lexical declaration of war, but, instead, a functionally equivalent, procedurally imperfect "authorization" from the Congress. The first of these was an *Authorization for the President to Employ the Armed Forces of the United States for Protecting the Security of Formosa ... of 1955*. The seventh and latest was the *Authorization of the Use of Force Against Iraq Resolution of 2002* (For a full list, see Hallett 2012, 133–4). This politically astute, but unconstitutional, solution was, of course, codified in the *War Powers Resolution of 1973*.

As already noted, if this unconstitutional solution were confined only to United States, one would probably be well served to ignore it. However, since the end of the Cold War, the world has seen an explosion of this type of misdirected "authorizing" legislation, especially in Europe. Thus, this false solution needs to be dealt with. One of the better ways to do so is to recall from Chapter 7 a curious feature of the relationship between ends and means. In particular, the way in which the ends and means do not "check and balance." Mindful of this, consider three curious dots. Is it possible to connect them?

1 Clausewitz *On War*

First off, one of the more curious features of Carl von Clausewitz's seminal book, *On War*, is how strongly he felt that the conduct of war required a doctrine of separation of powers. As he states in his "remarkable trinity" passage:

> The passions that are to be kindled in war must already be inherent in the people; the scope which the play of courage and talent will enjoy in the realm of probability and chance [i.e., in the contingent world of military operations] depends on the particular character of the commander and the army; but the political aims [of war] are the business of the government" (1976, 89).

Critically, Clausewitz does not propose his "remarkable trinity" doctrine for the purpose of establishing a system of "checks and balances" to buffer conflicting executive and legislative interests and powers. The business of the "government" is not to "check" or "balance" the commander of the nation's military means. Rather, under Clausewitz's "separation of powers" doctrine, the *decider* and *declarer* of the political ends of war does not and cannot "check" or "balance" the commander of the military means. To imagine such is to fundamentally misunderstand the command relationship. Stated more generally, the performative speech act of *intending, deciding,* and *declaring* the ends of an interaction guide, direct, and limit the number of coherent means. This occurs because only a limited number of means will accomplish the ends desired. In addition, the performative speech act of a legitimate *decider* and *declarer* of ends generates the transmissible authorities needed to legitimize the execution of the means chosen by the commander. This ends-means separation of powers is significantly different than a Madisonian playing of one interest or power against an opposing interest or power. In point of fact, playing a Madisonian game of "checks and balances" does not take one to the heart of the matter.

It follows, therefore, that, in order to maintain the separation of ends from means, the "government" must be reinterpreted to mean a small, *monofunction*, unicameral decision-making assembly employing committee-of-the-whole rules. Clausewitz would no doubt be appalled at this unnatural infringement on the King of Prussia's God-given, royal prerogatives. Yet, the force of his argument is unrelenting. If all human interactions, including war, are end-means problems, then the *decider* and *declarer* of the ends must be separated institutionally from the chooser of the means. Further, practical experience shows that non-executive decision-making assemblies employing parliamentary procedures are the more appropriate *deciders* and *declarers* of the ends, whereas single, individual executive officers and their staffs are the more appropriate *choosers* of the means. Republican governments are the natural result of Clausewitz's ends-means analysis of war, as the Romans of the Republic well knew.

2 The Just-Interaction Criteria

Before starting on this second dot, a word of introduction is needed: Over the millennia from Aristotle to Cicero, Augustine to Aquinas, and Grotius to the Hague and Geneva conventions, the laws of war have been built upon the moral and aesthetic criteria found in the traditional just-war criteria (Hallett. Forthcoming). As reproduced in Appendix F, these moral and aesthetic criteria are divided into two parts: The first part comprises the traditional *jus ad bellum* criteria, which enable one to come to a rigorous and balanced judgment concerning the *decision to war*. These criteria require one to ask whether the proposed ends and purposes are both justified and prudent. The second part comprises the traditional *jus in bello* criteria, which enable one to come to a rigorous and balanced judgment concerning the means to be employed *in the war*. These criteria require one to ask whether the proposed means—the weapons, means, and methods—are proportionate and discriminate.

However, war is a human interaction. And, every human interaction is an ends-means problem. Every human interaction requires a rigorous and balanced judgment concerning the *decision* to do the interaction. Likewise, every human interaction also requires a rigorous and balanced judgment concerning the means to be employed, once the *decision* has been made. Thus, the traditional just-war criteria possess a more general application than is usually recognized. This more general application may be spoken of as the *just-interaction criteria*, which is comprised the *jus ad interactionem* and the *jus in interactione*. This more general application allows one to conceive of and analyze all human interactions in terms of the moral and aesthetic coherence of the respective performative speech acts. Does the speech act 1) articulate coherent, well-*decided* and *declared* moral ends, and 2) will the authorities transmitted accomplish those ends by means of well-chosen, proportionate, and discriminate material means?

With that word of introduction, one of the more curious features of the just-interaction criteria is the way in which the criteria flesh out and are congruent with Clausewitz's separation of powers doctrine. The just-interaction criteria flesh out the relationship between ends and means by establishing a moral and aesthetic hierarchy. Operating separately, the *jus ad interactionem* criteria guide and justify the "government's" (*i.e.*, the small decision-making assembly's) *decision* and *declaration* of the political and moral ends. Next, the *jus in interactione* criteria guide and justify the commander's employment of coherent and practical military means to attain those ends. When coherence, especially, a high degree of an aesthetic and moral coherence is achieved between the two, the proposed interaction is most likely justified and prudent. When such a high degree of coherence is not achieved, the proposed interaction is most likely an unjustified, imprudent, an immoral perversion of war.

Of critical importance in achieving a high degree of aesthetic and moral coherence, one must signal out the "open and determined declaration of intention and purposes" criterion from among the *ad interactionem* procedural criteria. This criterion is, need it be said, the heart and soul of Hague Convention III. It is also a performative speech act. Consequently, the "open and determined declaration of intention and purposes" criterion makes clear two vital points: First, that the decision-making assembly's moral justification "determines" the validity of its political justification, not the other way around. Neither *realpolitik* nor *raison d'état* nor "national security interests" lead to just wars. This point is most easily verified by re-reading the *Declaration of Independence*.

Another of the more curious features of the just-interaction criteria is that a functionally equivalent "closed and undetermined" declaration made by the nation's war leader is an illegitimate *decision* and *declaration*. That is, when the nation's war leader, its commander-in-chief, substitutes a functionally equivalent speech act for a fully determined and open declaration by a decision-making assembly, his declaration is doubly illegitimate. It is illegitimate procedurally because it is self-justificatory, which taints the moral and legal quality of the transmissible authorities. It is illegitimate functionally because it violates the distinction between ends and means, between a small decision-making assembly voting on the political ends and a commander ordering the military means. The functional distinction having been violated, neither the public, nor the enemy, nor, most significantly, the subordinate commanders and the army have any good way of learning either the legitimate political objectives or the legitimate moral justification for the war, most especially, the moral justification (Grynaviski 2013).

To see this crucial point, imagine the American Revolution without the *Declaration of Independence*. Many people wonder about the legitimacy of and the moral justification for a variety of America's wars, the war in Vietnam or the 2003 invasion of Iraq, for example. Does anyone wonder about either the legitimacy of the political objectives or the moral justification for the American Revolution? Most especially, the moral justification? If anyone does, a quick glance at the *Declaration of Independence* will soon provide the needed explanation. In the first place, the Second Continental Congress respected the functional distinction between ends and means, between the "government" and the "commander and the army." In the second place, the *Declaration of Independence* transmitted procedurally legitimating authorities to Commander-in-Chief George Washington and his subordinates. In the third place, because of the first two, the authorities transmitted to Commander-in-Chief George Washington gave him clear and precise guidance and direction concerning the desired ends of the war. In short, Commander-in-Chief George Washington was put in a position where he could most easily separate appropriate from inappropriate military means.

The contrast with Vietnam and Iraq is stunning. In violation of the necessary functional distinction, Commander-in-Chief Lyndon Johnson's functionally equivalent *decisions* and *declarations* gave little or no direction or guidance to General William Westmoreland in Vietnam. Likewise, Commander-in-Chief George W. Bush's functionally equivalent *decisions* and *declarations* gave little or no guidance to General Tommy Franks in Iraq. The perverse consequential results of this violation of the functional distinction between ends and means should have been expected. In short, republican government is the natural result of a procedurally perfect ends-means analysis in accordance with the just-interaction evaluation of human interactions, most especially, of the social interact known as "war."

3   The Federal Convention of 1787

The third and final dot highlights one of the more curious features of the Federal Convention of 1787. This curiosity entails the way in which Madison's conception of the separation of powers doctrine is not congruent with either Clausewitz or the just-interaction criteria, as he wrote in *Federalist No. 51*:

> This policy of supplying, by opposite and rival interests, the defect of better motives, might be traced through the whole system of human affairs, private as well as public. We see it particularly displayed in all the subordinate distributions of power, where the constant aim is to divide and arrange the several offices in such a manner as that each may be a check on the other—that the private interest of every individual may be a sentinel over the public rights. These inventions of prudence cannot be less requisite in the distribution of the supreme powers of the State.

Managing political power, not the aesthetic and moral coherence of ends and means, was the unfortunate object of the Federal Convention. To no surprise, a most excellent example of the deleterious effects of Madison's misplaced emphasis on managing political power is found in the explosion of "authorizing" legislation since the end of the Cold War, beginning, of course, with the grandfather of them all, the *War Powers Resolution of 1973*.

4   Obscuring Agency by Authorizing War in the Unites States and Europe

On Wednesday, 7 November 1973, the Ninety-third United States Congress passed a *War Powers Resolution* over President Richard Nixon's veto. In doing so, it raised the false hope that the new law's procedures would "check and balance" any future president who might be "prone" to war. Instead, the *Resolution* only enhanced what Arthur Schlesinger called *The Imperial Presidency*. It did little to "check" and less to "balance" presidential "proneness" to war, while doing much to exacerbate and facilitate presidential war making (Glennon 1995; Fisher and Adler 1998)

Until recently, only the United States was subject to this false hope. Then, unexpectedly, shortly after the fall of the Berlin Wall in 1989, country after country in Europe passed enactments modeled loosely on the moribund American *Resolution of 1973*. For example, in the name of democratic accountability and transparency, *The Bundestag Participation Act of 18 March 2005* (BGBl. I 775) calls for legislative "consent" of executive *decisions* to employ the nation's armed forces. Or, the 23 July 2008 amendment of Article 35 of the French Constitution clarifies when and how the National Assembly would "authorize" the President of the Republic to declare war:

ARTICLE 35. A declaration of war shall be authorized by Parliament.

The Government shall inform Parliament of its decision to have the armed forces intervene abroad, at the latest three days after the beginning of said intervention. It shall detail the objectives of the said intervention. This information may give rise to a debate, which shall not be followed by a vote.

Where the said intervention shall exceed four months, the Government shall submit the extension to Parliament for authorization. It may ask the National Assembly to make the final decision.

If Parliament is not sitting at the end of the four-month period, it shall express its decision at the opening of the following session (*Conseil Constitutionnle* N.D.).

Superficially, the American, French, German, and similar legislative vetoes celebrate eminently democratic principles. After all, who can object to a process that begins with "consultation" between the commander of the nation's military means and the legislative branch and, then, concludes with an enactment of their "collective judgment?" This doctrine was first articulated in different words by Speaker Henry Clay in his *aide-mémoire* of Sunday, 15 March 1812, which was cited in Chapters 3 and 6. It has, however, found its fullest expression in Sections 2(a) and 3 of American *War Powers Resolution*:

PURPOSE AND POLICY
Sec. 2. (a) It is the purpose of this joint resolution to fulfill the intent of the framers of the Constitution of the United States and insure that the collective judgment of both the Congress and the President will apply to the introduction of United States Armed Forces into hostilities, or into situations where imminent involvement in hostilities is clearly indicated by the circumstances, and to the continued use of such forces in hostilities or in such situations.

CONSULTATION
Sec. 3. The President in every possible instance shall consult with Congress before introducing United States Armed Forces into hostilities or into situations where imminent involvement in hostilities is clearly indicated by the circumstances,. ... (Pub. L. 93-148; 87 Stat. 555).

Theoretically, to repeat, the "process" looks nicely participatory and democratic, as it no doubt is. It requires the nation's political elite—as represented by the two political branches of government—to come together in a participatory manner to "consult" on the question of war or peace so as to form a "collective (democratic?) judgment." Once the two political branches have come to a mutually acceptable agreement, who can object to a legislative "authorization?" Actually, of course, the "consultative" process is Gilgamesh's five-thousand-year-old *Scenario 3: An Unsolemn Functionally Equivalent Declarative Act by the Nation's Hereditary or Elected King that Involves a Legislature*.

Consequently, "consultation leading to collective judgment" does not "check or balance" executive war-making. Of even greater concern, it violates the separation of ends and means as understood by Clausewitz and the just-interaction criteria. Instead, what it really does is to obscure the role of the nation's war leader as the speaker/agent who is driving the process towards war behind an apparently "democratic" façade. In the first place, the issue is no longer a procedural question of how a small, *monofunctional*, decision-making assembly might articulate the political ends so as to give both guidance and transmissible authorities to the commander of the military means. Now, the issue has been redefined as a "mutually acceptable agreement" among the nation's political elite for the nation's war leader to do that which he has already *decided* to do. Interbranch concord and agreement is now the objective of the exercise, as Gilgamesh and all politically astute war leaders know.

In the second place, as noted, the whole "process" is clearly driven by the agency of the nations' war leader, the executive. He makes the initial, unilateral *decision* for war, not the legislature. The legislature does not "consult" with him. He "consults" with the legislature, but only for the purpose of aligning their "collective judgment" with his *decision*. Then, once the "collective judgment" of the legislature has been properly aligned, it obediently "authorizes" the commander of the nation's military means to do that which he has already *decided* to do. Needless to say, this obscuration of the war leader's agency has been systematically exploited by prime ministers, presidents, chancellors, kings, and emperors from Caesar and Octavian to Tony Blair and George W. Bush.

A good medieval example of this obscutantizing "process" of "consultation leading to a collective judgment" is that of Charles v of France, the Wise (1337–1380) is Christine de Pisan's "wel gaaf ensample the good wyse kyng charles the fythe of that name," which was cited in Chapter 1:

> ... assembled at parys [Paris] at his parliament the forsaid foure estates/ .../and to theym purposed his reasons ayenst thenglyssh men [against the English men] demaundyng theyr aduys/yf he had cause to bygynne warre/for without iuste cause/the regarde & deliberacion emonge theym/and the consente & wylle of his good subgetts in no wyse he wold doo it at whiche counseyl by long deliberacion was concluded that he

had good & iuste cause to begynne agayn the warre & thus the good wise kynge entreprysed it/(1937, I, v).

In passing, it is noteworthy that Charles v was considered the "legitimate" authority for *deciding* and *declaring* war in medieval France. Even more noteworthy, his successor, the President of the French Republic, is still considered the "legitimate" authority for *deciding* and *declaring* war in modern France. Little, it seems, has changed in six hundred years, except the justification for the legitimizing convention. For Charles v, his "legitimacy" fell out a matter of divine right. He had been chosen by god and consecrated by the Church. For the President of the French Republic, his "legitimacy" falls out as a matter of Article 35 of the French Constitution. In addition, he is chosen by the voters of France, if not god. In both cases, though, "legitimacy" is a matter of ancient custom or legal convention. "Legitimacy," one must therefore conclude, is not a question of *ought*, but of *is*, which is to say, of convention. Not coincidentally, one might add, this positive convention is based upon the solid material fact that both hereditary and elected monarchs command the nation's military means. Still, one might wonder, *ought* this positive, conventional understanding of "legitimate" authority be sustained forever? Should *ought* depend exclusively on *is* forever? But I digress.

And, finally, the obscuration of the true speaker/agent is not the only consequence of a doctrine of "consultation leading to a collective judgment." To it, one must add the way in which a legislative veto or "authorization" tends to eliminate Hague Convention III compliant, procedurally perfect, solemn, open and determined declarations of war altogether, substituting in their place a variety of simulacra or functionally equivalent televised speeches, documents, or reports written by the commander of the military means.

Foremost among these simulacra, one must highlight how these self-justifying "authorizations" are authored by the commander of the military means and exclude the moral reasoning of the just-interaction criteria. For example, consider the relevant passages in *The Bundestag Participation Act* and the *War Power Resolution*:

> Article 3 (Request) (2) The request of the Federal Government shall contain information, in particular, concerning:
>   the mandate of the deployment,
>   the operational area,
>   the legal bases of the deployment,
>   the maximum number of soldiers to be deployed,
>   the capabilities of the armed forces to be deployed,

the planned duration of the deployment, and

the envisaged costs and financing (BGBl. I 775; Translation Denza 2006).

The parallel instructions in the War Powers Resolution are:

> ... the President [of the United States] shall submit within 48 hours to the Speaker of the House of Representatives and to the President pro tempore of the Senate a report, in writing, setting forth-
> (A) the circumstances necessitating the introduction of United States Armed Forces;
> (B) the constitutional and legislative authority under which such introduction took place; and
> (C) the estimated scope and duration of the hostilities or involvement (Pub. L. 93-148; 87 Stat. 555, Section 4 (a) (3)).

In short, the "information" reported to the legislature by the nation's war leader is, at best, a budgetary and legal justification for the war. The crucial public reasoning is missing (Grynaviski, 2013; Cameron 2013). The critical aesthetic and moral coherence found in the *Declaration of Independence*, for example, is missing. Of course, this does make some sense, not much, but some. It makes some sense as soon as one recalls that the nation's war leader has already resolved all moral questions in his own mind on his own authority as the nation's war leader. All he requires from the legislature is a political accommodation and an "authorization." No more and no less.

Yet, of much greater importance, the critical functional distinction between ends and means is entirely lost in all of the recent legislative veto enactments. None are Hague Convention III compliant, in the first place, and, in the second place, all violate the functional distinction between ends and means, grievously. For, the commander of the armed forces himself cannot legitimately presume to declare the political objectives of the war or to generate the transmissible authorities from himself to himself. The conflict of both function and interest is too abundantly clear.

Appendices

APPENDIX A

The Declaration of Independence and Twelve Congressional Declarations of War

1. *The War for Independence*: An Absolute, Reasoned, Solemnly Perfect Declaration

Resolved, That it be recommended to the respective assemblies and conventions of the United Colonies, where no government sufficient to the exigencies of their affairs have been hitherto established, to adopt such government as shall, in the opinion of the representatives of the people, best conduce to the happiness and of safety of their constituents in particular, and America in general (*Journals of the Continental Congress* 1904–37, IV: 342).

Introduced by John Adams of Massachusetts,
seconded by Richard Henry Lee of Virginia,
Friday, 10 May 1776

The Virginia Resolutions:
Resolved, That these United Colonies are, and of Right ought to be, Free and Independent States, that they are absolved from all allegiance to the British Crown, and that all Political connection between them and the State of Great Britain is, and ought to be, totally dissolved.

Resolved, That it is expedient forthwith to take the most effectual measures for forming foreign Alliances.

Resolved, That a plan of confederation be prepared and transmitted to the respective Colonies for their consideration and approbation (Maier 1997, 41).

Introduced by Richard Henry Lee of Virginia,
seconded by John Adams of Massachusetts,
Friday, 7 June 1776

In CONGRESS, July 4, 1776.
A DECLARATION
By the REPRESENTATIVES of the
UNITED STATES OF AMERICA,
In GENERAL CONGRESS assembled.

WHEN in the Course of human Events, it becomes necessary for one People to dissolve the Political Bands which have connected them with another, and to assume among the Powers of the Earth, the separate and equal Station to which the Laws of

Nature and of Nature's God entitle them, a decent Respect to the Opinions of Mankind requires that they should declare the causes which impel them to the Separation.

We hold these Truths to be self-evident, that all Men are created equal, that they are endowed by their Creator with certain unalienable Rights, that among these are Life, Liberty, and the Pursuit of Happiness—That to secure these Rights, Governments are instituted among Men, deriving their just Powers from the Consent of the Governed, that whenever any Form of Government becomes destructive of these Ends, it is the Right of the People to alter or to abolish it, and to institute new Government, laying its Foundation on such Principles, and organizing its Powers in such Form, as to them shall seem most likely to effect their Safety and Happiness. Prudence, indeed, will dictate that Governments long established should not be changed for light and transient Causes; and accordingly all Experience hath shewn, that Mankind are more disposed to suffer, while Evils are sufferable, than to right themselves by abolishing the Forms to which they are accustomed. But when a long Train of Abuses and Usurpations, pursuing invariably the same Object, evinces a Design to reduce them under absolute Despotism, it is their Right, it is their Duty, to throw off such Government, and to provide new Guards for their future Security. Such has been the patient Sufferance of these Colonies; and such is now the Necessity which constrains them to alter their former Systems of Government. The History of the present King of Great Britain is a History of repeated injuries and Usurpations, all having in direct Object the Establishment of an absolute Tyranny over these States. To prove this, let Facts be submitted to a candid World.

[*indictment*]

He has refused his Assent to Laws, the most wholesome and necessary for the public Good.

He has forbidden his Governors to pass Laws of immediate and pressing Importance, unless suspended in their Operation till his Assent should be obtained; and when so suspended, he has utterly neglected to attend to them.

He has refused to pass other Laws for the Accommodation of large Districts of People, unless those People would relinquish the Right of Representation in the Legislature, a Right inestimable to them, and formidable to Tyrants only.

He has called together Legislative Bodies at Places unusual, uncomfortable, and distant from the Depository of their public Records, for the sole Purpose of fatiguing them into Compliance with his Measures.

He has dissolved Representative Houses repeatedly, for opposing with manly Firmness his Invasions on the Rights of the People.

He has refused for a long Time, after such Dissolutions, to cause others to be elected; whereby the Legislative Powers, incapable of Annihilation, have returned to the People at large for their exercise; the State remaining in the mean time exposed to all the Dangers of Invasion from without, and Convulsions within.

He has endeavoured to prevent the Population of these States; for that Purpose obstructing the Laws for Naturalization of Foreigners; refusing to pass others to encourage their Migrations hither, and raising the Conditions of new Appropriations of Lands.

He has obstructed the Administration of Justice, by refusing his Assent to Laws for establishing Judiciary Powers. He has made Judges dependent on his Will alone, for the Tenure of their Offices, and the Amount and Payment of their Salaries.

He has erected a Multitude of new Offices, and sent hither Swarms of Officers to harrass our People, and eat out their Substance.

He has kept among us, in Times of Peace, Standing Armies, without the consent of our Legislatures.

He has affected to render the Military independent of and superior to the Civil Power.

He has combined with others to subject us to a Jurisdiction foreign to our Constitution, and unacknowledged by our Laws; giving his Assent to their Acts of pretended Legislation:

For quartering large Bodies of Armed Troops among us: For protecting them, by a mock Trial, from Punishment for any Murders which they should commit on the Inhabitants of these States:

For cutting off our Trade with all Parts of the World:

For imposing Taxes on us without our Consent:

For depriving us, in many Cases, of the Benefits of Trial by Jury:

For transporting us beyond Seas to be tried for pretended Offences:

For abolishing the free System of English Laws in a neighbouring Province, establishing therein an arbitrary Government, and enlarging its Boundaries, so as to render it at once an Example and fit Instrument for introducing the same absolute Rule into these Colonies:

For taking away our Charters, abolishing our most valuable Laws, and altering fundamentally the Forms of our Governments:

For suspending our own Legislatures, and declaring themselves invested with Power to legislate for us in all Cases whatsoever.

He has abdicated Government here, by declaring us out of his Protection and waging War against us.

He has plundered our Seas, ravaged our Coasts, burnt our Towns, and destroyed the Lives of our People.

He is, at this Time, transporting large Armies of foreign Mercenaries to compleat the Works of Death, Desolation, and Tyranny, already begun with circumstances of Cruelty and Perfidy, scarcely paralleled in the most barbarous Ages, and totally unworthy the Head of a civilized Nation.

He has constrained our fellow Citizens taken Captive on the high Seas to bear Arms against their Country, to become the Executioners of their Friends and Brethren, or to fall themselves by their Hands.

He has excited domestic Insurrections amongst us, and has endeavoured to bring on the Inhabitants of our Frontiers, the merciless Indian Savages, whose known Rule of Warfare, is an undistinguished Destruction, of all Ages, Sexes and Conditions.

In every stage of these Oppressions we have Petitioned for Redress in the most humble Terms: Our repeated Petitions have been answered only by repeated Injury. A Prince, whose Character is thus marked by every act which may define a Tyrant, is unfit to be the Ruler of a free People.

Nor have we been wanting in Attentions to our British Brethren. We have warned them from Time to Time of Attempts by their Legislature to extend an unwarrantable Jurisdiction over us. We have reminded them of the Circumstances of our Emigration and Settlement here. We have appealed to their native Justice and Magnanimity, and we have conjured them by the Ties of our common Kindred to disavow these Usurpations, which, would inevitably interrupt our Connections and Correspondence. They too have been deaf to the Voice of Justice and of Consanguinity.

[denunciation of war]

We must, therefore, acquiesce in the Necessity, which denounces our Separation,

[declaration of war]

and hold them, as we hold the rest of Mankind, Enemies in War, in Peace, Friends.

[declaration of peace terms]

We, therefore, the Representatives of the UNITED STATES OF AMERICA, in General Congress, Assembled, appealing to the Supreme Judge of the World for the Rectitude of our Intentions, do, in the Name, and by Authority of the good People of these Colonies, solemnly Publish and Declare, That these United Colonies are, and of Right out (sic) to be, Free and Independent States; that they are absolved from all Allegiance to the British Crown, and that all political Connection between them and the State of Great-Britain, is and ought to be totally dissolved; and that as Free and Independent States, they have full Power to levy War, conclude Peace, contract Alliances, establish Commerce, and to do all other Acts and Things which Independent States may of right do. And for the support of this Declaration, with a firm Reliance on the Protection of divine Providence, we mutually pledge to each other our Lives, our Fortunes, and our sacred Honor.

[no authorization]

2. *The War of 1812*: An Absolute, Unreasoned, Solemnly Perfect Declaration

Be it enacted by the Senate and House of Representatives of the United States in Congress assembled,

[declaration of war]

That war be and the same is hereby declared to exist between the United Kingdom of Great Britain and Ireland and the dependencies thereof, and the United States of America and their Territories;

[authorization]

and that the President of the United States is hereby authorized to use the whole land and naval force of the United States to carry the same into effect, and to issue to private armed vessels of the United States commissions or letters of marque and general reprisal, in such form as he shall think proper, and under the seal of the United States, against the vessels, goods, and effects, of the Government of the said United Kingdom of Great Britain and Ireland, and the subjects thereof (Pub. L. No. 12–102, 2 Stat. 755).

3. *The Mexican-American War, 1846*: An Absolute, Unresaoned, Unsolemn, Imperfect Declaration

Whether this act counts as a declaration of war or not must be disputed. It is basically an appropriations bill that has had its title changed and a single recital pasted on. Certainly it is functionally equivalent to a formal declaration of war, but, precisely because it is functionally equivalent, good reason exists to discount it as declaration "in form." I have I reproduce only a select few sections of the act.

An Act providing for the Prosecution of the existing War between the United States and the Republic of Mexico.

[*indictment and denunciation of the enemy?*]

Whereas, by the act of the Republic of Mexico, a state of war exists between that Government and the United States:

Be it enacted by the Senate and House of Representatives of the United States of America in Congress assembled,

[*authorization*]

That, for the purpose of enabling the Government of the United States to prosecute said war to a speedy and successful termination, the President be, and he is hereby, authorized to employ the militia, naval, and military forces of the United States, and to call for and accept the services of any number of volunteers, not exceeding fifty thousand, who may offer their services, either as cavalry, artillery, infantry, or riflemen, to serve twelve months after they shall have arrived at the place of rendezvous, or to the end of the war, unless sooner discharged, according to the time for which they shall have been mustered into service; and that the sum of ten million dollars, out of any moneys in the treasury, or to come into the Treasury, not otherwise appropriated, be, and the same is hereby, appropriated, for the purpose of carrying the provisions of this act into effect.

[*appropriation*]

Sec. 5. *And be it further enacted*, That the said volunteers so offering their services shall be accepted by the President in companies, battalions, squadrons, and regiments, whose officers shall be appointed in the manner prescribed by law in the several States and Territories to which such companies, battalions, squadrons, and regiments shall respectively belong.

Sec. 6. *And be it further enacted*, That the President of the United States be, and he is hereby, authorized to organize companies so tendering their services into battalions or squadrons, battalions and squadrons into regiments, regiments into brigades, and brigades into divisions, as soon as the number of volunteers shall render such organization, in his judgment, expedient; and the President shall, if necessary, apportion the staff, field, and general officers among the respective States and Territories from which the volunteers shall tender their services, as he may deem proper.

Sec. 9. *And be it further enacted*, That whenever the militia or volunteers are called and received into the service of the United States, under the provisions of this act, they shall have the organization of the army of the United States, and shall have the same pay and allowances; and all mounted privates, non-commissioned officers, musicians and artificers, shall be allowed 40 cents per day for the use and risk of their horses, except of horses actually killed in action; and if any mounted volunteer, private, non-commissioned officer, musician, or artificer, shall not keep himself provided with a serviceable horse, said volunteer shall serve on foot. Approved 13 May 1846. (Pub. L. No. 29-16, 9 Stat. 9

4. *The Spanish-American War, 1898*: A Conditional, Reasoned, Solemnly Perfect Declaration

House Resolution 233 was introduced in the House on 13 April 1898 but completely revised by the Senate. The original resolution read as follows:

Joint resolution (H. Res. 233) authorizing and directing the President of the United States to intervene to stop the war in Cuba, and for the purpose of establishing a stable and independent government of the people therein.

[indictment and denunciation of the enemy]

Whereas the Government of Spain for three years past has been waging war on the Island of Cuba against a revolution by the inhabitants thereof without making any substantial progress towards the suppression of said revolution, and has conducted the warfare in a manner contrary to the laws of nations by methods inhuman and uncivilized, causing the death by starvation of more than 200,000 innocent noncombatants, the victims being for the most part helpless women and children, inflicting intolerable injury to the commercial interests of the United States, involving the destruction of the lives and property of many of our citizens, entailing the expenditure of millions of money in patrolling our coasts and policing the high seas in order to maintain our neutrality; and

Whereas this long series of losses, injuries, and burdens for which Spain is responsible has culminated in the destruction of the United States battle ship Maine in the harbor of Havana and the death of 260 of our seamen;

Resolved by the Senate and the House of Representatives of the United States of America in Congress assembled,

[declaration of peace terms]

That the President is hereby authorized and directed to intervene at once to stop the war in Cuba to the end and with the purpose of securing permanent peace and order there and establishing by the free action of the people thereof a stable and independent government of their own in the Island of Cuba;

[*authorization*]

and the President is hereby authorized and empowered to use the land and naval forces of the United States to execute the purpose of this resolution (*Cong. Rec.* (House) 18 April 1898, p. 4041, where the Senate amendments are also recorded.).

[*no declaration of war*]

4a. *The Spanish-American War, 1898:* A Conditional, Reasoned, Solemnly Perfect Declaration
The Senate Amendment of House Resolution 233:
Joint Resolution For the independence of the people of Cuba, demanding that the Government of Spain relinquish its authority and government in the Island of Cuba, and withdraw its land and naval forces from Cuba and Cuban waters, and directing the President of the United States to use the land and naval forces of the United States to carry these resolutions into effect.

[*indictment*]

Whereas the abhorrent conditions which have existed for more than three years in the Island of Cuba, so near our own borders, have shocked the moral sense of the people of the United States, have been a disgrace to Christian civilization, culminating, as they have, in the destruction of a United States battleship, with two hundred and sixty of its officers and crew, while on a friendly visit in the Harbor of Havana, and cannot longer be endured, as has been set forth by the President of the United States in his message to Congress of April eleventh, eighteen hundred and ninety-eight, upon which the action of Congress was invited: Therefore,

Resolved by the Senate and the House of Representatives of the United States of America, in Congress assembled, First. That the people of the Island of Cuba are, and of right ought to be free and independent.

[*denunciation of the enemy and declaration of peace terms*]

Second. That it is the duty of the United States to demand, and the Government of the United States does hereby demand, that the Government of Spain at once relinquish its authority and government in the Island of Cuba, and withdraw its land and naval forces from Cuba and Cuban waters.

[*authorization*]

Third. That the President of the United States be, and he hereby is, directed and empowered to use the entire land and naval forces of the United States, and to call into the actual service of the United States the militia of the several States to such extent as may be necessary to carry these resolutions into effect.

Fourth. That the United States hereby disclaims any disposition or intention to exercise sovereignty, jurisdiction, or control over said island except for the pacification thereof, and asserts its determination, when that is accomplished, to leave the government and control of the island to its people.

Approved, April 20, 1898. (The Joint Resolution was passed at 1:30am on 19 April 1898. Pub. Res. No. 55-24, 30 Stat. 738)

[*no declaration of war*]

4b. *The Spanish-American War, 1898* An Absolute, Unreasoned, Solemnly Perfect Declaration
An Act Declaring that war exists between the United States of America and the Kingdom of Spain.

[*no indictment and denunciation of the enemy*]

Be it enacted by the Senate and House of Representatives of the United States of America in Congress assembled,

[*declaration of war*]

First. That war be, and the same is hereby, declared to exist, and that war has existed since the twenty-first day of April, anno Domini eighteen hundred and ninety-eight, including said day, between the United States of America and the Kingdom of Spain.

[*authorization*]

Second. That the President of the United States be, and he hereby is, directed and empowered to use the entire land and naval forces of the United States, and to call into the actual service of the United States the militia of the several States, to such extent as may be necessary to carry this Act into effect.

[*no declaration of peace terms*]

Approved, April 25, 1898. (Pub. L. No. 55–189, 30 Stat. 364)

5. *World War I, 1917*: Two Absolute, Unreasoned, Solemnly Perfect Declarations
The State Department's draft as approved by President Woodrow Wilson and submitted to the House leadership on 2 April 1917:
JOINT RESOLUTION, *Declaring that a State of War Exists Between the Imperial German Government and the Government and People of the United States and Making Provisions to Prosecute the Same.*

[*indictment and denunciation of the enemy*]

Whereas. The recent acts of the Imperial German Government are acts of war against the Government and people of the United States:

Resolved. By the Senate and House of Representatives of the United States of America in Congress assembled,

[*declaration of war*]

that the state of war between the United States and the Imperial German Government which has thus been thrust upon the United States is hereby formally declared; and

[*authorization*]

That the President be, and is hereby, authorized and directed to take immediate steps not only to put the country in a thorough state of defense but also to exert all of its power and employ all of its resources to carry on war against the Imperial German Government
[no declaration of peace terms]
and bring the conflict to a successful termination (*The New York Times* 3 April 1917, 1).

After passing in the House, the State Department draft was amended in the Senate and, then, accepted by the House:

Joint Resolution Declaring that a state of war exists between the Imperial German Government and the Government and the People of the United States and making provision to prosecute the same.
[indictment and denunciation of the enemy]
Whereas the Imperial German Government has committed repeated acts of war against the Government and people of the United States of America: Therefore, be it

Resolved by the Senate and House of Representatives of the United States of America in Congress assembled,
[declaration of war]
That the state of war between the United States and the Imperial German Government which has thus been thrust upon the United States is hereby formally declared;
[authorization]
and that the President be, and he is hereby, authorized and directed to employ the entire naval and military forces of the United States and the resources of the Government to carry on war against the Imperial German Government;
[no declaration of peace terms]
and to bring the conflict to a successful termination all the resources of the country are hereby pledged by the Congress of the United States (Approved, April 6, 1917. Pub. Res. No. 65-1, 40 Stat. 1).

5a. The declaration of war against the Imperial and Royal Austro-Hungarian Government (Approved, 7 December 1917. Pub. L. No. 65-1, 40 Stat. 429) is identic with the declaration against the Imperial German Government.

6. *World War II, 1941*: Six Absolute, Unreasoned, Solemnly Perfect Declarations

Declaring that a state of war exists between the Imperial Government of Japan and the Government and the people of the United States and making provisions to prosecute the same:
[indictment and denunciation of the enemy]
Whereas the Imperial Government of Japan has committed unprovoked acts of war against the Government and the people of the United States of America; therefore, be it

Resolved by the Senate and the House of Representatives of the United States of America in Congress assembled,

[*declaration of war*]

That the state of war between the United States and the Imperial Government of Japan which has thus been thrust upon the United States is hereby formally declared;

[*authorization*]

and the President is hereby authorized and directed to employ the entire naval and military forces of the United States and the resources of the Government to carry on the war against the Imperial Government of Japan;

[*no declaration of peace terms*]

and, to bring the conflict to a successful termination, all of the resources of the country are hereby pledged by the Congress of the United States (Pub. L. No. (Pub. L. No. 77–328, 55 Stat. 795. Approved, 8 December 1941, 4:10pm, EST.).

The other five declarations are identic except for two changes: 1) the name of the country concerned and 2) where the "Whereas" clause reads "... has committed unprovoked acts of war ..." in the declaration against Japan and "... has formally declared war against ..." in the other five.

6a. A declaration against the Government of Germany (Pub. L. No. 77–331, 55 Stat. 796. Approved, 11 December 1941, 3:05pm, EST.).
6b. A declaration against the Government of Italy (Pub. L. No. 77–332, 55 Stat. 797. Approved 11 December 1941 3:06pm, EST.).
6c. A declaration against the Government of Bulgaria (Pub. L. No. 77–563, 56 Stat. 307. Approved, 5 June 1942.).
6d. A declaration against the Government of Hungary (Pub. L. No. 77–564, 56 Stat. 307. Approved, 5 June 1942.).
6e. A declaration against the Government of Rumania (Pub. L. No. 77–565, 56 Stat. 307. Approved, 5 June 1942.).

APPENDIX B

British Declaration of War against France, 7 May 1689

1689, May 7.
[Declaration of War against France.]
THEIR MAJESTIES DECLARATION
AGAINST THE FRENCH KING.

WILLIAM R.

It having pleased Almighty God to make Us the happy Instruments of Rescuing these Nations from Great and Imminent Dangers, and to place Us upon the Throne of these Kingdoms, We think Our Selves obliged to endeavour to the uttermost to Promote the Welfare of Our People, which can never be effectually secured, but by preventing the Miseries that threaten them from Abroad.

[*indictment*]

When we consider the many unjust Methods the French King hath of late Years taken to gratifie his Ambition, that he has not only Invaded the Territories of the Emperor, and of the Empire now in Amity with Us, laying Waste whole Countries, and destroying the Inhabitants by his Armies, but Declared War against Our Allies without any Provocation, in manifest Violation of the Treaties Confirmed by the Guaranty of the Crown of England; We can do no less then Join with Our Allies in opposing the Designs of the French King, as the Disturber of the Peace, and the Common Enemy of the Christian World.

And besides the Obligations We lie under by Treaties with Our Allies, which are a sufficient Justification of Us for taking up Arms at this time, since they have called upon Us so to do, the many Injuries done to Us and to Our Subjects, without any Reparation, by the French King, are such, that (however of late Years they were not taken Notice of, for Reasons well known to the World, nevertheless) We will not pass them over without a Publick and Just Resentment of such Outrages.

It is not long since the French took Licences from the English Governor of New-found-Land, to Fish in the Seas upon that Coast, and paid a Tribute for such Licences, as an Acknowledgment of the sole Right of the Crown of England to that Island; and yet of late, the Encroachments of the French upon Our said Island, and Our Subjects Trade and Fishery, have been more like the Invasions of an Enemy, then becoming Friends, who enjoy'd the Advantages of that Trade only by Permission.

But that the French King should Invade Our Charibbee Islands, and possess himself of Our Territories of the Province of New-York and of Hudson's-Bay in a Hostile manner, seizing Our Forts, burning Our Subjects Houses, and enriching his People with the Spoil of their Goods and Merchandizes, detaining some of Our Subjects under the Hardship of Imprisonment, causing others to be inhumanely kill'd, and driving the rest to Sea in a Small Vessel, without Food and Necessaries to support them, are Actions not becoming even an Enemy; and yet he was so far from declaring himself so, that at that very time he was Negotiating here in England by his Ministers, a Treaty of Neutrality and good Correspondence in America.

The Proceedings of the French King against Our Subjects in Europe are so Notorious, that We shall not need to enlarge upon them; His countenancing the Seizure of English Ships by French Privateers, forbidding the Importation of great part of the Product and Manufactures of Our Kingdom, and imposing exorbitant Customs upon the rest, notwithstanding the vast Advantage he and the French Nation reap by their Commerce with England, are sufficient Evidences of his Designs to destroy the Trade, and consequently to ruin the Navigation, upon which the Wealth and Safety of this Nation very much depends.

The Right of the Flag, Inherent in the Crown of England, has been Disputed by his Orders in Violation of Our Sovereignty of the Narrow Seas, which in all Ages has been Asserted by Our Predecessors, and We are resolv'd to Maintain for the Honour of Our Crown, and of the English Nation.

But that which must nearly touch Us, is his unchristian Prosecution of many of Our English Protestant Subjects in France, for matters of Religion, contrary to the Law of Nations, and express Treaties, forcing them to abjure their Religion by strange and unusual Cruelties, and Imprisoning some of the Masters and Seamen of Our Merchant Ships, and Condemning others to the Gallies, upon pretence of having on Board, either some of his own miserable Protestant Subjects, or their Effects; And Lastly, as he has for some years last past, endeavoured by insinuations and Promises of Assistance to overthrow the Government of England; So now by open and violent Methods, and the actual invasion of Our Kingdom of Ireland, in support of Our Subjects in Arms, and in Rebellion against Us, he is promoting the utter Extirpation of Our good and Loyal Subjects in that Our Kingdom.

[denunciation of war]

Being therefore thus necessitated to take up Arms, and Relying on the help of Almighty God in Our just undertaking,

[declaration of war]

We have thought fit to Declare, and do hereby Declare War against the French King, and that We will in Conjunction with Our Allies, Vigorously Prosecute the same by Sea and Land (since he hath so unrighteously begun it) being assured of the hearty Concurrence and Assistance of Our Subjects in support of so good a Cause;

[transmission of authorities]

Hereby Willing and Requiring Our General of Our Forces, Our Commissioners for Executing the Office of High Admiral, Our Lieutenants of Our several Counties, Governours of Our Forts and Garisons, and all other Officers and Soldiers under them, by Sea and Land, to do, and execute all acts of Hostility in the Prosecution of this War against the French King, his Vassals and Subjects, and to oppose their Attempts, Willing and Requiring all Our Subjects to take Notice of the same, whom We henceforth strictly forbid to hold any Correspondence or Communication with the said French King, or his Subjects; And because there are remaining in Our Kingdoms many of the Subjects of the French King; We do Declare and give Our Royal Word, that all such of the French Nation as shall demean themselves dutifully towards Us, and not Correspond with Our Enemies, shall be safe in their Persons and Estates, and free from all molestation and trouble of any Kind.

Given at Our Court at Hampton-Court, the Seventh Day of May, 1689. In the First Year of Our Reign.

GOD SAVE KING WILLIAM AND QUEEN MARY.

(Brigham 1968 (1911), 147–50)

APPENDIX C

Two Modern, Procedurally Imperfect Declarations of War

President George W. Bush's Addresses the Nation, 19 March 2003
and
The Prime Minister Tony Blair's Address To The Nation on the Iraq invasion, televised 20th March 2003

President Bush Addresses the Nation
The Oval Office 10:16 P.M. EST

THE PRESIDENT: My fellow citizens, at this hour, American and coalition forces are in the early stages of military operations to disarm Iraq, to free its people and to defend the world from grave danger.

On my orders, coalition forces have begun striking selected targets of military importance to undermine Saddam Hussein's ability to wage war. These are opening stages of what will be a broad and concerted campaign. More than 35 countries are giving crucial support—from the use of naval and air bases, to help with intelligence and logistics, to the deployment of combat units. Every nation in this coalition has chosen to bear the duty and share the honor of serving in our common defense.

To all the men and women of the United States Armed Forces now in the Middle East, the peace of a troubled world and the hopes of an oppressed people now depend on you. That trust is well placed.

The enemies you confront will come to know your skill and bravery. The people you liberate will witness the honorable and decent spirit of the American military. In this conflict, America faces an enemy who has no regard for conventions of war or rules of morality. Saddam Hussein has placed Iraqi troops and equipment in civilian areas, attempting to use innocent men, women and children as shields for his own military—a final atrocity against his people.

I want Americans and all the world to know that coalition forces will make every effort to spare innocent civilians from harm. A campaign on the harsh terrain of a nation as large as California could be longer and more difficult than some predict. And helping Iraqis achieve a united, stable and free country will require our sustained commitment.

We come to Iraq with respect for its citizens, for their great civilization and for the religious faiths they practice. We have no ambition in Iraq, except to remove a threat and restore control of that country to its own people.

I know that the families of our military are praying that all those who serve will return safely and soon. Millions of Americans are praying with you for the safety of your loved ones and for the protection of the innocent. For your sacrifice, you have the gratitude and respect of the American people. And you can know that our forces will be coming home as soon as their work is done.

Our nation enters this conflict reluctantly—yet, our purpose is sure. The people of the United States and our friends and allies will not live at the mercy of an outlaw regime that threatens the peace with weapons of mass murder. We will meet that threat now, with our Army, Air Force, Navy, Coast Guard and Marines, so that we do not have to meet it later with armies of fire fighters and police and doctors on the streets of our cities.

Now that conflict has come, the only way to limit its duration is to apply decisive force. And I assure you, this will not be a campaign of half measures, and we will accept no outcome but victory.

My fellow citizens, the dangers to our country and the world will be overcome. We will pass through this time of peril and carry on the work of peace. We will defend our freedom. We will bring freedom to others and we will prevail.

May God bless our country and all who defend her.

END 10:20 P.M. EST

STATEMENT *televised 20th March 2003*

The Prime Minister's [Tony Blair's] Address to The Nation on the Iraq invasion

On Tuesday night I gave the order for British forces to take part in military action in Iraq. Tonight, British servicemen and women are engaged from air, land and sea. Their mission: to remove Saddam Hussein from power, and disarm Iraq of its weapons of mass destruction. I know this course of action has produced deep divisions of opinion in our country. But I know also the British people will now be united in sending our armed forces our thoughts and prayers. They are the finest in the world and their families and all of Britain can have great pride in them. The threat to Britain today is not that of my father's generation. War between the big powers is unlikely. Europe is at peace. The Cold War already a memory. But this new world faces a new threat: of disorder and chaos born either of brutal states like Iraq, armed with weapons of mass destruction; or of extreme terrorist groups. Both hate our way of life, our freedom, our democracy.

My fear, deeply held, based in part on the intelligence that I see, is that these threats come together and deliver catastrophe to our country and world. These tyrannical states do not care for the sanctity of human life. The terrorists delight in destroying it.

Some say if we act, we become a target. The truth is, all nations are targets. Bali was never in the front line of action against terrorism. America didn't attack Al Qaeda. They attacked America.

Britain has never been a nation to hide at the back. But even if we were, it wouldn't avail us.

Should terrorists obtain these weapons now being manufactured and traded round the world, the carnage they could inflict to our economies, our security, to world peace, would be beyond our most vivid imagination.

My judgement, as Prime Minister, is that this threat is real, growing and of an entirely different nature to any conventional threat to our security that Britain has faced before.

For 12 years, the world tried to disarm Saddam; after his wars in which hundreds of thousands died. UN weapons inspectors say vast amounts of chemical and biological poisons, such as anthrax, VX nerve agent, and mustard gas remain unaccounted for in Iraq.

So our choice is clear: back down and leave Saddam hugely strengthened; or proceed to disarm him by force. Retreat might give us a moment of respite but years of repentance at our weakness would I believe follow.

It is true Saddam is not the only threat. But it is true also- as we British know- that the best way to deal with future threats peacefully, is to deal with present threats with resolve.

Removing Saddam will be a blessing to the Iraqi people. Four million Iraqis are in exile. 60% of the population dependent on food aid. Thousands of children die every year through malnutrition and disease. Hundreds of thousands have been driven from their homes or murdered.

I hope the Iraqi people hear this message. We are with you. Our enemy is not you, but your barbarous rulers.

APPENDIX D

A Model Constitutional Amendment

Sect. 1. The fœderative power of the United States shall be vested in a Council on War and Peace.

Sect. 2. The fœderative power shall extend to the ratification of treaties, on behalf of the nation, by majority vote; to the undivided and unshared power to decide the question of public war, both domestic and foreign, on behalf of the nation, by majority vote, and to declare and publish same; and to the undivided and unshared power to decide the question of private war, both secret and open, on behalf of the nation, by majority vote, by means of a grant of a letter of marque or reprisal, and to publish same, either immediately or with delay to preserve secrecy.

Sect. 3. The aforesaid power to ratify treaties shall be exercised in accordance with the Circular 175[1] process to distinguish executive agreements from treaties. Only acknowledged treaties shall go forward to the Council on War and Peace for ratification. In case of disagreement over whether an international instrument is a treaty or an executive agreement, the opinion of the Council on War and Peace shall be binding on the executive branch.

Sect. 4. The aforesaid power to decide and declare public war, both domestic and foreign, on behalf of the nation, shall include the imposition of diplomatic, economic, or military sanctions.

The aforesaid power to decide and declare public war, both domestic and foreign, on behalf of the nation, shall be exercised in accordance with Hague Convention III of 1907, both conditionally and absolutely, with a text modeled on the Declaration of Independence. The text shall not take the style of a resolution.

When made conditionally, the public declaration shall indict the gravamina as well as declare the nation's preferred peace terms. The decision to affix a time limit to a conditional declaration of war is an executive decision of the president.

When made absolutely, the public declaration shall indict the gravamina, declare the nation's preferred peace terms as well as denounce the termination of the state and condition of peace and declare the unfortunate, but necessary, existence of the state and condition of war.

An unreasoned, absolute, public declaration is appropriate when negotiations over the preferred peace terms previously declared conditionally have failed in the estimation of a majority of the members of the Council on War and Peace.

---

1 The Circular 175 process is a State Department process for clearing Executive Agreements with the Senate Foreign Relations Committee staff (Krutz and Peake 2009).

An unreasoned, absolute, public declaration is appropriate when the nation is in such imminent danger as will not admit of delay, or when novel circumstances arise suddenly such that no time exists for the Council on War and Peace to deliberate more extensively.

In cases where either imminent danger or novel circumstances require an unreasoned, absolute, public declaration, the responsibility of the Council on War and Peace to make a fully reasoned, public declaration of war is not lessened. A fully reasoned, absolute, public declaration is still required as soon as time and circumstances permit to ensure that the President as Commander-in-Chief has not exceeded his command authority to employ diplomatic, economic, or military sanctions when not called for.

Sect. 5. The aforesaid power to decide upon and grant authority to the President for private war by means of a letter of marque or reprisal shall be exercised through carefully circumscribed grants in terms of geographic extent, time, and the means employed.

Sect. 6. The purpose of public declarations for public war or of grants of a letter of marque or reprisal for private war is to express that it is the best and most prudent judgment of the Council on War and Peace, with the president's approval, that the gravamina indicted combined with the declaration of peace, when declared conditionally, and the denunciation and declaration of war, when declared absolutely, constitute true *casus belli*.

Sect. 7. The intention of this amendment is, on the one hand, to make procedurally imperfect declarations or authorizations of public war by either the Congress or president illegitimate, illegal, and unconstitutional; and, on the other hand, to make procedurally imperfect presidential or congressional finding or commissions for private war illegitimate, illegal, and unconstitutional.

Sect. 8. The Council on War and Peace may seek injunctive relief in the Appellate Court against either the Congress or the President for infringing, by means of unconstitutional declarations or authorizations of public war or grants for private war, the Council's right and power to decide and declare public war or to grant a letter of marque or reprisal for private war.

Sect. 9. The Council on War and Peace may submit a petition for impeachment of the President to the House of Representatives for the waging of a procedurally imperfect public or private war without a procedurally perfect public declaration for public war or a grant for private war from the Council on War and Peace.

Sect. 10. The Council on War and Peace of the United States shall be no greater than fifty Councilors, chosen by the legislatures of the several States, for eight years; and each Councilor shall have one vote. Should the number of States exceed fifty, the votes of the legislatures of two or more States shall be combined to elect one Councilor, preserving the fifty-member limit on the number of Councilors.

No person shall be a Councilor who shall not have attained to the age of forty years, and been nine years a citizen of the United States, and who shall, when elected, be an inhabitant of that State or States from which he shall be chosen.

The Council on War and Peace should represent a mix of diplomatic, political, and military experience and expertise.

No Councilor may receive confidential or secret information that is material to a decision for public war. The work of the Council on War and Peace with regard to declarations of public war shall be confined to publically available documents and testimony.

Exceptionally, Councilors may receive confidential or secret information material to the granting of a secret letter of marque or reprisal, when absolutely unavoidable.

Sect. 11. Immediately after they shall be assembled in consequence of the first election, they shall be divided as equally as may be into four classes. The seats of the Councilors of the first class shall be vacated at the expiration of the second year, of the second class at the expiration of the fourth year, of the third class at the expiration of the sixth year, and of the fourth class at the expiration of the eighth year, so that one-fourth may be chosen every second year; and if vacancies happen by resignation, or otherwise, during the recess of the Legislature or Legislatures of the State or States that elected the Councilor, the Executive or Executives of the States may make temporary appointments until the next meeting of the Legislature or Legislatures, which shall then fill such vacancies. Councilors shall be eligible for reelection to multiple terms.

Sect. 12. The times, places and manner of holding elections for Councilors, shall be prescribed by the Legislature or Legislatures thereof; but the United States Congress may at any time by law make or alter such regulations, except as to the places of choosing Councilors.

The Council on War and Peace shall assemble at least once in every year, as prescribed by law.

Sect. 13. The Council on War and Peace shall be the judge of the elections, returns, and qualifications of its own members, and a majority shall constitute a quorum to do business; but a smaller number may adjourn from day to day, and may be authorized to compel the attendance of absent members, in such manner, and under such penalties as law may provide.

The Council on War and Peace shall choose its own officers.

The Council on War and Peace may determine the rules of its proceedings, punish its members for disorderly behavior, and, with the concurrence of two-thirds, expel a member.

The Council on War and Peace shall keep a journal of its proceedings, and from time to time publish the same; and the yeas and nays of the members on any question shall be entered on the journal.

Sect. 14. The councilors shall receive a compensation for their services, to be ascertained by law, and paid out of the treasury of the United States. They shall in all cases, except treason, felony and breach of the peace, be privileged from arrest during their attendance at the session, and in going to and returning from the same; and for any speech or debate in the Council on War and Peace, they shall not be questioned in any other place.

No Councilor shall, during the time for which he was elected, be appointed to any civil or military office under the authority of the United States, which shall have been created, or the emoluments whereof shall have been increased during such time; and no person holding any office under the United States, shall be a member during his continuance in office.

Sect. 15. Every declaration of war or letter of marque or reprisal which shall have passed the Council on War and Peace, shall, before it become a law, be presented to the President of the United States; if he approve he shall sign it, but if not he shall return it, with his objections to that Council on War and Peace, who shall enter the objections at large on their journal, and proceed to reconsider it.

The Council on War and Peace may not override a presidential negative. It may, after mature consideration, present a revised declaration of war or letter of marque or reprisal to the President for his approval.

If any declaration of war or letter of marque or reprisal shall not be returned by the President within ten days (Sundays excepted) after it shall have been presented to him, the same shall be a law, in like manner as if he had signed it, unless the Council on War and Peace by their adjournment prevent its return, in which case it shall not be a law. (Reprinted with permission of Cambridge University Press, Hallett 2012, 175–179. Slightly modified.)

APPENDIX E

A Joint Resolution to Establish a Joint Congressional Drafting Committee of 20xx

WHEREAS, Article I, Section 8, Clause 11 of the Constitution empowers the Congress alone to effect, establish, and create the state and condition of public war by declaring war solemnly and of private war by granting letters of marque or reprisal; and

WHEREAS, Article I, Section 8, Clause 11 of the Constitution does not condition this sole power with any qualification whatsoever, such as exercising this congressional power as "the collective judgment of both the Congress and the President," as is suggested in the preamble of the War Powers Resolution of 1973; and,

WHEREAS, despite the silence of Article I, Section 8, Clause 11 of the Constitution, the procedurally imperfect declaring of public war by either the Congress or the president undermines the republican and democratic character of the nation and its Constitution, just as executive findings or authorizations of private war undermines the congressional power to grant letters of marque or reprisal. Consequently, procedurally imperfect acts by either the Congress or the president must be considered illegitimate and unconstitutional; and,

WHEREAS, in accordance with Hague Convention III, *Relative to the Opening of Hostilities,* one of the larger purposes of the congressional power to declare war and grant letters of marque or reprisal is to take the first necessary steps toward resolving a conflict. This is achieved in the case of public war by declaring war conditionally before declaring war absolutely with fully reasoned declarations. This is achieved in the case of private war by carefully circumscribing the commissions granted in letters of marque or reprisal; and,

WHEREAS, the proper relationship between the congressional powers found in Article I, Section 8, Clause 11 of the Constitution and the presidential powers as commander-in-chief found in Article II, Section 2, Clause 1 of the Constitution is that of a coherent, organic ends-means/ideal-in-process relationship, wherein the congressional declaration of public war or its grant of letters of marque or reprisal for private war articulates the nation's political desires or purposes, while the operational control of the diplomatic, economic, or military means rests with the president as commander-in-chief.

NOW THEREFORE BE IT RESOLVED:

Section 1. Short Title.

The War Powers Resolution of 1973, Pub. L. No. 93-148, is hereby repealed. This Resolution shall be cited as the Joint Congressional Drafting Resolution of 20XX.

Section 2. Purpose and Intention.

2(A). The purpose of this resolution is to establish a joint committee of the Congress dedicated solely to the preparation and drafting of fully reasoned, conditional and absolute declarations of public war and carefully circumscribed letters of marque or reprisal for private war.

2(B) The intention of this resolution is to make procedurally imperfect declarations of public war by either the Congress or president illegitimate, illegal, and unconstitutional, as well as making procedurally imperfect executive findings or authorizations for private war illegitimate, illegal, and unconstitutional.

Section 3. Definitions.

3(A). The "Joint Congressional Drafting Committee" consists of:
- (i) The Speaker of the U.S. House of Representatives and the Majority Leader of the Senate;
- (ii) The Minority Leaders of the House of Representatives and the Senate.

3(B). The Chairmanship and Vice Chairmanship of the Joint Congressional Drafting Committee shall alternate between the Speaker of the House of Representatives and the Majority Leader of the Senate, with the former serving as the Chairman in each odd-numbered Congress and the latter serving as the Chairman in each even-numbered Congress.

Section 4. Staffing.

4(A). The Joint Congressional Drafting Committee shall have two staffs:
- (i) The support staff consists of administrative, clerical, and research assistants as need.
- (ii) The Special staff consists of no greater than fifty members.
- (iii) Qualifications for service on the Special staff are:
    - (a) to have attained to the age of forty years, and
    - (b) to have been nine years a citizen of the United States.
- (iv) The Special staff is chosen by the members of the Senate and House of Representatives by secret ballot from a slate recommended by the Joint Congressional Drafting Committee,
    - (a) for eight years, and
    - (b) representing a mix of diplomatic, political, and military experience and expertise.
- (v) Immediately after they are assembled in consequence of the first election, the Special staff shall be divided as equally as may be into four classes.
    - (a) The seats of the first class shall be vacated at the expiration of the second year,
    - (b) of the second class at the expiration of the fourth year,

(c) of the third class at the expiration of the sixth year, and
(d) of the fourth class at the expiration of the eighth year,
(e) so that one-fourth may be chosen every second year; and
(f) if vacancies happen by resignation, or otherwise, a special election by the members of the Senate and House of Representatives voting by secret ballot shall be held, which shall then fill such vacancies for the remainder of the Special staff member's term.
(vi) The Special staff assembles at least once in every year at the same time as the Congress.
(vii) A majority of the Special staff constitutes a quorum to do business;
(a) but a smaller number may adjourn from day to day, and
(b) may compel the attendance of absent members, in such manner, and under such penalties as law may provide.
(viii) The Special staff chooses its own officers.
(ix) The Special staff determines the rules of its proceedings,
(a) punishes its members for disorderly behavior, and,
(b) with the concurrence of two-thirds, expels a member.
(x) Each Special staff shall have one vote.
(xi) The Special staff keeps a journal of its proceedings, and from time to time publishes the same; and the yeas and nays of the members on any question shall be entered on the journal.
(xii) The special staff shall in all cases, except treason, felony and breach of the peace, be privileged from arrest during their attendance at the session, and in going to and returning from the same; and for any speech or debate in the Council on War and Peace, they shall not be questioned in any other place.
(xiii) The Special staff receives no confidential or secret information material to the declaring of public war.
(a) The work of the Special staff relative to the declaring of public war is confined to publically available documents and testimony.
(xiv) Exceptionally, the Special staff may receives confidential or secret information material to the granting of letters of marque or reprisal for secret private wars.
(a) Normally, the work of the Special staff relative to the granting of letters of marque or reprisal shall be confined to publically available documents and testimony.

4(B). The Special staff receives compensation equal to the greater as between the Senate or the House of Representatives.
(i) No Special staff, during the time for which he is elected, is appointed to any civil or military office under the authority of the United States,

(a) which shall have been created, or the emoluments whereof shall have been increased during such time; and
(b) no person holding any office under the United States, shall be a member during his continuance in office.

Section 5. Duties of the Special Staff.

5(A). The duties of the Special staff are
- (i) to draft, debate, amend, and vote fully reasoned declarations of public war for both
  - (a) domestic and
  - (b) foreign wars, and
- (ii) to draft, debate, amend, and vote carefully circumscribed letters of marque or reprisal for private war.
- (iii) For declarations of public war, the draft will be a bill, modeled on the Declaration of Independence. The text shall not take the style of a resolution.

(5B). The duties found in 5(A) are exercised in accordance with Hague Convention III of 1907 both
- (i) conditionally by
  - (a) indicting the gravamina as well as
  - (b) declaring the nation's preferred peace terms or
- (ii) absolutely by
  - (a) indicting the gravamina
  - (b) declaring the nation's preferred peace terms
  - (c) denouncing the termination of the state and condition of peace and
  - (d) declaring and declaring the existence of the state and condition of war as well.
- (iii) An unreasoned absolute, public declaration of war is appropriate,
  - (a) when negotiations over the preferred peace terms declared conditionally have failed in the estimation of the Special staff, or
  - (b) when the nation is in such imminent danger as will not admit of delay, or
  - (c) when novel circumstances arise suddenly.
- (iv) In cases where either imminent danger or novel circumstances require an unreasoned, absolute, public declaration, the responsibility of the Joint Drafting Committee to make a fully reasoned, public declaration of war is not lessened. A fully reasoned, absolute, public declaration is still required as soon as time and circumstances permit to ensure that the President as Commander-in-Chief has not exceeded his command authority to employ diplomatic, economic, or military sanctions when not called for.

(v) The decision to affix a time limit to a conditional declaration of war is an executive decision of the president.

5(C). The draft declarations of public war or the draft grants of letters of marque or reprisal for private war passed by the Special staff represent the best and most prudent judgment of the Special staff that
    (i) the gravamina indicted
    (ii) combined with the declaration of peace constitute true *casus belli*.

5(D). The Special staff may recommend that the Joint Congressional Drafting Committee seek injunctive relief in the Appellate Court against the president
    (i) whenever a presidential declaration infringes upon the congressional right to declare public war, or
    (ii) whenever a presidential act or finding infringes upon the congressional right to grant letters of marque or reprisal for private war.

5(E). The Special staff may submit a petition for the impeachment of the chair to the Joint Congressional Drafting Committee for the waging of either public or private war unconstitutionally.

Section 6. Congressional Approval or Disapproval.

6(A). Once the Special staff have drafted, debated, amended, and voted either a fully reasoned declaration of public war, or a letter of marque or reprisal for private war,
    (i) the Chairman and Vice Chairman of the Joint Congressional Drafting Committee shall introduce identical versions of the Special staff's draft in the Senate and House of Representatives as a bill, calling for approval without amendment.
    (ii) Voting shall be by secret ballot. The clerks of each chamber shall collect and tally the ballot slips from the members before announcing the totals for and against. The ballots will remain secret in the care of the clerks for five years at which time the clerks will publish the names of the persons voting for and against the draft declaration or letter of marque or reprisal and shall entered the names and votes on the journal of each chamber respectively.

6(B). Once introduced, the Special Staff's bill may be called up by any Senator or Representative, shall be highly privileged, shall become the pending business of both chambers, shall be voted on within 5 calendar days thereafter, and shall not be susceptible to intervening motions, except that each chamber may adjourn from day to day.
    (i) If the bill is approved, it is presented to the president for his approval or disapproval.
    (ii) If the bill is disapproved by the president, the bill dies; no attempt shall be made to override a presidential disapproval. The bill is returned to the Special staff of the Joint Drafting Committee, with his objections, for review and revision.

6(C). The Special staff's bill is debated in both chamber without amendment out of respect for the acknowledged stature and expertise of the Special staff.
- (i) A vote of approval by either chamber represents the members' best and most prudent judgment that
    - (a) the gravamina indicted
    - (b) combined with the declaration of peace constitute true *casus belli*.
- (ii) A vote of disapproval by either Chamber represents the members' best and most prudent judgment that
    - (a) the gravamina indicted
    - (b) combined with the declaration of peace do not constitute true *casus belli*.

Section 7. Severability.

If any provision of this Resolution is held invalid, the remainder of the Act shall not be affected thereby. (Reprinted with permission of Cambridge University Press, Hallett 2012, 198-202. Slightly modified.)

APPENDIX F

Re-evaluating the Traditional Just-War Criteria

The Internal organization of the Just-Interaction criteria
I. *jus ad interactionem*
    A. The Necessary Conditions
        1. Procedural Criteria: Who? and How?
            i. Competent authority
            ii. An open and determined declaration
        2. Justificatory Criteria: What and Why?
            i. Justified cause
            ii. Right Intention
    B. The Sufficient Conditions
        1. Prudential Criteria: Whether?
            i. Comparative justification
            ii. Proportionality of ends
            iii. Probability of success
            iiii. Last resort
II. *jus in interactione*
    A. Proportionality
    B. Discrimination
    C. Right intention
(Hallett. Forthcoming)

The relationship between performative speech acts and the traditional just-war criteria is not at all clear. The relationship is intimate and complex, but not at all clear. The traditional just-war criteria have always been looked on as, at best, a specialized checklist useful when talking about war, but of no greater use or utility. This absence of any greater utility is reinforced by the fact that the four, unreasoned, absolute congressional declarations reproduced in Appendix A are accepted as praiseworthy paradigms. But what if the congressional declarations are not praiseworthy paradigms? What if, instead, the *Declaration of Independence* is the only praiseworthy paradigm?

The reason one might suggest that the congressional declarations are not praiseworthy paradigms is the fact that they are not Hague Convention III compliant, whereas the *Declaration of Independence* is. None of the congressional declarations is "a reasoned declaration of war," unlike the *Declaration of Independence*, which is "reasoned." But to say that a praiseworthy paradigmatic declaration must be "reasoned" does not tell one much. How can one tell a "reasoned" from an "unreasoned" declaration of war? What is meant by "reasoned?"

What is meant, a close reading of the *Declaration of Independence* soon reveals, is that the text of the declaration addresses most, if not all, of the traditional *ad bellum* criteria. As is outlined just above, the text must meet the necessary procedural criteria: A reasoned or determined declaration must be declared by a competent authority with an open and determined declaration. The text must also articulate the required justificatory criteria: It must not only indict the gravamina that justify the resort to war, but also demonstrate a right intention by articulating feasible peace terms/war aims. In addition, the text must meet the sufficient prudential conditions: It must demonstrate that its peace terms/war aims are comparatively more justified than those of its conflict partner's. It must show that primary and secondary consequences of armed hostilities are not disproportional to the primary and secondary consequences of not resorting to arms. It must establish that military means are not incoherent with the ends sought. And, it must vindicate that negotiations have failed.

In sum, "reasoned" declarative speech acts are Hague compliant because they meet the traditional *ad bellum* criteria. This means that meeting the traditional *ad bellum* criteria is, in part, how one does war with words, to paraphrase John Austin. Yet, declarations of war are only one species of the genus performative speech acts. Might it not be the case that the other species must also meet the traditional *ad bellum* criteria, in part?

For example, might the pronouncement of marriage also need to meet the necessary procedural criteria, namely, that the pronouncement must be made by a competent authority with an open and solemn pronouncement. Might the pronouncement also need to articulate justificatory criteria with solemn vows justifying both the decision to marry and a right intention to marry. In addition, might the pronouncement need to meet the sufficient prudential conditions: Namely, that marriage is comparatively more justified than not marrying for the couple; that the primary and secondary consequences of marriage are not disproportional; that the ends sought by the couple's vows pre-exist in a pronouncement of marriage as the means to attain the ends sought in the vows; and that marriage is a last resort.

But, if, not just war, but all other performative speech acts must meet the traditional *ad bellum* criteria, then the traditional just-war criteria possess a greater use or utility. This greater utility covers all human interactions that are done with words. On this assumption, then the narrowly focused traditional just-war criteria are better conceived of as just-interaction criteria.

Bibliography

Académie Française. 1932–1935. *Dictionnaire de L Académie Française, 8e édition.* Paris: Hachette.

Adams, John. 1850–56. *The Works of John Adams, Second President of the United States: with A Life of the Author, by his grandson Charles Francis Adams,* x Vols. Boston: Charles C. Little and James Brown.

Arendt, Hannah. 1963. *On Revolution.* New York: Viking Press.

Auerswald, David P. and Colton C. Campbell, eds. 2012. *Congress and the Politics of National Security.* New York: Cambridge University Press.

Austin, J. L. (John Langshaw). 1979. *Philosophical Papers,* 3rd ed. Eds. J. O. Urmson and G. J. Warnock. Oxford: Oxford University Press.

Austin, J. L. (John Langshaw). 1975 (1962). *How To Do Things With Words.* Ed. J.O. Urmsom and Marina Sbisa. Cambridge, MA: Harvard University Press.

Beaumanoir, Philippe de. 1899–1900 [1286]. *Coutumes De Beauvaisis. Texte critique publié avec une introduction, un glossaire et une table analytique par Am. Salmon.* Paris: A. Picard et fils. [Amédée Salmon, ed.] Address for Tome 2 http://gallica.bnf.fr/ark:/12148/bpt6k220827p.image.r=philippe+de+Beaumanoir.langFR.f3.pagination Accessed 15 July 2009.

Beaumanoir, Philippe de Remi, sire de. 1992. *The Coutumes de Beauvaisis of Philippe de Beaumoir.* Trans. F. R. P. Akehurst. Philadelphia, PA: University or Pennsylvania Press.

Blackstone, William. 1769. *Commentaries on the laws of England.* Oxford at the Clarendon Press.

Blair, Tony. 2003. The Prime Minister's Address To The Nation on the Iraq invasion televised 20th March 2003. http://www.pm.gov.uk/output/Page3327.asp Accessed 16 Dec 2007.

Blanco, Kathleen Babineaux. 2005. Letter to President George W. Bush of 28 August 2005 Requesting an Expedited Major Disaster Declaration. http://www.yuricareport.com/Disaster/GovBlancoAsksReliefFromPresLtr.pdf Accessed 10 February 2014.

Bodin, Jean. 1992. *Jean Bodin: On Sovereignty: Four Chapters from "The Six Books of the Commonwealth."* Ed. and trans. Julian H. Franklin. New York: Cambridge University Press.

Bradbury, Jim. 1998. *Philip Augustus: King of France 1180–1223,* London: Longmans.

Brant, Irving. 1941–1961. *James Madison.* 6 vols. Indianapolis, IN: Bobbs-Merrill, Co.

Brigham, Clarence S., ed. 1968 (1911). *British Royal Proclamations Relating to North America, 1603–1783.* New York: Burt Franklin.

Bronner, Ethan and David E. Sanger. 2011. Arab League Endorses No-Flight Zone Over Libya. *New York Times,* 12 March, pA1.

Bush, George H. 1990. *Public Papers Of The Presidents Of The United States: George Bush 1989*, (In Two Books) Book II—July 1 To December 31, 1989. Washington, DC: United States Government Printing Office.

Bush, George H. W. 1992. *Public Papers Of The Presidents Of The United States: George Bush 1991*, (In Two Books) Book I—January 1 To June 30, 1991. Washington, DC: United States Government Printing Office.

Bush, George W. 2001. "Address to the Nation Announcing Strikes Against Al Qaida Training Camps and Taliban Military Installations in Afghanistan," October 7, 2001. Online by Gerhard Peters and John T. Woolley, *The American Presidency Project*. http ://www.presidency.ucsb.edu/ws/?pid=65088. Accessed 18 February 2014.

Bush, George W. 2003. *President Bush Addresses the Nation The Oval Office* (The Commencement of Operation Iraqi Freedom), 19 March. http://www.whitehouse.gov/news/releases/2003/03/20030319-17.htm Accessed 25 May 2008.

Bush, George W. 2006. *President Nominates Rob Portman as OMB Director and Susan Schwab for USTR, 18 April*. http://www.whitehouse.gov/news/releases/2006/04/20060418-1.html Accessed 7 July 2006.

Butler, Judith. 1999. Performative Acts and Gender Constitution: An Essay in Phenomenology and Feminist Theory. In Sue-Ellen Case, ed. *Performing Feminisms: Feminist Critical Theory and Theatre*. Baltimore, MD: The Johns Hopkins University Press.

Cameron, Maxwell A. 2013. *Strong Constitutions: Social-Cognitive Origins of the Separation of Powers*. New York: Oxford University Press.

Cicero, Marcus Tullius. 1928. *De Officiis*. Trans. Walter Miller. New York: G. P. Putnam's Sons.

Cicero, Marcus Tullius. 1928. *De Re Publica, De Legibus*. Trans. Clinton Walker Keyes. Cambridge, MA: Harvard University Press. London: William Heinemann.

Cicero. 1969. *Cicero in Twenty-Eight Volumes, XV, "Philippics."* Trans. Walter A. Ker. The Loeb Classical Library. Cambridge, MA: Harvard University Press.

Clausewitz, Carl von. 1976. *On War*. Michael Howard and Peter Paret, eds. and trans. Princeton, NJ: Princeton University Press.

Calvin, John. 1845 (1553). *Institutes of the Christian Religion*. Trans. Henry Beveridge. Edinburgh: Calvin Translation Society. https://www.ccel.org/ccel/calvin/institutes.vi.xxi.html Accessed 1 May 2020.

Clay, Henry. 1959–1984. *The Papers of Henry Clay*. James H Hopkins, ed.; Mary W.M. Hargreares, assoc. ed. Lexington, KY: University of Kentucky Press.

Congressional Record. 1873-. Washington, DC.: USGPO.

Congressional Research Service. 2005. Memorandum to The Honorable John Conyers, Jr. of September 12, 2005, Hurricane Katrina-Stafford Act Authorities and the Actions by Governor Blanco and President Bush to Trigger Them, CRS-53576. http://fpc.state.gov/documents/organization/53576.pdf Accessed 9 February 2014.

Conseil Constitutionnle N.D. http://www.conseil-constitutionnel.fr/conseil-constitutionnel/root/bank_mm/anglais/constitution_anglais.pdf Accessed 26 May 2013.

Cooper, Joseph. 1965. Jeffersonian Attitudes toward Executive Leadership and Committee Development in the House of Representatives, 1789–1829. *The Western Political Quarterly* XVII (1), 45–63.

Denza, Eileen. 2006. *Memorandum for the Select Committee on Constitution, House of Lords, 29 March.* http://www.publications.parliament.uk/pa/ld200506/ldselect/ldconst/236/6032912.htm Accessed 5 February 2012.

Department of Justice. 2011. *Opinions of the Office of Legal Counsel in Volume 35 8 Authority to Use Military Force in Libya.* http://www.justice.gov/olc/2011/authority-military-use-in-libya.pdf Accessed 10 April 2011.

Eagleton, Clyde. 1938. The Form and Function of the Declaration of War. *The American Journal of International Law* 32 (1) January, 19–35.

Fazal, Tanisha M. 2018. *Wars of Law: Unintended Consequences in Regulation of Armed Conflict.* Ithaca, NY: Cornell University Press.

Fisher, Louis and David Gray Adler. 1998. The War Powers Resolution: Time to Say Goodbye. *Political Science Quarterly* 113 (1), 1–20.

Fisher, Louis. 1995. *Presidential War Power.* Lawrence, KS: University Press of Kansas.

Fisher, Louis. 2012. Military Operations in Libya: No War? No Hostilities? *Presidential Studies Quarterly* 45 (1), 176–88.

Fisher, Roger and William L. Ury. 1991. *Getting to Yes.* New York: Penguin Books.

Glennon, Michael J. 1995. Too Far Apart: Repeal the War Powers Resolution. *University of Miami Law Review* 50 (1) October, 17–31.

Glennon, Michael J. 2011. The Cost of 'Empty Words': A Comment on the Justice Department's Libya Opinion. *Harvard National Security Journal Forum.* http://ssrn.com/abstract=1810922 Accessed 19 May 2012.

Grimmett, Richard F. 2007. *Congressional Use of Funding Cutoffs since 1970 Involving U.S. Military Forces and Overseas Deployments.* Library of Congress, Congressional Research Service RS20775, 16 January.

Grimmett, Richard F. 2012. *War Powers Resolution: Presidential Compliance.* Washington, DC: Congressional Research Service, February 1, 2012, RL33532.

Grynaviski, Eric. 2013. The bloodstained spear: public reason and declarations of war. *International Theory* 5 (2), 238–72.

Hallett, Brien. 1998. *The Lost Art of Declaring War.* Urbana, IL: University of Illinois Press.

Hallett, Brien. 2012. *Declaring War: Congress, the President, and What the Constitution Does Not Say.* New York: Cambridge University Press.

Hallett, Brien. Forthcoming. Just-War Criteria. In *Encyclopedia of Violence, Peace, and Conflict, 3rd ed.* Kurtz, Lester R., ed. San Diego, CA: Academic Press.

Hamilton, Alexander. 1961–87. *The Papers of Alexander Hamilton*. 27 vols. Ed. Harold C. Syrett. New York: Columbia University Press.

Hamilton, Alexander and James Madison. 1976 [1845]. *The Letters of Pacificus and Helvidius (1845) with The Letters of Americanus*. A Facsimile Reproduction with an Introduction by Richard Loss. Delmar, NY: Scholars' Facsimilies and Reprints.

Harbom, Lotta and Peter Wallensteen. 2010. Armed Conflicts, 1946—2009. *Journal of Peace Research*, July 2010 47, 501–509.

Hendrickson, Ryan C. 2013. Libya and American war powers: war-making decisions in the United States, *Global Change, Peace & Security*, 2–15.

Hill, George. 1940–48. *A History of Cyprus*. Cambridge at the University Press.

Johnson, Robert David. 2012. In David P. Auerswald and Colton C. Campbell, eds. *Congress and the Politics of National Security*. New York: Cambridge University Press.

Johnson, Samuel, 1709–1784. *Dictionary of the English Language*. Publisher: New York: Arno Press, 1979. Reprint of the 1755 ed. printed by W. Strahan, London.

Joseph, Rosara. 2013. *The War Prerogative: History, Reform, and Constitutional Design*. Oxford: Oxford University Press.

Journals of the Continental Congress, 1774–1789. 1904–37. Ed. Worthington C. Ford et al. Washington, D.C.: GPO.

Koh, Harold Hongju. 2012. *Address by the Legal Adviser, U.S. State Department, to the American Society of International Law Midyear Meeting*, University of Georgia Law School, Athens, GA, 20 October 2012. http://www.asil.org/activities_calendar.cfm?action=detail&rec=239 Accessed 18 Nov 2012.

Krasner, Stephen D. 1999. *Sovereignty: Organized Hypocrisy*. Princeton, NJ: Princeton University Press.

Kriesberg, Louis. 1998. *Constructive Conflicts: From Escalation to Resolution*. Lantham, MD: Rowan & Littlefield.

Kriner, Douglas L. 2010. *After the Rubicon: Congress, Presidents, and the Politics of Waging War*. Chicago, IL: University of Chicago Press.

Krutz, Glen S. and Jeffrey S. Peake. 2009. *Treaty Politics and the Rise of Executive Agreements: International Commitments in a System of Shared Power*. Ann Arbor, MI: University of Michigan Press.

Locke, John. 1764 [1690]. *Two Treatise of Government*. London. http://www.constitution.org/jl/2ndtr00.htm Accessed 7 June 2009.

Livy. 1919. *Livy in Fourteen Volumes*. Trans. B.O. Foster. The Loeb Classical Library. London: William Heinemann.

Madison, James. 1900–1910. *The Writings of James Madison*. 9 vols. Ed. Gaillard Hunt. New York: G.P. Putnam's Sons.

Madison, James. 1966. *Notes of Debates in the Federal Convention of 1787 Reported by James Madison*. Ed. Adrienne Koch. Athens, Ohio: Ohio University Press.

Maier, Pauline. 1997. *American Scripture: Making the Declaration of Independence.* New York: Alfred A. Knopf.

Malone, Dumas. 1948–81. *Jefferson and His Time.* 6 vols. Boston: Little, Brown and Company.

Mandela, Nelson. 1964. *Nelson Mandela's Statement From The Dock At The Opening Of The Defence Case In The Rivonia Trial: "I am Prepared to Die."* Pretoria Supreme Court, 20 April 1964. http://www.anc.org.za/ancdocs/history/mandela/1960s/rivonia.html Accessed 9 May 2000.

Maurice, J.F. Brevet-Lt. Col. 1883. *Hostilities Without Declaration of War: From 1700 to 1870: An Historical Abstract Of The Cases In Which Hostilities Have Occurred Between Civilized Powers Prior To Declaration Or Warning.* London: H.M. Stationery Office.

Mill, John Stuart. 1867. A Few Words on Non-intervention. In *Dissertations and Discussions: Political, Philosophical, and Historical, vol. 3*. London: Green, Reader, and Dyer.

Moe, Terry and William G. Howell. 1999. Unilateral Action and Presidential Power: A Theory. *Presidential Studies Quarterly* 29 (4) December, 850–72.

Monroe, James. 1960. *James Monroe Papers 1960.* Presidential Papers Microfilm. Washington, DC: Library of Congress (Microfilm S91026).

Montesquieu, Charles de Secondat, Baron de. 1914. *The Spirit of the Laws.* Trans. Thomas Nugent, revised J. V. Prichard. London: G. Bell & Sons, Ltd.

Nelson, Eric. 2014. *The Royalist Revolution: Monarchy and the American Founding.* Cambridge, MA: Belknap Press of Harvard University Press.

New Oxford American Dictionary, 3rd Ed. 2010. Eds. Angus Stevenson and Christine A. Lindberg. Oxford: Oxford University Press.

Nixon, Richard. 1973. "Address to the Nation About Vietnam and Domestic Problems," March 29, 1973. Online by Gerhard Peters and John T. Woolley, *The American Presidency Project.* http://www.presidency.ucsb.edu/ws/?pid=4161 Accessed 24 March 2013.

Obama, Barak. 2011. *Remarks by the President on the Situation in Libya, 18 March 2011.* http://www.whitehouse.gov/the-press-office/2011/03/18/remarks-president-situation-libya Accessed 20 May 2012.

Obama, Barak. 2011a. *Letter from the President regarding the commencement of operations in Libya of March 21, 2011.* http://www.whitehouse.gov/the-press-office/2011/03/21/letter-president-regarding-commencement-operations-libya Accessed 18 May 2011.

Pictet, Jean, ed. 1958. *Commentary on the Geneva Convention of 12 August 1949, vol. III.* Geneva: International Committee of the Red Cross.

Pisan, Christine de. 1937 [c. 1434]. *The Book of Fayttes of Armes and of Chyualrye (Le Livre des Faits d'Armes et de Chevalerie).* Trans. William Caxton (*1489*). Ed. A.T.P. Byles. Published by the Early English Text Society. London: Humphrey Milford, Oxford University Press.

Pritchard, James B., ed. 1955. Gilgamesh and Agga. In *Ancient Near Eastern Texts, Relating to the Old Testament. Second Edition, Corrected and Enlarged.* Princeton, NJ: Princeton University Press.

Rudalevige, Andrew. 2005. *The new imperial presidency renewing presidential power after Watergate.* Ann Arbor, Mich.: University of Michigan Press.

Scarry, Eliane. 2014. *Thermonuclear Monarchy: Choosing between Democracy and Doom.* New York: W.W. Norton.

Schelling, Thomas C. 1966. *Arms and Influence.* New Haven, CT: Yale University Press.

Schlesinger, Arthur M., Jr. 1973. *The Imperial Presidency.* Boston: Houghton Mifflin, Co.

Schooten, Hanneke van. 2007. The Legal Abolition Of War: Lip-Service To The Cause Of Peace? *Tilburg Law Review* 14, 363–78.

Searle, John R. 2010. *Making the Social World.* Oxford University Press.

Sidak, J. Gregory. 1991. "To Declare War." *Duke Law Journal* 41 (1), 27–121.

Thatcher, Oliver J., ed. 1907. *The Library of Original Sources: Vol. V: 9th to 16th Centuries.* Milwaukee: University Research Extension Co.

United States Department of Justice, Office of Legal Counsel. 2001. The President's Constitutional Authority To Conduct Military Operations Against Terrorists And Nations Supporting Them, September 25. http://www.justice.gov/olc/warpowers925.htm Accessed 30 June 2012.

Ward, Robert. 1805. *An Enquiry into the manner in which the different Wars of Europe have commenced during the last two centuries. ...* London: J. Butterworth and J. Stockdale.

Watson, Alan. 1993. *International Law in Archaic Rome: War and Religion.* Baltimore, MD: The Johns Hopkins University Press.

White House. 2002. *White House Discussion Draft of September 19, 2002, Joint Resolution To authorize the use of United States Armed Forces against Iraq.* http://usinfo.state.gov/topical/pol/terror/02091914.htm Accessed 24 September 2002.

White House. 2011. *United States Activities in Libya*, 15 June 2011. http://www.foreignpolicy.com/files/fp_uploaded_documents/110615_United_States_Activities_in_Libya_--_6_15_11.pdf Accessed 16 June 2011.

White, Leonard D. 1951. *The Jeffersonians: A Study in Administrative History 1801–1829.* New York: Macmillian.

Wilson, Woodrow. 1966–1993. *The Papers of Woodrow Wilson.* 69 vols. Ed. Arthur S. Link, et al. Princeton, NJ: Princeton University Press.

Wilson, Woodrow. 1917. "Address to a Joint Session of Congress: "Request for Authority,"" February 26, 1917. Online by Gerhard Peters and John T. Woolley, The American Presidency Project. http://www.presidency.ucsb.edu/ws/index.php?pid=65398 Accessed 25 July 2013.

Wormuth, Francis D. and Edwin B. Firmage. 1989. *To Chain the Dog of War: The War Power of Congress in History and Law.* Urbana, IL: University of Illinois Press.

Wright, Quincy. 1932. When Does War Exist? *American Journal of International Law* 26 (2) April, 362–8.

Yoo, John C. 1996. The Continuation of Politics by Other Means: The Original Understanding of War Powers. *California Law Review.* 84 (2), March, 167–305.

Yoo, John. 2002. War and the Constitutional Text. *University of Chicago Law Review* 69 (4), 1639–84.

Yoo, John. 2005. *The Powers of War and Peace: The Constitution and Foreign Affairs after 9/11.* Chicago, IL: University of Chicago Press.

Yoshihashi, Takehiko. 1963. *Conspiracy at Mukden: The Rise of the Japanese Military.* New Haven, CT: Yale University Press.

Zeisberg, Mariah. 2013. *War Powers: The Politics of Constitutional Authority.* Princeton, NJ: Princeton University Press.

Index

Adams, John   133, 139, 143
   Constitution of Massachusetts   131, 134
   seconds independence motion   51
Afghanistan   89
African National Congress   3, 101, 129
Agga and Gilgamesh   19, 34, 94
Antiochus IV Epiphanes   39
Aquinas   148
Arab League 2011   54
Arab Spring 2011   55
Arendt, Hannah   107
armed conflict   6, 9, 74–75
   a euphemism for war   80
   two definitions   75
Article I, Section 8, Clause 11   34, 75
   cited   xi, 18, 20, 70, 116
   values of   16
Article II, Section 2, Clause 1
   cited   70
asymmetric structure. *See* Constitution
asynchronic decision-making   104–105, 109, 140
Athens   109
   of Pericles   50
Augustine   148
Austin, John   5, 13, 76, 143, 186
   total speech situations   21, 85
   transmissible authorities   21
authority   59, 86, 130, 141, 155
   collective   15
   in War Powers Res.   56
   of Security Council   54
   personal   14, 21
   procedural   138
   tracing schematics   9, 137
Authorization for the President to Employ the Armed Forces of the United States for Protecting the Security of Formosa … of 1955   147
Authorization of the Use of Force Against Iraq Resolution of 2002   147
authorization to use military force (AUMF)   154
   for Iraq 2002   61

Beaumanoir, Philippe de   43–44
   Coutumes De Beauvaisis   41

Bebler, Ales   123
Ben Ali, Sine El Abidine, President   55
bicameral institution   30, 52, 110, 117, 122
Blackstone, William   82, 112, 117
Blair, Tony   1, 10, 12, 90, 99, 153
Blanco, Kathleen Babineaux   85
Bodin, Jean   43, 47–48
   governmental functions   44
Boener, John, Speaker   61
Boland amendment, 1982   115
Bundestag Participation Act   151
   partial text   154
Bush, George H. W.   10, 35, 39
   on inherent powers   32
   on Locke   46
Bush, George W.   1, 10, 12, 50, 55, 68, 82, 150, 153
   2002 AUMF for Iraq   61–62
   announces *Operation Enduring Freedom* 2001   89
   announces *Operation Iraqi Freedom* 2003   90
   disaster declaration   85
   the decider   99
Butler, Judith   131
Butler, Pierce   134, 143

Caesar, Julius   108, 153
   crossing the Rubicon   16, 39
Cambodia
   Congress ends funding   114
Cameron, Maxwell   137
Chang Kai-shek   118
Chang, John M., Korean Ambassador   120
Charles I   3, 37, 45, 114
   Bishop's War, 1639–1640   114
Charles V of France   15, 153
Charles V of France   25, 34
Chinese Communist Party   3, 129
Cicero   40, 108–109, 148
Clausewitz, Carl von   109, 150
   and republics   148
   and separation of power   149
   ends and means   148
   remarkable trinity   147
   two definitions of war   108

INDEX 195

Clay, Henry
   aide-mémoire 67
   War of 1812 66
Cleveland, Grover 1
collective action problem 30, 58, 61, 98,
   117–118, 121, 123
collective decision making 8, 50, 97, 142
   Scenario 4 9, 14, 30, 98
collective decision-making 8, 12, 137, 144
committee-of-the-whole system 19, 29, 48,
   65, 110, 119–120, 123, 125, 148
   and Second Continental Congress 51, 54
   and Security Council 53, 119
   schematically 138
Confederal Congress 139
Congress. *See* power of the purse
   Authorization for Use of Military Force
      Against Iraq Resolution of 14 January
      1991 33
   incapacity to declare war 16, 29, 48, 63,
      65, 67, 76, 143
   explained 11, 23, 50, 58, 101, 117, 121
   three causes 30
   not to be kept unnecessarily in the
      dark 33, 35, 46, 55, 61, 65, 68, 115
   president convenes and gives
      information 118
   primary function of, lawmaking 11, 18
   the *exercise* of the *power.* ... to declare
      war 13, 18, 20, 23, 64, 82
Congresses
   107th Congress 50, 55, 61, 68
   112th Congress 50, 55, 57
      House Concurrent Resolution 32, 2011
         on Libya 59
      House Concurrent Resolution 51, 2011
         on Libya 59
      House Concurrent Resolution 53, 2011
         on Libya 59
      House Concurrent Resolution 57, 2011
         on Libya 59
      House Joint Resolution 67, 2011 on
         Libya 60
      House Joint Resolution 68, 2011 on
         Libya 60
      House Joint Resolution 74, 2011 on
         Libya 60
      House Resolution 2278, 2011 on Libya 59
      House Resolution 292, 2011 on
         Libya 60

      Senate Joint Resolution 14, 2011 on
         Libya 59
      Senate Joint Resolution 16, 2011 on
         Libya 59
      Senate Joint Resolution 20, 2011 on
         Libya 60
      Senate Resolution 85, 2011 on Libya 58
   Eighty-first Congress 35, 122
      and Korean War 118, 124
   Fifty-fifth 26, 28
   Ninety-third Congress
      and *War Powers Resolution* 116
      ends funding for Vietnam 115
      passes War Powers Res. 151
   Seventy-seventh Congress for WW II 81
   Sixty-fifth Congress and WW I 104
   Twenty-ninth 25
Constitution
   asymmetric structure 32, 48, 126, 134
   checks and balance 19, 33, 39, 46, 112, 114,
      140, 144, 153
   and Clausewitz 147
   and Madison 147
   enhanced executive powers 111–112
   of three branches 134
   original intent 113, 118
   original understanding 116–117
   power of the purse 114
   separation of powers 33, 38, 111
      in Clausewitz 147
   symmetric structure 134, 138, 141
   unitary executive 111
Constitution, French 154
   Article 35, text 151
constitutional monarchy 125, *See* monarch
Cuba 26, 72
Cyprus, conquest of 1571 97

Dayton-Paris Agreement for Bosnia, 1995 101
decision-making
   an individual's private mental act 83, 85, 137
decision-making assembly 5, 7, 29, 48, 50,
   54, 79, 98, 102, 110, 124, 135, 139, 141, 143,
   148–149, 153
declaration
   disaster, federal-level text 86
   disaster, Katrina 84
   disaster, state-level text 85
   lexical definition 20, 23, 26, 82
   ontology of 86

Declaration Against The French King 77
Declaration of Independence 12, 27, 29, 77, 96, 103, 122, 131, 149, 155, 175, 182
    compared with televised address 100
    introduced 7 June 1776 51
declaration of war. 177
    a royal prerogative 29, 35, 65, 112, 118, 124–125, 127, 148
    absolute 15, 25, 110
    against Perseus 96
    against Venice, 1570 97
    as objective expression of parliamentary procedures (policy by other means) 121, 124
    as subjective expression of single individual (compellence) 124
    codepedent and causative of war 80, 84, 89
    conditional 6, 25–26, 28, 110
        scenarios 10
        Security Council 122
    dictionary definitions 20
    drafted by State Department 105
    earliest 34
    functionally equivalent 6, 9, 14, 21, 24, 50, 54, 56, 65, 81, 86, 90, 101, 124
    imperfect 81, 90, 138
    lexical 15, 24, 27, 31, 68, 79, 82, 90, 94, 102, 146
    Mexican-American 24
    perfect 63, 81, 138
        misunderstood 112
    reasoned 6, 12, 28, 70, 94
    scenarios 98, 102, 104, 118, 146, 152
    solemn 13, 81
    Spanish-American War 26
    sui generis 69
    text 21, 25
    unreasoned 94
    unsolemn 81
    World War I text cited 103
Declaration on Taking Arms 97
declarer of war 3, 56, 67, 71, 73, 82, 101, 109, 148
    collective 6, 9, 12
    individual 6, 9, 12
    legitimate and competent 6, 76, 81, 86, 138
    of the political ends 147
    scenarios 21

democracy 152, 173
    and authorization to use military force 151
    and Constitution 17
    values of 19, 152
Dutch Act of Abjuration of 1581 127, 131
Dutch Estates General 3, 128, 130, 133

Edward III of England 15
ends-means 133, 137–138, 141, 144, 147, 149, 151, 153, 155
English Civil War 37, 42, 45, 114, 127
executive decision-making 5, 12, 97–98, 137, 140, 142, 151, 153
    asynchronic 137

Fawzi, Mahmoud Bey 123
Fazal, Tanisha 73–74, 79
Federal Convention 4, 63, 73, 75–76, 107, 130, 134, 143
    aspirations of 34, 46, 48, 143
    governmental functions 47
Federalist No. 25 112
Federalist No. 51
    partial text 150
Fisher, Roger 109
foederative powers. *See* Locke, John
Franco-American Treaty of Amity and Commerce of 1778 63
Franklin, Benjamin 139
Franks, Tommy, General 150
French *États-Généraux* 45
French National Assembly 3, 151
French Revolution 45, 65, 127
functionally equivalent speech acts 13–14, 35, 53, 73, 75, 79, 83, 97, 109–110, 119, 121–122, 124, 146, 149–150, 154
    ontological guillotine 88

Gaddafi, Maummar 54–55
Garrett, Scott, Rep. 59
George III 4, 131
Germanic tribes and consultation 37, 40, 48
Germany 102
Gerry, Elbridge 63, 143
Gilgamesh 38, 46, 48, 55, 57, 62, 65–66, 68, 104–105, 112, 115, 127, 152–153
governmental functions
    Bodin 44

Federal Convention   47
Locke   45
Montesquieu   46
Great Britain   51, 64
   constitution   34, 46, 112
   independence from   52, 94, 138
   Korean War   120
   number of wars declared   114
   War of 1812   66
Gross, Earnest A.   119
Grotius   148

Hague Convention III, *Relative to the Opening of Hostilities*   8, 11, 27, 73, 75, 77, 80–81, 91, 93–95, 100, 102–103, 107, 110–111, 119, 122, 140, 149, 154, 175, 179, 182
   cited   71
   text   6, 70
Hamilton, Alexander   67
   and *Federalist No. 25*   112
   legislative function   58
   Letters of Pacificus   64, 70
Hanaya Tadashi Major   88
Hastings, Alcee, Rep.   60
Hayashi, Hissjiro Consul General   87
Helvidius Priscus   64
Hoar, George F. Senator   28
Hobbes, Thomas   105
Honjo, Shigeru Lieutenant General   86, 89
Howell, William   19
Hurricane Katrina   84
Hussein, Saddam   32

Imada Shintaro Captain   88
imperia in imperium   41, 43
Imperial Presidency   14
impium   6, 13–14
Indian National Congress   3, 129
Iraq   61, 90, 150
Ishihara Kanji Lieutenant Colonel   88
Itagaki Seishiro Colonel   88

Japan   81, 86, 119
Jefferson, Thomas   64, 101, 139
Johnson, Lyndon   150
Johnson, Samuel   19, 82
Joseph, Rosara   37, 74
jus ad interactionem   139, 149
jus fetiale   94, 105, 109, 111

jus gentium   105, 107
jus in interactione   149
jus naturale   105
justice, procedural   13–14, 105, 110
justice, substantive   13
just-interaction criteria   28, 150
   and separation of powers   149
just-war criteria   148

Kellogg-Briand Pact of 1928
   cited   79
   outlaws war   73
Kerry, John, Sen.   60
King John   37
   Magna Carta   40
King William   77, 98
Koh, Harold   71, 112
Korea   33, 35, 110, 119
   North invades   119
Krasner, Stephen   40
Kriesberg, Louis   93, 105
Kucinich, Dennis, Rep.   59
Kumanovo Agreement for Kosovo, 1999   101
Kuwait   32
Kwantung Army
   Army Special Services Agency   86
   Mukden Incident   86

Laenas, Gaius Popillius and *majestas*   39
Lansing, Robert, Secretary of State   104
League of Nations   88
Lee, Richard Henry   138
   introduces independence motion   51
legislative veto   152, 154–155
legitimacy   137, 143
   conventional   154
   legitimating parliamentary procedures   121, 124
   ought not *is*   154
   procedural   149
   procedural, no longer an issue   153
   procedural, Second Continental Congress   138
   textually legitimate   109
Lesser Magistrates Doctrine   127, 131, 134, 138
Libya   50, 55, 58, 60
   no-fly zone   16, 54, 110
Lie, Trygve, Secretary General   119

Livingston, Robert R.   139
Livy, and fetial code   96
Locke, John   2, 46, 118, 130, 143
   and fœderative powers   4, 45, 48, 54, 112, 127, 134
      mal-distribution of   143
     governmental functions   45
   Second Treatise   45
Louis VI   4
Louis XIII   45
Louis XIV   42, 45

Madison, James   11, 15, 19, 50, 53, 63, 65, 67, 87, 101, 116, 118, 143, 146–147
   Federalist No. 51, partial text   150
   Letters of Helvidius   64, 69
   power to declare war sui generis   69
Magna Carta   37
majestas (majesty)   39, 42, 45
   and Laenas, Gaius Popillius   39
   embodiment of   43
Mandela, Nelson   101
manifestive moment   96, 98, 103, 105, 110, 137
manifestive speech act   9, 83–84, 93, 101, 109, 138
Mao Tse-tung   3, 17, 118
Massachusetts, Constitution of the Commonwealth of   131
Mau Mau Movement   3, 129
Mazarin, Jules, Cardinal   45
McKinley, William   11, 15, 26, 72
Menendez, Robert, Senator   57
Mill, John Stuart   7, 106
Milosevic, Slobodan   101
Moe, Terry   19
monarch   29, 32, 36, 40, 48, 55, 95, 141
   absolute   17, 45, 126
   astute   65
   constitutional monarchy   29, 34, 45, 48, 50, 70, 102, 104, 111, 125
   elected   4
   elected constitutional   39, 46, 48, 55, 66, 112–113, 117–118, 126, 130, 132–134, 143, 145, 154
   hereditary   2, 4, 45, 48, 113, 117, 130, 154
   imposes his will on world   140
   non-absolute   42
   Roman antipathy   108

Monroe, James, Secretary of State   66
Montesquieu, Charles Louis de Secondat   2, 127
   governmental functions   46
Morgenthau, Hans   105
Mubarak, Hosni, President   55
Mukden Incident   86

Nero, Emperor   64
New Orleans   84
Nincitch, Djuro   120
Nixon, Richard   115
   vetoes War Powers Res.   151
non-executive decision-making   76, 148

Obama, Barak   50, 58, 110
   letter to Congress, Libya 2011   55
   report on Libya 2011   56
Octavian, Gaius   108, 153
Office of Legal Counsel
   memo of 2001   82
   memo on Libya 2011   56
Operation Enduring Freedom, Afghanistan, 2001   89
Operation Iraqi Freedom, 2003   90
Operation Odyssey Dawn, Libya, 2011   55

Parliament
   Long   3, 114
   Short   114
parliamentary government, rise of   127
Paul, Rand, Sen.   59
performative speech acts   5, 12–13, 19, 21, 52, 76, 79, 133, 148
   and transmissible authorities   76, 79, 85, 88–89, 138, 141–143, 149, 153, 155
   and transmissible authority   21, 77, 137–138, 147
   codependent, causative   76, 78, 80, 84–85, 87, 89
   felicitous performance   83, 86
   ontological guillotine   76, 78, 81, 83–84, 86, 88, 93, 96, 99, 101, 103, 131, 137
   ontology   84
   to define declaration of war   76
   total speech situations   21, 85
performativity   131, 133
Perseus   72, 96
Philip II Augustus   37, 40, 42

INDEX

Philip II of Spain 3, 128, 131
Pisan, Christine de 15, 153
pium 6, 11, 13–14, 107
Polk, James 25
power of the purse 32, 36, 38, 40, 48, 113, 115, 127
    Congress ends funding for Cambodia 114
    Congress ends funding for Vietnam 114
    restrains presidential war making 112
presidential war making 5, 97
    executive leadership and agenda setting 31, 53, 65, 67, 72, 76
    Scenario 1 9, 14, 98, 145
    Scenario 2 9, 14, 50, 55–57, 98, 145
    Scenario 3 9, 14, 21, 24, 27, 50, 53, 55, 61, 65, 98, 100, 102, 104, 118, 145–146, 152
Proclamation of Neutrality 63

Rau, Benegal Sir 119, 123
Reagan, Ronald 56
rebus repetitis 72, 95, 108
republic 124, 134, 141, 143–144
    and Clausewitz 148
    and just-interaction criteria 150
    and sovereignty 48
    and *War Powers Resolution* 17
    as symmetrical 138
    Second Continental Congress republican-like 50
    Security Council republican-like 50
    structures 19
    transformation of 34, 125, 145
    values of 19, 48
Roman Republic 3, 29, 42, 50, 94, 107, 109
Roman Senate 42
Rooney, Thomas, Rep. 59
Roosevelt, Franklin
    and declaring WWII 81
rule of law 39, 79
Russo-Japanese War 86

Scenario 1, 2, 3. See presidential war-making
Scenario 4. See collective decision-making
Schelling, Thomas C. 109
Schlesinger, Arthur 5, 17, 23, 35, 50, 75, 101, 110, 116–117, 144, 151
Schmitt, Carl 105
Schooten, Hanneke van 80
Schumer, Chuck, Senator 57

Second Continental Congress 3, 11–12, 25, 28–29, 50, 54, 61–63, 96, 110, 118, 131, 144, 150
    Committee of Five 139
    compared to Security Council 120
    procedures for *Declaration of Independence* 138
    republican-like 51
Security Council 11, 35, 50, 54, 58, 110, 118–119, 121–122, 124, 144, 146
    and presidential war-making 33
    as model 124
    republican-like 50, 53–54
    Resolution 1970 on Libya, 2011 54
    Resolution 1973 on Libya, 2011 54
    Resolution 678, on Kuwait, 1990 33
    Resolution 82 on Korea 121
    Resolution 83 on Korea 123
Selim II, Sultan 97, 104
Sherman, Roger 139
Smith, Adam, Rep. 60
social contract 135, 143
Southern Christian Leadership Conference 3, 129
sovereign people 133
sovereignty 42, 48
    embodiment of 43
Spain 72, 131
Stafford Act 85
standing-committee system 30, 52, 65, 110, 117, 125
Stimson, Henry, Secretary of State 88
substantive justice 105
symmetric structure. *See* Constitution
synchronic decision-making 102, 104, 109, 137, 140

Tarquinius, Superbus 108
Taylor, John 66
Taylor, Zachary 25
Thucydides 105
Truman, Harry 118, 122, 124, 146
    Security Council 35
    Security Council authorization 33

unicameral institution 29–30, 48, 51, 53–54, 110, 121, 124–125, 148
United Nations 54, 119, *See* Security Council
    war outlawed 73, 146

United Nations (cont.)
    cited   80
Ury, William L.   109

Vietnam War   150
    Congress ends funding   114
    end of combat   114
Vietnamese Workers Party   3, 129

war
    a thought experiment   78
    as social phenomenon   85–86, 99, 104, 140
    defined as performative speech act   76
    imperfect   112
    in the legal sense   87
    in the material sense   87
    perfect   82, 112
War Hawks and War of 1812   66
war leader, national   1, 3, 6, 9, 14–16, 19, 21, 23, 31–32, 35, 38, 48, 54, 61, 67, 97, 101, 109, 124, 135
    astute   27, 35, 55, 65, 104, 115, 146, 153

War Powers Resolution   18, 30, 147, 151
    60-day grace period   58
    consultation for collective judgment   118, 152–153
    consultation for collective judgment, text   116
    Obama letter for Libya 2011   56
    partial text   116, 152, 154
Warren, Austin R.   119
Washington, George   34, 138, 144, 150
    Proclamation of Neutrality, 1793   63
Watson, Alan   107
Westmoreland, William, General   150
Wilson, Woodrow   103, 105
    on inherent powers   34
Wright, Quincy   87

Yoo, John   20, 34, 71, 82, 89, 111–112, 117, 125, 145
    and original understanding   111

Zeisberg, Mariah   137

Printed in the United States
By Bookmasters